Diplomacy and Revolution: The Soviet Mission to Switzerland, 1918. Alfred Erich Senn.

America in Change: Reflections on the 60's and 70's. Ronald Weber, ed.

Social Change in the Soviet Union. Boris Meissner, ed.

Foreign Assistance: A View from the Private Sector. Kenneth W. Thompson.

Hispanismo, 1898-1936: Spanish Conservatives and 'Liberals and Their Relations with Spanish America. Fredrick B. Pike.

Democracy in Crisis: New Challenges to Constitutional Democracy in the Atlantic Area. E. A. Goerner, ed.

The Task of Universities in a Changing World. Stephen D. Kertesz, ed.

The Church and Social Change in Latin America. Henry A. Landsberger, ed.

Revolution and Church: The Early History of Christian Democracy, 1789-1901. Hans Maier.

The Overall Development of Chile. Mario Zañartu, S.J., and John J. Kennedy, eds.

The Catholic Church Today: Western Europe. M. A. Fitzsimons, ed.

Contemporary Catholicism in the United States. Philip Gleason, ed.

The Major Works of Peter Chaadaev. Raymond T. McNally.

A Russian European: Paul Miliukov in Russian Politics. Thomas Riha.

A Search for Stability: U.S. Diplomacy Toward Nicaragua, 1925-1933. William Kamman.

Freedom and Authority in the West. George N. Shuster, ed.

Theory and Practice: History of a Concept from Aristotle to Marx. Nicholas Lobkowicz.

Coexistence: Communism and Its Practice in Bologna, 1945-1965. Robert H. Evans.

Marx and the Western World. Nicholas Lobkowicz, ed.

INTERNATIONAL STUDIES OF THE
COMMITTEE ON INTERNATIONAL RELATIONS
UNIVERSITY OF NOTRE DAME

THE NEW CORPORATISM

The New Corporatism
Social-Political Structures
in the Iberian World

Fredrick B. Pike
and
Thomas Stritch
EDITORS

UNIVERSITY OF NOTRE DAME PRESS
Notre Dame   **London**

Library of Congress Cataloging in Publication Data

Pike, Fredrick B.
    The new corporatism.

    (International studies of the Committee on International
Relations, University of Notre Dame)
    Includes bibliographical references.
    1. Corporate state — Addresses, essays, lectures. 2. Latin
America — Politics — 1948- — Addresses, essays, lectures.
3. Spain — Politics and government — 1939- — Addresses, essays,
lectures. I. Stritch, Thomas, joint author. II. Title. III. Series:
Notre Dame, Ind. University. Committee on International Rela-
tions. International studies.
JC478.P45   320.5'31   73-22583
ISBN 0-268-00538-9
ISBN 0-268-00539-7 (pbk.)

Manufactured in the United States of America

To
Stephen D. Kertesz

Contents

Contributors

James M. Malloy is Associate Professor of Political Science at the University of Pittsburgh.

Ronald C. Newton is on the history faculty of Simon Fraser University (B.C.).

Fredrick B. Pike is Professor of History at the University of Notre Dame.

Philippe C. Schmitter is on the faculty of The University of Chicago and the faculty of the Université de Genève.

Thomas Stritch is Professor of American Studies at the University of Notre Dame.

Howard J. Wiarda teaches at the University of Massachusetts (Amherst).

Introduction

Thomas Stritch

The arguments in this book flow like planets around the idea of the nature of the state. Corporatism is a very old concept of community, if not of the state proper, but as a theory it never got any hold on the native imagination of the United States. Although our two greatest sources of legend, the ranch and the plantation, are suggestive of corporatism, they did not inspire dreams of a corporate state. Neither John Quincy Adams nor John C. Calhoun, both claimed for corporatism, made any dent in the ethos of individualism that swept the country almost from its beginnings to the rumblings of the great depression. As Victor C. Ferkiss puts it, "The American republic had a strong and lasting agrarian tradition based not on feudalism but on the yeoman farmer, and it was a tradition to which most American thinkers related . . . along with its agrarianism the new nation was imbued with liberalism, Whig to the bone. Neither throne nor altar, nor above all reverence for the past existed as barriers to the new leveling forces unleashed by industrial technology."[1]

Not so the Iberian world. What underlies this book is its history of corporatism, what prompts it is a sense of its contemporary revival there. Elsewhere, too, perhaps, but only by extension; largely the book sticks to its subtitle, "Social-Political Structures in the Iberian World." James Malloy, of the University of Pittsburgh, focuses on the new corporatism in contemporary Peru, giving us a blueprint of a brand-new corporatist state trying to carve out a successful future. Robert Newton, of Simon Fraser University, describes the phenomenon of *natural* corporatism, a spontaneous linkage of social groups especially in the absence of strong state power. Howard Wiarda, of the University of Massachusetts (Amherst), develops his concept of Portuguese-Brazilian corporatism largely from Portuguese history. Fredrick Pike, of the University of Notre Dame, ties Latin-American corporatism first to the United States and second to the *madre patria*, Spain, in related but separate articles. Philippe Schmitter, of The University of Chicago, ponders the nature and longevity of corporatism.

---

[1] Victor C. Ferkiss, *Technological Man* (New York, 1969), p. 65.

xiii

Schmitter distinguishes two main varieties of corporatism, state and societal. Some modern states seem almost by nature attracted to corporatism, Sweden, Portugal and Austria among them.[2] And some societies and nationalities reveal the same characteristic. Both at home and abroad Greeks and Italians seem naturally to build communities. Of our authors, Ronald Newton and Fredrick Pike make most of this same propensity among the Iberians.

Robert Newton, indeed, almost makes this the basis of his concept of natural corporatism. But this must be carefully distinguished from the surface voluntary clubbism North Americans go in for so heartily. Natural corporatism derives from class, from family, from tradition. These, allied with the classical triad of landowners, ecclesiastics and soldiers, kept civil life going behind the scenes of what Newton charmingly calls the melodrama of party politics. Such enduring relationships are of the blood, and differ greatly not only from the shifting brotherhood of Rotary and the Knights of Columbus in the United States, but also inspire a much deeper loyalty and devotion than most United States interest-group associations of business and labor. The numerous attempts to make labor unions in the United States ideological, let alone into some sort of mystique a la the Soviet Union, have all failed.[3]

But what Newton describes as natural corporatism is not wholly unknown to the United States. Much of it is true of society in the south both before and after the Civil War; some of it is almost interchangeable with parts of W. J. Cash's *The Mind of the South*.[4] More recent writers say that the south has retained this cast of character throughout its relatively recent industrialization.[5] If this is true, the example may shed some light on Newton's doubts about the continuation of natural corporatism in Latin America.

For Newton says that corporatism of the natural sort can't keep going under conditions of headlong economic growth. Just this has kept the English-speaking people, the French and most of the

---

[2] The Austrian People's Party (OVP) formally has no members at all. One can join the party only through membership in one of its corporate groups. See Ronald Rogowski and Lois Wasserspring, *Does Political Development Exist? Corporatism in Old and New Societies* (Beverly Hills: Sage Professional Papers, Series 01-024, Vol. 2, 1971).

[3] Editors of *Fortune, The Permanent Revolution,* February, 1951.

[4] W. J. Cash, *The Mind of the South* (New York, 1941).

[5] C. Vann Woodward, *The Burden of Southern History* (Baton Rouge, 1960), and David Potter, *The South and the Sectional Conflict* (Baton Rouge, 1968).

German-speaking people relatively innocent of corporatism, which is why Howard Wiarda seems to me to claim too much for the influence of Portuguese history on present-day Portuguese corporatism. That is, if the industrial revolution hadn't come first and strongest to England it, too, might have developed a modern corporatist state. This is one reason why Philippe Schmitter emphatically parts company with Wiarda on this point. Preferring to link corporatism to modern industrialism, he sees it as much more secular and much less ingrained than does Wiarda. Setting aside Nazi Germany, whose corporatism he dubs ambiguous (and most scholars call the Italian corporate state a mere facade, its ambitious 1934 program never actually put into practice), Schmitter believes corporatism evolved as a *tertium quid* out of the inadequacy of liberal pluralism on the one hand and the rigors of the Soviet model on the other. More than any of our authors Schmitter ranges beyond the Iberian world. He argues that it is a mistake to confine corporatism to its Iberian exemplars, citing Sweden, Belgium, Greece and Yugoslavia, among many others, as modern states with corporatist institutions owing little or nothing to Iberia. Moreover, he takes emphatic exception to the fairly widespread tendency to associate corporatism largely with the Roman Catholic Church. There are, of course, many connections, and they have been emphasized by the corporate cast of the modern papal encyclicals on problems of state and society. But Schmitter points to some Catholic intellectuals like Maritain who argued against corporatism, and finds its intellectual parenthood predominately German, Belgian, French, Austrian, English, Italian and Rumanian rather than Iberian. But Fredrick Pike thinks Schmitter exaggerates such influences on the Iberian variety of corporatism, pointing not only to a long list of Spanish corporatist theorists who did not borrow from abroad, but also importantly to the temperamental affinities between the theory and the Spanish character. This is, indeed, a unifying theme throughout Pike's articles.

Set also against Newton's point about Latin American natural corporatism being an arrangement for keeping civil life going (nothing so elegant as a system, he says), certain reservations arise. For all its dazzling scope and intellectual subtlety, Schmitter's argument may claim too much. We may yet reflect, as he himself admits, that Belgium is not Bolivia, nor the Netherlands Peru, even as we yield to certain of his criticisms of both narrowness and looseness in thinking about corporatism. The Netherlandish cycle described by Schmitter as developing corporatism sounds little like the Peruvian model so neatly unveiled by James Malloy. Much depends, of course, on what you want to emphasize, but I rather think that the corporatism of the New Deal and the New Federalism[6] and that of contemporary Greece and Sweden have a different flavor from what Malloy tells us is happening in Peru.

What the United States and other highly developed countries did is to channel some of their abounding wealth into hands hitherto largely deprived of its natural flow, and to create, through government, power countervailing to that of the private economic sector. Malloy describes a very different process: corporate structures designed to evoke wealth, and government designed to lay the specter of incipient popular revolution. Anything as sweeping as the SINAMOS he analyzes wouldn't have a chance in most developed countries.

The sort of chance it has had in South America generally is superbly documented in Fredrick Pike's first essay on Latin American corporatism's relations with the United States. The larger sweep of Pike's view makes it possible for him to emphasize the ebb and flow of Latin American corporatism, arising he thinks more from its own historical changes than from such outside pressure as the United States brought to bear. In times of prosperity many states veered toward liberalism, only to return to structures more corporate when times got hard. Pike wryly documents the inability of the North American ethos to understand Latin America's traditional corporatism, from John Quincy Adams to and beyond John F. Kennedy, both of whom had leanings toward some corporate structures in their own country. But he is wary of attributing overwhelming influence to the United States. Despite historical ups and downs, Iberian culture everywhere, Pike thinks, retained throughout a dichotomized society, with the leading classes relatively independent and capitalistic, while the masses remained dependent and subsistence-oriented.

This is the main thrust of Pike's second article which is focused on Spain. The remarkable Spanish prosperity of 1950-1970 continues, Pike thinks, this dichotomy in the face of increasing industrialization. It does so largely through the pattern described by

---

[6] The name Max Ways gave Lyndon Johnson's program. See Max Ways, "The New Federalism," *Fortune,* January, 1966, p. 121.

John Kenneth Galbraith in his *The New Industrial State,* a manipulation of the masses into a consumerism which leaves them unable to accumulate any capital of their own on the one hand, and dependent on the state on the other for steady employment, and welfare and old age benefits.[7] Galbraith, a defender along with Arthur Schlesinger, Jr., of interest-group liberalism, argues for channeling consumption of luxury goods into improved housing, health and welfare services and suchlike, but he does not propose corporate structures for this purpose.

What the Spanish leadership has done is a neat trick, if it is a trick. Pike documents the acquiescence of the Spanish masses even including rebellious youth outside the universities. Corporatism means above all harmony, integralism; and it depends for its success, as Pike notes, on the ability of the state to moderate the goals and demands of the various vertical corporations it has created or sanctioned, like the twenty-six labor syndicates in contemporary Spain. But what really counts is popular support. Schmitter notes that corporatism in Portugal is full of holes; Malloy gravely doubts the viability of the new corporate structures of Peru. Even in Portugal, as Schmitter notes, corporatism abjures statism. If this is to be the rule of state corporatism of the future, and if time has indeed dispelled the foul atmosphere generated by certain aspects of fascist Italy and Nazi Germany, corporatism will prosper or wane depending on what popular support it can win. As Talleyrand is said to have told Napoleon, you can do everything with bayonets except sit on them.

Of our authors only Philippe Schmitter turns prophet. He is impatient for the inequities of corporatism to run their course so that a new age of syndicalism may come into being. Howard Wiarda, stressing the resurgence of corporatism, also stresses the repudiation of United States-style liberalism, suggesting throughout his essay that corporatism is indigenous to the Iberian world. Fredrick Pike thinks it likely that the relative success of corporatism in Spain, in comparison to much of its pre-Civil War history, will continue so long as the forces that make it go continue, and that this might influence the Latin American states to implement their development of corporatist institutions. Ronald Newton agrees with this latter point. Noting the decline of natural corporatism, he thinks it at

---

[7] John Kenneth Galbraith, *The New Industrial State,* especially Chapter XX (Boston, 1967).

least possible that corporatism may be a useful element in ideology. But he joins with Wiarda against trying to transform scholarship into policy, in his words, or in Wiarda's, of trying to explain the whole of the Iberian world in terms of corporatism. Similarly, James Malloy cautions against too great confidence in models such as the one he sets forth with such great skill. Raising the question of the future of corporatism in Peru, he notes the success of the model in Mexico and its failure in Bolivia. There is more to social and economic life than the structures this book speaks of, most of all, perhaps, the *elan vital*, the sense of life itself. Our intellectual generation has perhaps inherited too much of this sort of thing from Marx and from such contemporary writers as Levi-Strauss. As our authors insist, the structures are worth examining, but they are not everything.

This is also true of liberal pluralism. There is a general agreement in this book that this hasn't and won't work in Latin America, and that efforts on the part of the United States to urge, even to impose it, have been mistakes. Despite their doubts and differences, our authors agree that some kind of corporatism seems congenial to the Iberian national character, and they see it as flexible and adaptable. It is hard for me to say whether they imply by this agreement with the analysis of the United States by Theodore Lowi in his *The End of Liberalism*, a book whose thesis is in its title.[8] It is interesting to note that Lowi (p. 70) dismisses corporatism as succinctly as Philippe Schmitter, in this book, dismisses Lowi's own rather mechanical approach to shoring up government in the United States. Liberalism has been under attack since it came into being. The valuable bibliography that Schmitter appends to his article represents a symphony of discontent with it, and even so it does not include such classics as the works of William Morris and John Ruskin, both embryo corporatists, nor the criticism of the new theology.[9]

Nor do our authors, except for Schmitter's heralding of syndicalism, push corporatism as world ideal. Many note the increase of

---

[8] Theodore Lowi, *The End of Liberalism* (New York, 1969).

[9] For example, "The goal of the bourgeois principle is the radical dissolution of the bonds of original, organic community life, the dissolution of the powers of origins into elements to be conquered rationally." James Luther Adams, "Tillich's Concept of the Protestant Era," in Paul Tillich, *The Protestant Era*, translated and with a concluding essay by James Luther Adams (Chicago, 1948).

societal corporatism in such liberal strongholds as the United States and Great Britain, and Fredrick Pike suggests a turnabout that would shock classical liberalists in both countries: that Iberian corporatism may profitably teach the rest of the world something about government. But perhaps government is the wrong word. I sense that our authors align themselves with the long quest for community since the advent of industrialism, and only in this sense are they inimical to liberalism.[10] They view the state as community writ large, something to love or to hate, the mother of virtue or the father of vice, the benevolent maker of good citizens or a vicious barrier to their making—in any case, something organic rather than mechanical.

The larger implications of this attitude, though they lie beyond the scope of this book, seem to me cloudy and complex. How does it apply to the new nationalisms of Africa, and to some degree, India? This book deals with the Iberian world, and with all its troubles and problems it is still a much more cohesive world than any comparable part of the globe, excepting possibly China. Mihaïl Manoïlesco, much quoted in this book, said that the twentieth century would be one of conflict among states rather than classes. This prediction is much less true of the Iberian than the rest of the world. It is hard to think that corporatism, however much it may promote harmony within the state, can promote it among states. Liberalism may be dying, but there is so far on the horizon no alternative to the diplomacy it spawned.

But even more important are the implications of technology. That word turns up quite often in this book; our authors note that one of the desirable features of corporatist structures is greater access to technical expertise and increased use of it. Very well, if you're talking about increasing agricultural productivity or predicting consumer demand. But what of the larger technology, the world of Galbraith's technostructure[11] or Brzezinski's technetronics?[12] What of the often predicted postindustrial world, with its computers directing such an abundance of goods that nobody will need to work, or be able to find it in these magic halls of automation? What of the happy visions of Marshall McLuhan and Buckminster

[10] So excellently documented in Robert Nisbet, *The Quest for Community* (Glencoe, 1954).

[11] John Kenneth Galbraith, *The New Industrial State*, see footnote 7.

[12] Zbiegniew Brzezinski, *Between Two Ages* (New York, 1970).

Fuller, of Herman Kahn and and Dennis Gabor? What of the terrible ones of Henry Adams, who surely invented the energy crisis, and Jacques Ellul?

These questions, too, lie outside the scope of this book. Yet they haunt its periphery. Wherever one begins, the history of corporatism is a long one.[13] Postindustrial technology has scarcely any history. It has instead projections into the future, history in reverse. These projections almost unanimously reject liberal pluralism as a possible form of governing the postindustrial state. Typical is the comment of Irene Taviss, "Classical theories of democracy and pluralism are, like classical economics, 'insufficient in the postindustrial society' . . . The increasing orientation of government toward planning must lead political scientists to question whether a system of federated and separated powers can cope with the demands of modern government."[14]

Can corporatism cope with them? The case of Sweden may be instructive. That country has the stablest society and the longest-lived government of this century. Its statistics of all sorts, excepting alcoholism and suicide, are most impressive: scarcely any unemployment, no labor unrest, excellent medical and welfare services, highly technicized and efficient industry, much else that can be indexed. And it is thoroughly corporate. But the alcoholism and suicide rate are suggestive of what may be wrong, not only with Sweden but with other corporate states. "When you turn all this (economic, military and other big problems) over to the government, as is done in Sweden," said Scott Buchanan, "you get a very dull, not necessarily stupid, kind of society."[15] In short, the trouble with corporatism that works may be banality.

This is the judgment of British journalist Roland Huntford, who has lived in Stockholm for many years.[16] It is also the judgment I apply to the commune described by B. F. Skinner in his famous novel, *Walden II,* as well as to many another commune. It seems

[13] Speros Vryonis refers to the corporations of tenth-century Byzantium in his *Byzantium and Europe* (New York, 1967), p. 98.

[14] Irene Taviss, "The Technological Society: Some Challenges for Social Science," *Social Research,* Autumn, 1968, abstracted in *Harvard University Program on Technology and Society, 1964-1972, A Final Review,* p. 201.

[15] Quoted in Hal Draper, "Neo-Corporatists and Neo-Reformers," *New Politics,* Fall, 1961, p. 94.

[16] Roland Huntford, *The New Totalitarians* (New York, 1972).

to me that only deeply held religion can hold members of such communes together.

Failing that, I wonder about the quality of life in a highly developed corporate state. There is a strain of romantic utopianism in corporatism, documented in some of these essays, that is worth questioning. The question runs like this: does the tightness of such states as Sweden, whose present government came to power the same year that Franklin D. Roosevelt did and is still in power, go well with human nature as we know it, as it is set forth in the Gospel of St. Matthew and the works of Shakespeare and Tolstoy, the human nature I must take as a constant in shaping human affairs, utopians from Plato to Skinner to the contrary?[17] Does the corporate state give enough rein to the imagination, powers, chances and even the engaging idiosyncrasies of the human person? It is a question usually asked by skeptics of state power, and it is worth asking once again.

Roosevelt's New Deal brought the United States many corporate institutions, some of which have endured and some of which haven't.[18] Yet despite the persistence of some of the same problems Roosevelt faced, and the appearance of many new ones, corporatism lies lightly on us. A new book on United States corporatism, *Corporate Power and Social Responsibility*, by Neil H. Jacoby, gives the corporatism described in this book short shrift.[19] If pluralism is dead, nobody told Mr. Jacoby; he describes it in much the same terms Pendleton Herring did back in the 1930's and 1940's.[20] And he concludes that the contemporary American business corporation is losing rather than gaining in direct political power.

I believe that Jacoby's viewpoint is still the dominant one in American thinking, both economic and political. The old American dream persists, pace Kurt Vonnegut, Jr., and Philippe Schmitter, who quotes him in this book.

Concluding his first article in this book, Fredrick Pike says, "For the moment corporatism lives anew—or still—in the Iberian world

---

[17] Of course it must be remembered that power in Sweden resides more with the corporations than with the government. But still, this is a mighty long run for one party in a country that is still technically a democracy.

[18] There was little that was original about this, to be sure. See William Appleman Williams, *The Great Evasion* (Chicago, 1974), especially pp. 147-166.

[19] Neil H. Jacoby, *Corporate Power and Social Responsibility* (New York, 1973).

[20] Pendleton Herring, *The Politics of Democracy* (New York, 1940).

in part because it is perceived to be the best method for containing social revolution." It is a pet theory of mine that the United States developed as it has in part because its principal crop, corn, exports badly and hence came to be used in an organic cycle of corn-animals-manures-pork and beef-more corn, and so on. Perhaps the political system that developed along with this isn't very exportable, either, despite the faith of its adherents. That faith is waning, too. Most Americans no longer expect Chile and Bolivia to be like Kansas and Missouri. This book shows how different they are. Despite much they can learn from one another, I believe they will go on being different.

THE NEW CORPORATISM

Corporatism and Development in the Iberic-Latin World: Persistent Strains and New Variations *

Howard J. Wiarda

Wherever one looks in the Iberic-Latin world, corporatist or neocorporatist forms of authority and sociopolitical organization appear to have staged a resurgence. One is used to thinking about such traditional states and societies as Nicaragua, Ecuador, and Paraguay in terms of their authoritarian and corporatist structures, and Portugal has by now been a self-proclaimed corporatist state for some 40 years. We shall have more to say regarding these "persistent strains" later on; what concerns us now is the apparent reemergence of corporatist ideology and organization in a variety of rapidly modernizing systems. Brazil, for instance, has always been less corporatist than Portugal in theory and in law, but today is probably just as corporatist in actual practice.[1] Research on Mexico has by this time largely abandoned the approach that stressed that country's quasi-democratic character or its supposed democratic aspirations in favor of an approach that takes Mexico on its own terms and analyzes its frankly authoritarian and corporatist structures.[2] The resurgence of *Peronismo* in Argentina clearly carries with it echoes of the corporatist, in this case "justicialist," solutions of the 1930's and 1940's. In Peru the military elite has vowed to carry through a "revolution from above" employing

* The field research on which this assessment is based was conducted in Latin America, chiefly Brazil, from May to November, 1972, and in Spain and Portugal, mainly the latter, from November, 1972, until July, 1973. The research was assisted by a grant from the Foreign Area Fellowship Program, Joint Committee on Latin American Studies of the American Council of Learned Societies and the Social Science Research Council. The assessment here presented also draws heavily on previous field research, principally in the Dominican Republic and Brazil, and is part of a larger ongoing study dealing with development in the Iberic-Latin tradition. Iêda Siqueira Wiarda assisted in the research and offered numerous useful comments on the draft of this article.

[1] See Philippe C. Schmitter, "The 'Portugalization' of Brazil?" in Alfred Stepan, ed., *Authoritarian Brazil* (New Haven, 1973); and Riordan Roett, *Brazil: Politics in a Patrimonialist Society* (Boston, 1972).

[2] See especially Susan Kaufman Purcell, "Decision-Making in an Authoritarian Regime: Mexico" (Paper presented at the 1971 Annual Meeting of the American Political Science Association, Chicago, September 7-11).

corporatist ideas and organizations to structure popular participation at the grass-roots and intermediary levels and reaching up to the Council of Ministers and the central state apparatus.[3] And of course in Chile we have seen both Allende's abortive design to install a unicameral legislature based on corporative functional representation, as well as the plans by the generals that overthrew him to inaugurate a similarly functionally representative congress (though obviously the groups represented and their weights would be significantly different in these two designs) and to deal with price, wage, and production issues through a government regulated and controlled system of *gremio-sindicato* relations.

What is occurring? Is there really a resurgence of corporatist theory and organization, not only in those countries mentioned but elsewhere in the Iberic-Latin world as well? How is that possible, given the general discrediting of corporatist and integralist ideas during the war and in the Nuremberg Trials, and also given the fact that we generally associate corporatism with a specific time and historical period, whose high point had already come—and apparently gone!—in Latin America? Perhaps most disturbing is the fact that corporatism, which we identify with right-wing and reactionary regimes, has, in Chile under Allende, the revolutionary military regime in Peru, and maybe even in Castro's Cuba, provided a form of organization and a strong ideological component for the Left. Corporatism, thus, can be identified not just with traditional and conservative regimes but with a great variety of diversely modernizing ones. How then does one begin sorting out these conflicting currents, the "persistent strains" and the "new variations" of corporatism, the seeming reemergence of a system we had previously thought to be discredited or consigned to the ash cans of history? This essay attempts to respond to some of these issues. Although it draws illustrative materials chiefly from the Luso-Brazilian world, the theme has important implications for the Hispanic one as well.

The Corporative Framework: Approaches and Definitions

In 1936 Mihaïl Manoïlesco proclaimed that the twentieth century would be "the century of corporatism," just as the nine-

---

[3] David Scott Palmer, *"Revolution from Above": Military Government and Popular Participation in Peru* (Ithaca, N.Y., 1973).

teenth had been the century of liberalism,[4] a fact that has in-spired the title Philippe Schmitter gives to his essay in this·collec-tion. That prediction has not been borne out by subsequent history, although in the context of the 1930's, with the apparent breakdown of liberalism and capitalism and the unacceptability of Stalinist socialism, it was more understandable than it is now. The 1930's were probably the high point of corporatist ideas and movements, not just in the Iberic-Latin world and in the fascist systems of Italy and Germany, but throughout much of Europe and even North America. In such diverse nations as Holland, Belgium, Switzerland, France, Norway, Austria, Poland, Sweden, and the United States (clearly not just the Latin and Catholic countries) a great variety of corporatist agencies and institutions were created. These in-cluded wage and price agencies, labor relations boards and tri-bunals, councils of state, and functionally representative organs of various sorts; and while none of these countries ever became full-fledged corporative states, as occurred in southern Europe, their corporative structures have both persisted and expanded. Indeed it is one of Portugal's arguments in response to European criticism of its corporative system that in fact the other European countries have since the war been practicing a disguised form of corporatism, and that even in the United States, though the labels are different, corporatism finds expression in the Wage and Price Board, the Cost of Living Council, and a variety of other agencies.[5]

In the Iberic-Latin context corporatism found an even more hospitable environment. In Spain the Falange provided some of the initial rationalizations for the Franco regime, and while by this time the Falange as a political movement and corporatism as an ideology have been relegated to distinctly secondary roles in the Spanish system, corporatist ideas and organizations still lie at the

---

[4] Mihaïl Manoïlesco, *Le siècle du corporatisme* (Paris, 1938).

[5] See especially Philippe C. Schmitter, "Corporatist Interest Representation and Public Policy-Making in Portugal" (Paper presented at the 1972 Annual Meeting of the American Political Science Association, Washington, Septem-ber 5-9). See also Matthew H. Elbow, *French Corporative Theory, 1789-1948* (New York, 1953); Samuel H. Beer, *Modern British Politics* (London, 1965); Stein Rokkan, "Norway: Numerical Democracy and Corporate Pluralism" in R. Dahl, ed., *Political Opposition in Western Democracies* (New Haven, 1966) pp. 70-115. Nor should one forget the NLRB, the WPA, and other corpora-tive agencies born in the U.S. in the 1930's.

heart of the system of labor relations, representation, and the like.[6] Portugal remains the only openly and often proudly corporatist system extant, the only one of the numerous corporatist experiments initiated in the interwar period to have been carried through to full fruition—though more recently corporatism in Portugal has evolved in ways not altogether different from the Spanish system. In Brazil under Vargas the operative agencies of the *Estado Novo* and the structure of labor relations, social assistance, and the like were all patterned after the model of a corporate state. In Argentina, Mexico, Chile, the Dominican Republic, and elsewhere, similar forms of corporatist organization were attempted, though in the American context they seldom called themselves by that name. It shows how pervasive corporatism was in the 1930's and 1940's indeed (and also how confusing for foreign observers) that even such left-of-center movements as APRA (Alianza Popular Revolucionaria Americana) in Peru and the MNR (Movimiento Nacionalista Revolucionario) in Bolivia embraced some of its principal ideas and were hence often stamped—mistakenly and often ludicrously— with the fascist label.

It should be made clear at the outset that when we use the term corporatism, we are using it in two distinct, but often interrelated, senses. The first refers to the manifestly corporatist experiments and regimes of the 1930's and 1940's and may be defined as a system of authority and interest representation, derived chiefly (though not exclusively) from Catholic social thought, stressing functional representation, the integration of labor and capital into a vast web of hierarchically ordered, "harmonious," monopolistic, and functionally determined units (or *corporations*), and guided and directed by the state.[7] The second sense in which we use the term corporatism is broader, encompassing a far longer cultural-historic tradition stretching back to the origins of the Iberic-Latin systems and embodying a dominant form of sociopolitical organization that is similarly hierarchical, elitist, authoritarian, bureaucratic, Catholic, patrimonialist, and corporatist to its core.[8]

---

[6] See especially Martín Bugarola, *Entidades Intermedias y Representación Política* (Madrid, 1970); and *Desarrollo Político: Estado, Movimiento y Sociedad* (Madrid, 1968).

[7] This definition derives from Schmitter, "Portugalization of Brazil?" p. 3; and Elbow, *Corporative Theory*, p. 11-12.

[8] This tradition is emphasized in Howard J. Wiarda, "Toward a Framework for the Study of Political Change in the Iberic-Latin Tradition: The Corporative Model," *World Politics*, XXV (January, 1973), 206-35; see also

Naturally, these two definitions and perspectives on corporatism overlap and are interconnected at various points. For one thing, many of the corporatist theorists of the interwar period sought to ground their systems in the historic structures and forms of organizations which had their roots in Roman and canon law, the Thomistic tradition, the feudal system of guilds and professional associations, and the characteristic, Suárezian sixteenth-century political forms which persisted so long.[9] For another, the corporatist experiments of the 1930's may be looked upon as a twentieth-century extension of that historic tradition, a way of handling the new "social question," of absorbing the rising labor elements into the system, in the same characteristic hierarchical, elitist, and corporatist fashion that the Iberic-Latin systems had been absorbing new elites for centuries.[10] Despite these overlaps, what makes the distinction between these two definitions and senses of corporatism useful for our purposes is that it helps us understand what occurred in the Iberic-Latin world in the postwar period. It should be emphasized thus that while the discredited forms or labels of corporatism associated with fascism were submerged or rebaptized under different names, the older *corporatist tradition* remained both intact and paramount. And it goes a long way toward explaining the supposed present resurgence of corporatism if we understand that beneath the democratic façades of the postwar constitutions and the liberal posturing, frequently so as to qualify for Alliance for Progress assistance, the historic political culture of corporatist values and organization was present all the time, disguised to be sure, but still extant and indeed dominant. Corporatism has now reemerged full-blown to the surface.

There are a series of neglected hypotheses, really at this stage mere suggestions, relating to the evolution of corporatist ideology and institutions in Latin America in the postwar period, and the United States presence there, that ought to be explored. For if, as the Peruvians argue and the analysis presented here implies,

---

the edited volume brought together by the same author, *Politics and Social Change in Latin America: The Distinct Tradition* (Amherst, 1974).

[9] See for instance João Pinto da Costa Leite, *A Doutrina Corporativa em Portugal* (Lisbon, 1966); Fernando Campos, *A Solução Corporativa* (Lisbon, 1939); and Marcello Caetano, *O Sistema Corporativa* (Lisbon, 1938).

[10] Howard J. Wiarda, "The Portuguese Corporative System: Basic Structures and Current Functions" (Paper presented at Workshop on Modern Portugal, University of New Hampshire, October 10-14, 1973).

corporatism is a dominant sociopolitical tradition in Latin America and about the only one of the three great isms that correspond closely to her history and political culture, then why, in Octavio Paz's words, is Latin America in 1973 still a continent "in search of a system"? Why is it that neither liberalism nor socialism has effectively taken hold, why does Latin America remain a "heap of ruined [liberal and social-democratic] ideas and victims' bones" (Paz), why has it failed to develop its own patterns of political thought and to evolve, at least up to now, its own indigenous developmental models?[11]

A key reason, it may be suggested, is that World War II, the Nazi experience and Nuremberg so poisoned our thinking, not only as regards the manifest atrocities of the Italian and German regimes but also as regards all corporatist and integralist experiments, that Latin America was largely forced to set aside or submerge the one ism that was true to its own traditions and with which it could function effectively. This is, in essence, a new twist on the Cold War-dependency thesis. For by totally and indiscriminately discrediting corporatism in World War II's aftermath, we forced Latin America to choose artificially between democracy and liberalism, United States style, on the one hand (the Alliance for Progress, the Peace Corps, United States-conceived developmentalism), which was hardly in accord with Latin America's own character and tradition, and revolutionary socialism à la the Soviet Union on the other, which was equally unacceptable. In other words, the United States forced Latin America to select between false alternatives by ruling out a middle way, an indigenous solution, that might have enabled the continent to escape some of the upheavals and chaotic civil-military alternations of the postwar period. Furthermore, the development literature then gaining currency supported this thesis by positing that modernization and pluralism were closely correlated, that development and the growth of a liberal democratic polity went hand in hand.

But corporatism, we already know, is an infinitely flexible and adaptable system, not nearly so rigid or impenetrable as the development literature suggests; and left to her own modes of organization, Latin America would likely have bridged the gap between the traditionalism of the pre-1930 period and the participatory demands of the present in greater peace and order. But our dis-

---

[11] See his "Op-Ed" essay in *New York Times*, October 21, 1973.

crediting of corporatism, together with the unilinear, ethnocentric developmental models we used, disallowed that possibility and thus helped precipitate the violent oscillation and swinging of the political pendulum during this period. It is only now in the 1970's, with the decline of the United States cultural, economic and political influence throughout the hemisphere, along with the general discrediting of the United States-based developmentalist model, that Latin America is again, as it did in the 1930's, searching for indigenous solutions to its own social and developmental problems. It is probably no accident that it is precisely at this time that corporatist and neocorporatist solutions should reemerge.[12]

Corporatism, thus, is not to be equated with naziism or fascism, nor are the Latin experiments in this direction to be considered as merely less developed versions of the fascist model. The interpretation that the Latins "just aren't up to it" reflects a typically Northern European and North American prejudice toward the Southern Europeans and especially the Latin countries, and finds expression in a host of anthologies and studies, all compiled by North Americans or Northern Europeans, attempting to look at Iberic-Latin *fascism* in this biased perspective.[13] For despite some rather obvious and usually superficial parallels, corporatism in the Iberic-Latin tradition is a distinct and separate type, fundamentally different from the fascism and naziism of the popular stereotypes. Authoritarian surely, as in the Linz formulation regarding Spain, which posits that authoritarianism is a distinct political form, neither liberal nor totalitarian, with dynamics and characteristics of its own, and without necessarily implying a transition to the one or the other of these other ideal types; but fascist not.[14] *Fascism* and *fascist* may still be

---

[12] For a fuller discussion of corporatism and U.S.-Latin American relations see Fredrick B. Pike's essay in this volume; also Glen Dealy, "The Tradition of Monistic Democracy in Latin America," *Journal of the History of Ideas* (July, 1974) and reprinted in Wiarda, *Politics and Social Change*. On the biases of "developmentalism" see Susanne Bodenheimer, *The Ideology of Developmentalism: The American Paradigm-Surrogate for Latin American Studies* (Beverly Hills, Cal., 1971); Douglas Chalmers, "The Demystification of Development" in Chalmers, ed., *Changing Latin America* (New York, 1972) pp. 109-22; and Howard J. Wiarda, "Elites in Crisis: The Decline of the Old Order and the Fragmentation of the New in Latin America" (Unpublished ms.: Ohio State University, Mershon Center, 1970), esp. pp. 33-46.

[13] Especially Ernst Nolte, *Three Faces of Fascism* (New York, 1966).

[14] Juan Linz, "An Authoritarian Regime: Spain" in Erik Allardt and Stein Rokkan, eds., *Mass Politics* (New York, 1970), pp. 251-83. Linz's formulation has recently been applied successfully to Mexico and Brazil; it could be

useful labels but they can hardly be applied in the Iberic-Latin context with any precision or accuracy. As an analytic term *fascism,* like *totalitarianism,* may have outlived its usefulness.

But if corporatism is not to be equated with fascism, it cannot be seen as a wholly or necessarily reactionary, backward-looking ideology either. That idea too comes out of the fascism studies, the belief that corporatism represents a turning back of the clock on the part of elite and bourgeois elements, an effort to restore the status quo ante, a reaction to unstable chaotic republicanism and liberalism, a means of preserving or restoring traditional privileges and of keeping the rising lower classes from overthrowing the system from below. There is some degree of truth in these allegations, of course, but we have already seen that corporatism may take a distinctly modernizing and leftist bent and in fact there is a great variety of options and alternatives open within the corporatist framework.

Philippe Schmitter, for example, has identified four schools of corporatist thought, and by this time in actual practice there are undoubtedly several more. Schmitter distinguishes between (1) a social Christian form as exemplified by such thinkers as Albert de Mun, the Marquis de la Tour du Pin, and Joaquín Azpiazu, and whose ideas found expression in the encyclicals *Rerum Novarum* of Leo XIII and *Quadragesimo Anno* of Pius XI, and later in a variety of Catholic and Christian democratic movements;[15] (2) an authoritarian, bureaucratic, nationalist, secular, *modernizing* school whose theorists include Manoïlesco and many of the Italian corporatist ideologues;[16] (3) a radical (in the French sense), parliamentary, bourgeois, "solidarist" tradition as exemplified by Léon Bourgeois, Charles Gide, and Emile Durkheim;[17] and (4) a leftist, socialist, "syndicalist" line of thought whose spokesmen

---

suggested that with some modification his model of the "authoritarian system" could be applied to all the Iberic-Latin nations.

[15] For this tradition, in English, see especially Elbow, *Corporative Theory;* and Azpiazu, *The Corporative State* (London, 1951). Also, Michael Fogarty, *Christian Democracy in Western Europe, 1820-1953* (Notre Dame, 1957).

[16] Manoïlesco, *Le siècle du corporatisme,* is the classic statement of this position. See also Roland Sarti, "Fascist Modernization in Italy: Traditional or Modern?" *American Historical Review,* LXXV (April, 1970), 1029-45.

[17] For Durkheim's argument see his "The Solidarity of Occupational Groups" in Talcott Parsons *et al., Theories of Society* (New York, 1965), pp. 356-63.

would include Saint-Simon, Sorel, and perhaps the guild social-ists.[18] For illustrative purposes, we could say that the Spanish and Portuguese systems represent perhaps a combination of the first and second types, while the Allende regime in Chile and perhaps that of Bosch in the Dominican Republic and of Goulart in Brazil were closer to categories three and four. The Peruvian regime may not fit any of these categories very well and may necessitate still a fifth type. In any case, what this categorization illustrates is both the diversity of the corporative approach, as well as the great variety of regimes that can fit under this rubric. Clearly there is abundant room here for progressive, leftist corporatist regimes as well as for regressive rightist ones, and many shades in between.

Corporatism, thus, is not a mere throwback to an earlier and conservative model of society and polity, nor can it be lumped together with the fascist and nazi regimes in a blanket condemna-tion. Rather what we are looking at in the corporatist model is a complex and varied form, distinct from both liberalism and totalitarianism, with a long tradition of its own and a great body of political thought and sociology, and with which, because we have condemned it out of hand or rendered it outmoded in our socio-logical analyses, we are almost wholly unfamiliar. Moreover, corporatism can be and has been a progressive, modernizing tradi-tion, not only in the type three and four categories but also in the type one category as exemplified by Chilean Christian Democracy and the type two category as exemplified in part by present-day Brazil. Overall, given our deep-rooted prejudices regarding corpo-ratism, what needs emphasis is the distinctiveness and viability of the corporative routes to development as opposed to the liberal and socialist ones, the diversity and complexity of its forms, and the fact that what we are dealing with here is literally "a fourth world of development" in the Iberic-Latin tradition, or a third "great ism," which requires analysis and understanding on its own terms and in its own context, not through some frame of reference derived from another tradition and inapplicable to the Iberic-Latin one.[19]

---

[18] For example, G. D. H. Cole, *Guild Socialism* (New York, 1921).

[19] See the contrasting but complementary comments in Philippe C. Schmit-ter, "Paths to Political Development in Latin America" in Chalmers, *Changing Latin America,* pp. 83-105; Wiarda, "Change in Iberic-Latin Tradition"; and Dealy, "Democracy in Latin America."

Origins and Antecedents: The Corporative Tradition in
Historic Perspective

Within the confines of the present essay, no detailed tracing
of the corporative tradition and its present-day expressions can be
attempted. Nonetheless, some of the origins and broad lines of
this tradition can be delineated and some of its contemporary ramifications noted. In the conclusion we shall be looking at some of
the implications and problems of the corporative approach.

The political-cultural origins of the Iberic-Latin tradition of
corporatism lie in the Roman period.[20] Indeed, one might argue
that any effort to understand present-day development issues in
the Iberic-Latin world must recognize and come to grips with the
pattern and imprint that Roman civilization indelibly stamped on
its far-flung empire. Rome gave Iberia a degree of unity it had
never had before, a system (and model) of central administration
and of state bureaucracy, and its most characteristic forms of
politico-military organization. Unity and a certain cultural coher-
ence were also forged through a common language and law, and
eventually through Christianity. Moreover, the Romans gave to
Iberia its prevailing conception of citizenship, its system of group
rights and charters, its organization of social hierarchy and class,
its similarly hierarchical structure of laws and orders, its stoic emphasis upon "virtue" rather than material gain, its patrimonialist
state apparatus, its conception of the "civilizing" mission of empire.[21] And if later ideologues like Salazar and Caetano are cor-

---

[20] Roman rule in Iberia is summarized in Rafael Altamira, *A History of
Spain,* trans. Muna Lee (New York, 1949), chap. 3.

[21] Although by present standards this provides small consolation to many
of those affected, it is interesting to note that Portugal treats its African subjects in much the same way it has historically treated its own aspiring classes.
In the corporative system it is characteristic that successive groups have been
successively "civilized" into the prevailing hierarchical system under the tutelage of the patrimonial state. First, the nobility was civilized in this way and
taught the proper elitist values, then the rising business and merchant class,
then the emergent middle sectors, then urban labor groups, and eventually
the rural peasants. In this seemingly inherently hierarchical and continuously
tutelary system, it has now become, from the Portuguese perspective, the
turn of the native Africans. That is, they may be accepted to full citizenship
and accommodated to the system, but only if they accept that system's values
and givens. In this sense the Portuguese colonies—first in Brazil and now in
Africa—represent a direct extension of the Portuguese metropole, a condition
which many in these "extensions" are no longer willing to accept. On this
theme see Laurence S. Graham, "Portugal: The Bureaucracy of Empire"

rect, Rome also laid the basis for the philosophical, legal, and organizational structure of the corporative state.

Over four centuries of close association with Rome and as a part of its empire helped make the Roman influence in the peninsula permanent and provided it with the foundations on which future Iberian civilization would develop. Moreover, the long-lasting success and logical clarity of the administrative structure strongly impressed the statesmen and jurists of later centuries, especially when, as Roman law and the achievements of its empire were rediscovered, it was fused and blended with the Christian, Thomistic-Suárezian conception to serve as the model for the modern, fifteenth- and sixteenth-century structures of the Spanish and Portuguese states. The Roman system not only served as the basis for modern, state-building royal authority and for the extension of that system to the New World, but it also served as the form of organization toward which virtually all monarchs and, later, *caudillos* and perhaps even republicans aspired.[22]

In the meantime, other characteristic forms and modes of behavior emerged which, in terms of coming to grips with contemporary Iberic-Latin development issues, merit far more detailed attention than they have thus far received. The collapse of the Roman Empire had paved the way for a Visigothic conquest of Iberia, which represented more an overlay on the Roman tradition than a submerging of it. The Visigoths helped institutionalize Christianity through an official state church; their rule led also to a hardening of absolutism and of authoritarian, centralized rule. The centuries-long Reconquest of the Peninsula from the Moors was also crucial in terms of institutionalizing some other characteristic forms of sociopolitical organization, but that is a subject area that few social scientists have explored.[23] During the Reconquest the church became more than ever an arm of the civil authority and the civil and military realms were fused (perhaps never again to be separated, as we imply in our use of the hyphenated term civil-military relations). And as the Reconquest proceeded,

(Paper presented at the Workshop on Modern Portugal, University of New Hampshire, Durham, October 10-14, 1973). The Roman and Thomistic conceptions underlying this approach and conception are striking.

[22] Brian Chapman, *The Profession of Government* '(London, 1959), Chap. 1; and John Henry Merryman, *The Civil Law Tradition: An Introduction to the Legal Systems of Western Europe and Latin America* (Stanford, 1969).

[23] Except for the flawed but still interesting work by Ronald Glassman, *Political History of Latin America* (New York, 1969).

the power of the nobility and military orders frequently became territorial, often as a result of acquisitions by or grants to them of the lands and peoples they had reconquered. Each lord was sovereign in his own realm, and an elaborate network of vassalage and *patrão*-dependent relations began tardily to grow up. The system of special *foros,* or "rights," which defined the relationship of the citizen individually and of the community collectively to its overlord, who could be the monarch, noble, church, military order, or even municipality, thus became the means by which political obligation was defined. The forms of authority were organized hierarchically and in a traditional patrimonialist fashion in which the wealth and lands of the area, as well as the persons living in it, were considered a part of the overlord's private preserve. No separation existed between the private and public domains.[24]

It is out of this matrix of forces that the separate kingdom of Portugal began to emerge in the twelfth century and from which stem some of the dominant characteristics of the Luso-Brazilian corporative-patrimonialist tradition. This period of nation-building and consolidation is also woefully understudied, but it is critical in shaping the future course of political relations, both in the Iberian Old World and in the New.

As Portugal emerged, wresting more and more territory from the Moors on the one hand and fending off León and Spain on the other, its internal politics were dominated chiefly by the struggle between the king and his nobles, *os senhores territoriais.* In return for loyalty and service, the king was obliged to grant land, titles, privileges, and *foros.* The landed aristocrats hence derived their positions from the king and in turn they owed him allegiance. The church, the military, the nobility also surrounded the king like a

---

[24] Patrimonialism is one of Weber's forms of traditional authority; see the discussion in Reinhard Bendix, *Max Weber: An Intellectual Portrait* (Garden City, 1960), pp. 329-81. The Iberic-Latin systems, in a sense, have turned Weber on his head, for not only have they remained cast in the patrimonialist mold without evolving other forms of authority in the Weberian scheme, but patrimonialism itself has proved infinitely flexible, adaptive, and capable of modernization. It should perhaps be noted that at this point the focus of the article shifts to Portugal and to the use of Portuguese terms; although much of the emphasis here is on an *Iberian* tradition and though the parallels and differences with Spain are well worth developing, it was my assignment in this collection to focus on the Luso-Brazilian world, leaving the Spanish and Hispanic to other contributors. Nonetheless the thrust of the article remains toward exploring corporatism and development in the broader Iberic-Latin world.

"college of influentials"; all came to be a part of the same centralizing, bureaucratic state apparatus. Governance came to be exercised through a number of consulting organs and councils, and through the king's ministers who served as his personal agents. The system remained one of rule from above, of elite or royal protection of those below them in the hierarchy, in return for fealty and certain obligations. As it emerged, the system was classically patrimonialist.[25]

Among the nobles, corporate entities, municipalities, and the like existent in the emerging Portuguese system, the state became overwhelmingly preeminent. The state was the regulator of both social structure and economic life. It was the state, specifically the crown, that granted the privileges, titles, and monopolies that bought the loyalty of the nobles, that helped centralize royal power, and that made the system work. Using this model of a patronage-patrimonialist system, a succession of kings helped make Portugal the first centralized nation-state in Europe and probably the most developed institutionally of that time.[26]

It was a system based on status, hierarchy, and royal favor. Each class, as well as each individual, was bound to accept its assigned place in society. Eventually a commercial-mercantile elite would grow up in Portugal alongside and overlapping with the landed nobility, and it was they, along with the crown, who in the fourteenth century launched the conquest of the vast Portuguese empire. The patrimonialist state apparatus continued to regulate the entire process of economic and political infrastructure building, however, and hence as a class system began to emerge in Portugal, the structure of state patrimonialism continued to coexist along with it and even superior to and independent from the various elite rivalries and class changes occurring below. Commerce, war, and colonization were all a part of the same extension of royal

---

[25] The discussion here is derived chiefly from Manuel Paulo Merêa, *O Poder Real e as Cortes* (Coimbra, 1923); Raymundo Faoro, *Os Donos do Poder: Formação do Patronato Político Brasileiro* (Porto Alegre, 1958); and Henrique de Gama Barros, *Historia da Administração Pública em Portugal nos Séculos XII-XV* (Lisbon, 1945).

[26] Anthropologist Sidney M. Greenfield has carried out some very exciting research in Portugal on the origins of this elaborate national patronage system, perhaps the first and most highly developed of its kind. I am indebted to Professor Greenfield for sharing his insights with me; for the approach see also Arnold Stricken and Sidney M. Greenfield, eds., *Structure and Process in Latin America: Patronage, Clientage, and Power Systems* (Albuquerque, New Mexico, 1972).

authority and of an ever more elaborate model of corporate-patri-
monialist state organization. In the promotion of trade and commerce overseas, hence, Portugal never developed a full-fledged
capitalist system, nor was capitalism the motor force driving Portuguese colonization and development: state capitalism or mer-
cantilism, yes; but capitalism in the sense of individual entrepre-
neurship, laissez-faire, and free enterprise, no. Hence while commerce and capitalism of a sort grew up alongside the traditional
agrarian and feudal structure, the former never replaced the latter.
The economic variable remained subordinate to the political one,
and in the Iberic-Latin tradition that probably remains true today.
Meanwhile, the one constant remained the patrimonialist state apparatus, around which all classes and individuals revolved and
from which they derived their legitimacy.[27]

Because this system is so strong and so omnipresent, it merits
further description. One can say thus that the Portuguese state is
modeled after that of the imperial Roman Caesars, overlain with
Visigothic, Thomistic, and feudal influences. It is absolutist and
administrative. The sovereign exercises power in the name of the
general interest, the res publica. He requires all powers and pre-
rogatives for his superior mission of governance. Society remains
dominated by the idea and presence of the state. The land of the
realm, its wealth, as well as its individual members, "belong to" the
monarch (or, in present-day parlance, the state). The crown or
the state may give part of its patrimony in the form of land, favors,
or monopoly to certain groups or individuals in return for a *jura-
mento a fidelidade*. The system thus remains highly personal and
vassalistic. But these relations, it should be emphasized, are not
wholly one way; rather, they are governed by rules of reciprocal
favors and loyalties in the classic *patrão*-client pattern.[28]

The crown or the sovereign exercises power in an authoritarian
fashion, but that power can never be "total" without violating the
system of mutual obligations and restraints. Power is also limited
by natural law in the Catholic-Thomistic tradition. It is limited
further by the traditional rights and *foros* of the orders and munic-

---

[27] Faoro, *Os Donos do Poder;* and José Calvet de Magalhães, *Historia do
Pensamento Econômico em Portugal: Da Idade Média ao Mercantilismo*
(Coimbra, 1967). For the contrast with an emerging capitalist system see
George Masselman's study of the Dutch empire, *The Cradle of Colonialism*
(New Haven, 1963).

[28] Faoro, *Os Donos do Poder;* and Gama Barros.

ipalities. When the king overstepped his authority, when he violated the charters and pacts that governed vassalage relations, he was likely to face a revolt on the part of the nobility, whose bloody uprisings continued throughout the twelfth and thirteenth centuries.[29] Custom, tradition, and the family also served as constraints on absolute authority.

The king had the supreme *fiscalizing* power, to regulate and pass on all contracts and agreements. He also garnered the power to confirm the acts of the *senhor*, for example, his military service or his right to a place in the *cortes*. Thus the king was not only supreme in his own right, but his sovereignty was enhanced by his ability almost literally to handpick those who sat in his parliament or tribunal. It is not hard to understand, thus, why the principle of separation of powers never became firmly established in the Iberic-Latin tradition as it did in the Anglo-American. Another royal lever came from the fact that the same individual would frequently be the recipient of grants of land or monopoly from the crown, while at the same time serving as the king's personal agent in that territory or municipality. The political evolution of Portugal during this period thus served to develop and unify the state, through the king and his patrimonialist state apparatus.[30]

The rediscovery of Roman law during this period gave special impetus to these trends. The *corpus juris civis* provided the model of a powerful state, absolutist in character, in which administration, not politics, assured order and justice. The Roman law favored the consolidation of the state against excesses, violence, and feudal rights. It contributed to the growth of royal power and also made it absolutist. The monarch became the focus of the *direito positivo*. He was the defender of "the public interest" in return for which the nation granted him broad, virtually absolute power. This then emerges as the Iberic concept of popular sovereignty, and it finds powerful echoes in the rule of Salazar and other such Caesarist regimes.[31]

The progress of royal power resulted in the weakening of the nobility and independent military orders, in the development of

---

[29] Later corporatist theorists, in harking back to the supposed order, stability, and unity of this era, largely ignored its violence, terror, conflict, and misery. In fact the medieval era and guild system, which the corporatists so romanticized, was not always very pleasant; see Gama Barros, IV, 113-72.

[30] Faoro, *Os Donos do Poder;* Merêa, *O Poder Real.*

[31] Merêa, *O Poder Real,* p. 9.

general power, in limits on seignorial power, in the affirmation of civilian authority over the church and its inclusion as still another arm of governance, in the development of central administrative organs, in the intervention of the crown in all phases of political and economic life, and in the widening delegation of certain goods and services in return for support and loyalty. Eventually the doctrine of the illegality of usurping royal authority emerged, that the king is not only superior in relation to other authorities but that he or his delegated agents have a true monopoly. The doctrine as evolved asserts that the rights and *foros* of the various societal and corporate units come only through concessions from the king and not from any inherent right. In the sixteenth century the extension of this idea and the full consolidation of the crown's power led to royal absolutism. It is this conflict between royal authority on the one hand and the rights of the classes on the other that determined so much of Portuguese history—until the nineteenth century added a new, liberal, and republican idea on top of that older conflict. This complicated political relations somewhat and forced the ancient patrimonialist state model to further adapt and accommodate, but it by no means destroyed the model itself.[32]

In contrast to the emerging absolutist doctrines and practices, the nobles and *homens bons* continued to assert the crown's obligation to defend their traditional rights, to guard good customs, and to protect the rights of the people. This gave rise to the concept that the relation between the crown and the classes was governed by a kind of pact and maintained by mutual accords. It is this system of the *magistratura judicial* that the contemporary corporate state tried to resurrect in its extension of the patrimonialist state apparatus and its "protective tutelage" over the rising labor classes. In the earlier period, just as at present, the inviolability of these *foros* was always invoked in conflicts with the king, or the state, and with varying degrees of success. The various "colleges," orders, brotherhoods, *gremios*, municipalities, and corporations all claimed to be governed by such pacts or charters, and they sought to reserve the right to withdraw their loyalty or foment rebellion if these norms were violated. At the same time the king and later the state reserved the right to pass on the charters of these groups, to grant

---

[32] *Ibid.* See also Richard M. Morse, "The Heritage of Latin America" in Louis Hartz *et al., The Founding of New Societies* (New York, 1964), pp. 123-77; reprinted in Wiarda, *Politics and Social Change.*

or withhold recognition and thus regulate and control the group's participation in the national life, and even to refuse to respect these privileges when the sovereign had just cause (one can see how this pattern is still characteristic of the relations of the state to the university in contemporary Latin America, for example). Throughout Portuguese history, indeed, this remained the dominant conflict: between the centralizing, absolutist forces and tendencies on the one hand, and the defenders of corporate privilege and group *foros* on the other. Those privileges and rights could be extended, to be sure—first to broaden the elite, then to the aspiring middle sectors, more recently to labor and the peasants. But again it is the system of paternalism, patronage, and privilege, exercised through an evolving corporate structure, that remains dominant. *Never* in any of this long history of conflict, even up to the present, was there a strong force arguing for genuine popular sovereignty, democratization, or participation in the Anglo-American mold.[33]

Implied in the above is the fact that the Portuguese *cortes* would never become an effective agent for popular representation, and it is purely wishful thinking that leads particularly English and American writers to see the seeds of democracy there. The *cortes* originated in the royal curia or council of the king. Its chief functions were consultative and in the administration of the laws, not the making of them. Although the *cortes* at several points accumulated some modicum of authority, no real separation of powers existed and the *cortes* always remained secondary to the real centers of patronage and influence. The *cortes* existed largely at the king's pleasure and call. Represented in it were the nobles and *homens bons;* the church was also represented along with the masters of the major military orders, the *procuradores* of the principal cities, and other corporate interests. The *cortes* could only be called into session by the king, and its members were required to heed this call as an obligation of their vassalage.[34]

The ordinary *curia* became an administrative arm of the king; however, the extraordinary curia gradually devolved some modest economic and legislative functions and was involved in the great political questions of that time. But as the *cortes* sought to expand its powers, it was called less and less frequently. The major *inter-*

---

[33] Merêa, *O Poder Real.* An excellent contemporary analysis of "o sistema" is Philippe C. Schmitter, *Interest Conflict and Political Change in Brazil* (Stanford, 1971).

[34] Merêa, *O Poder Real.*

esses, church, nobility, and military, were all represented, as were some persons who were there because of their elevated positions. The franchise was always limited or entirely nonexistent; the *povo* were represented by their "betters." Municipalities also tended to choose local notables that *andam no governo,* that "went along with the government" (just as they do today in a system of "party" representation). What vote existed was ordinarily for an assigned list of the *homens bons,* the elite; and the king would often suggest for whom one should vote, naturally those he trusted and those who enjoyed his *confiança.*

The *cortes* met by separate estates, each jealous of guarding its own privileges. It would meet irregularly and generally for about a month when it met at all. It gradually acquired a modicum of power over the purse and in 1372 refused a request of the king for the first time. It might be consulted by the king on war, gained some limited authority to suggest and modify laws, and could even exercise some choice in the selection of a monarch in cases where the dynasty had ended. The *cortes* remained limited, however, never employing the supremacist doctrine that a handful of its members occasionally advocated. The king most often legislated without the *cortes* through decree-law. The power of the people thus remained virtually nil, and the sovereign reserved the right to revoke the rights even of the elites. It was the popular sectors, as Gama Barros shows, beginning to emerge in the fifteenth century, which probably had the most interest in the meeting of the *cortes,* but they were the weakest and had virtually no direct representation. The elites and *homens bons* did have representation, but they had no more interest in promoting popular government than had the monarch. Hence in the great, evolving conflicts between royal authority and the power of the state on the one hand and the nobles and corporate interests on the other, whose relative influence varied over time depending on the force of each and the vicissitudes of politics, the people never had any voice at all.[35]

Was the *cortes* ever representative of society or the nation? Emphatically not, at least in the Anglo-American sense of representation. In the Portuguese sense the *cortes* was roughly representative, however, for when a Spaniard or Portuguese speaks of society or the nation, he tends to think of it in terms of its component corporate units: the religious institutions, the munici-

---

[35] *Ibid.*

palities, the corporations and *sindicatos*, the *gremios*, the army, the grand foundations and autarchies, and the like.[36] Not included in this conception of course is the general public or public opinion, for interpreting the *general will* out of the conglomerate of *interesses* is the special province of the ruler. Hence at best we can say that the *cortes* was occasionally an imperfect representation of the classes —as most parliaments in Latin America are today. Its membership was limited only to certain elites and it was their rights that were protected. The general public was not represented, and individual rights were protected only insofar as they corresponded to those of the *interesses* or to "the common good" (as defined of course by the king). The *cortes* was restrictive also in its elective character, local notables or the king's choices. However the *cortes* was representative of society's major corporate elements and, more than that, it sometimes presumed to speak in defense of the common interests. But the king also claimed that power, and in the long run he won out—at least up to the nineteenth century. The *cortes* met for the last time in this earlier period in 1696-98. Then divine right monarchy triumphed and the *cortes* was replaced by nonelective secretaries of the state and superior tribunals. The *cortes* hence never acquired the power of the British parliament, nor was the idea of popular sovereignty (and all its accompanying paraphernalia—elections, party government, separation of powers, popular rights, etc.) ever secured or to become a fundamental principle of public law.[37]

We have devoted all this space to these historic themes for several reasons. First, it is clear that the fundamental foundations of the Portuguese system show a close correspondence to the model of corporative society and of the patrimonialist political order outlined previously.[38] Second, it is important because this structure served as the base and model on which the modern Portuguese state system was erected from the fifteenth century on—not only in the Old World but also in the New. These ideas were probably most clearly articulated by the Infante Dom Pedro, brother of Henry the Navigator, who artfully constructed perhaps the first full-blown theoretical and practical guide (model?) for a patronage-patrimonialist system organized on a national basis; by Alvaro Pais, the

---

[36] Gama Barros, III, 104 and 129 ff.
[37] Merêa, *O Poder Real.*
[38] In Wiarda, "Change in Iberic-Latin Tradition."

Franciscan bishop of Elvas, who articulated many of the same themes; and later by Francisco Suárez, the great Spanish jurist (who also taught at Coimbra), who joined the traditions of Thomism and Spanish customary law with the newer imperatives of state-building royal authority and who in large measure stands in the Iberic-Latin tradition where Locke does in the Anglo-American.[39] In their rationalizations of emerging power relationships in Iberia, the king (or president, in modern parlance) holds superior power; he rules authoritarianly but justly, exercising tutelage over his people and using his power to promote the general welfare. The true king is thus distinguished from a tyrant (or fascist or totalitarian) in that his power rests on a popular base through his knowledge of the general will (elections thus are not the only or even very important means for expressing that general will). Moreover, the ruler is obligated to respect the rights of society and of the *interesses*. The pacts and charters by which the nation and society are governed are tentative, however, and can be dissolved if the rights, obligations, and loyalties of each party are violated. For Portugal, it is Dom Pedro who puts these formulations all together, who shows the king how to grasp and exercise all the levers of power and patronage, and who fashions a dynamic, even modernizing model of the patrimonialist state apparatus. It is no accident that the king he instructed, João II (1481-1495), is recognized by all historians as the best ruler Portugal ever had. It is no accident either that the model he fashioned sounds remarkably similar to the present-day formulation of the Latin American political process of Charles W. Anderson and others.[40]

---

[39] For an introduction to the ideas of Dom Pedro see Merêa, *O Poder Real;* for the importance of Suárez see Morse, "Heritage of Latin America"; Peggy K. Liss, "Jesuit Contributions to the Ideology of Spanish Empire in Mexico, Part I," *The Americas,* XXIX (1973), esp. 320; and Ronald C. Newton, "On 'Functional Groups,' 'Fragmentation,' and 'Pluralism' in Spanish-American Political Society," *Hispanic American Historical Review,* L (February, 1970) 1-27, reprinted in Wiarda, *Politics and Social Change.* A consideration of the way Suárez stands in the Iberic-Latin tradition of development as compared with Locke in the Anglo-American one—along with a consideration of the contemporary critiques of both these models—would make a fascinating study.

[40] In Anderson's terms, a key to understanding Latin American politics lies in the ongoing competition among various "power contenders" and in their relations with the authoritarian state apparatus—see his "Toward a Theory of Latin American Politics," incorporated as chapter 4 in his book *Politics and Economic Change in Latin America* (Princeton, 1967); reprinted in Wiarda, *Politics and Social Change.* Also Merle Kling, "Toward a Theory of Power

The third reason for this historical survey is to show the parallels between the fifteenth century ideas and structures and the *Estado Novo* of Salazar and Caetano or the military regime that came to power in Brazil in 1964. In terms of the authoritarian but tutelary role of the state, the restricted functions of the legislature, the treatment of the opposition, the fiscalizing and confirming functions of the government, the respect for traditional interests, the erection of a corporative system of social organization and representation (more formally defined in Portugal than in Brazil, but still strongly present in the latter), the low place of public opinion and popular sovereignty, the controlled and regulated way of promoting development, the leadership of the patrimonialist state apparatus, etc., the parallels are remarkable.[41] To some extent this is so because Salazar consciously tried to resurrect in his corporative state a model derived at least in part from this older semifeudal, semimodern tradition. But it also represents the continuity of a powerful and dominant historical pattern and tradition, the extension in twentieth-century form of a historic model and order which have always been characteristic of Portuguese society and polity.

The patrimonialist state apparatus, put together so painstakingly and with so much struggle from the twelfth century through the fifteenth, remained the dominant form of Portuguese political organization. The system was based upon an organic, authoritarian, hierarchical, and corporate conception of society and polity that, due to the absence of a genuinely revolutionary transformation anywhere in the Iberic-Latin world (except in Mexico in 1910, Cuba in 1959, and perhaps one or two others), served to lock Iberic-Latin civilization into the patrimonialist-corporate mold and to perpetuate it to the present. The system was further elaborated and refined in the sixteenth century into a form that was particularly durable and long-lasting, not only in the Iberian metropolis but in their New World colonies as well. Through the grants of land and authority (*donatários*), through the *ordenações,* and through the creation of a number of royal councils to help govern this far-flung empire, what Faoro calls the "estamento burocrático" was extended overseas. In this way the Portuguese (and Spanish) col-

---

and Political Instability in Latin America," *Western Political Quarterly,* IX (March, 1956), 21-35.

    [41] Though approaching the subject area from a somewhat different perspective, Philippe C. Schmitter analyzes some of the same phenomena in his "The Portugalization of Brazil?"

onies, allowing for local variations, came to represent smaller-scale models of society and polity in the mother countries, with the church, the military, and the civil administration all a part of the bureaucratic state apparatus and with all the lines, however tenuously and ambiguously at times, centering in the crown.[42]

The Evolving National Systems: Portugal, Brazil, Peru

It is not our purpose here to present more than a gloss of the national histories of these systems. However, recent scholarship has forced us to reinterpret some of these national histories in a new light and to analyze some of these newer interpretations as a means of suggesting further lines of investigation.

Portugal. In the nineteenth century Portugal represented a blending of the traditional form of *monarquia moderada* with a newer (and confused and mistakenly understood) form of British parliamentarism. The forms were constitutional and republican, but the operating realities were continuous with Portugal's earlier history. The two parties were in fact rival elite factions vying for control of the same patrimonialist state apparatus. Elections were the expression of classic vassalage and *patrão*-client relations and had little to do with democratic choice in the Anglo-American model. *Caciquismo* flourished, with the local notables delivering votes and loyalty in return for favors and patronage. Rather than implying any genuine democratization, politics served as a means for the newer urban bourgeoisie to rise to positions of wealth and power; the elite was thus expanded to accommodate nineteenth-century pressures, but the elitist system was retained intact. Although the remnants of feudal privileges were legally abolished, the power

---

[42] The best study of the development of the patrimonialist state apparatus in Portugal *and* its extension to Brazil is Faoro. See also Graham, "Portugal." For the Spanish system see especially Magali Sarfatti, *Spanish Bureaucratic-Patrimonialism in America* (Berkeley, 1966); Francisco José Moreno, "The Spanish Colonial System: A Functional Approach," *The Western Political Quarterly,* XX (1967), 308-320; and John Leddy Phelan, "Authority and Flexibility in the Spanish Imperial Bureaucracy," *Administrative Science Quarterly,* V (June, 1960) 47-64. By way of clarification it may be noted that in my earlier work on corporative political society based chiefly on research in Latin America, I had naturally stressed this sixteenth-century model. More recent research in the Old World systems of Spain and Portugal, however, has obviously, as indicated in the above discussion, forced me to trace the model's origins and antecedents farther back historically.

of strong vested interests was perpetuated while the same *homens bons* continued to govern.[43]

It is tempting, as the corporatist ideologues of the 1920's and 1930's sought, to dismiss the entire century of Portuguese liberalism and parliamentarism from 1822 until 1926 as an aberration, a temporary break in what was in fact a far longer and stronger authoritarian tradition, a set of institutions solely "for the English to see." That interpretation is clearly wrong and misleading, but so too is the opposite and liberal one which sees the republican era as the steady march of progress, as the inevitable growth of liberalism and pluralism, as the historical unfolding of an evolutionary but unilinear, democratizing development process.[44] First, it is clear that the progress of the period can easily be exaggerated and would have have come anyway no matter the nature of the regime. Second, the liberalizing and democratizing influences of the period have been overstated, for we have already indicated that Portugal remained an elitist system without any genuine popular rule. Third, it is important to see that even in the most liberal of regimes and documents, such as the numerous constitutions of the period and in the 1891 "magna carta" of Portuguese associational life, the authoritarian, elitist, patrimonialist, and carefully regulatory features of the Portuguese tradition were preserved, thus implying that Portugal was consistently far less democratic *even in intention* than republican historians like Oliveira Marques care to admit. Indeed, as Oliveira Marques' own research has shown, the only time the parliamentary regime worked at all effectively is when it was least parliamentary, that is, when it was governed by a strong monarch or president.[45] Finally, it must also be said that some new currents and social forces had emerged in Portugal during this period, that a new elite had grown up, and that alongside the traditional pyramid of power and only partially integrated with it there had grown up a parallel structure, nascently liberal in character, in some sense assimilated into the traditional system but in

---

[43] Charles E. Nowell, *A History of Portugal* (Princeton, 1962); Francisco Sarsfield Cabral, *Uma perspectiva sobre Portugal* (Lisbon, 1973); and Joel Serrão, "Decadencia e Regeneração no Portugal Contemporaneo" (Paper presented at the Workshop on Modern Portugal, University of New Hampshire, Durham, October 10-14, 1973).

[44] Especially A. H. de Oliveira Marques, *A History of Portugal Vol. II: From Empire to Corporate State* (New York, 1972).

[45] *Ibid.*, p. 48.

another representing a challenge to it.[46] The liberal current was, and remains still, a minority current, still secondary to the dominant elitist, authoritarian, and patrimonialist tradition. Hence, as the republican regime broke down into disorder and chaos in the 1920's, the army stepped in with its "moderating" function paving the way for the coming to power of the corporatists, who promised a means of dealing with the rising "social question," of responding to twentieth-century urgencies without sacrificing traditional institutions.

All the superficial suppositions to the contrary, the Portuguese *Estado Novo* was not just a poorer, atrophied version of European fascism, nor was the Salazar regime merely a reactionary effort to turn back the clock or to preserve the status quo ante. Rather, it represented an effort to come to grips with the new social forces emerging in Portugal but without sacrificing its traditional institutions, to correct the false starts and excesses of the republican period and to prevent the currents it had let loose from getting completely out of hand. Its intention was not to reverse the process by which the ruling elites had been expanded or that under which the working class had achieved certain benefits. The *Estado Novo* hence stood for change and development, but only those features of it that could be carefully controlled and regulated. Thus, if the nineteenth century was not nearly so liberal as we have often assumed, so the corporative system was not nearly so reactionary. In fact, one might argue that those who see the issues in terms of a struggle between liberal and reactionary forces may be fundamentally misunderstanding the nature of the Portuguese system, which even to this day remains elitist and hierarchical and has always dealt with change in that same characteristic manner.

In practice, the harmonious and coequal status of employers and workers, which the corporative ideology posited, remained a myth, for as one would expect the *homens bons* and the already established interests dominated right from the beginning. Moreover in the classic patrimonialist fashion, both labor *and* capital

---

[46] A balanced treatment is Douglas L. Wheeler, "The Portuguese Revolution of 1910," *Journal of Modern History*, XLIV (June, 1972) 172-94. An account of how the Portuguese elitist system has been broadened without this implying much fundamental change in the way Portugal continued to be ruled is Henry Keith, "Point-Counter-point in Portuguese Educational Reform" (Paper presented at the Workshop on Modern Portugal, University of New Hampshire, Durham, October 10-14, 1973).

and indeed the entire corporative institutional network were sub-ordinate to the central state apparatus. Furthermore, by this time it was no longer possible to resurrect a fully corporative system in the classic pattern, since new groups had already grown up organized around principles distinct from those previously considered the only right or legitimate ones. Cast in the rigid Catholic-corporatist mold of the 1930's, the *Estado Novo* could only deal with those elements who rejected the system through repression, because by definition they were subversive, heretical, and pernicious and had to be destroyed to preserve the "natural" order. That this repression also helped to maintain the regime in power and to protect those elites profiting from it was not merely coincidental. The same rigidities served to prevent Portugal from modernizing more rapidly in the post-World War II period during which all such corporate-integralist solutions had been discredited and when the Portuguese concept clearly required reformulation and reconstruction. That, indeed, is precisely what Marcelo Caetano has been attempting, to provide for the evolution and restructuring of the Portuguese system, a further broadening of the elites and greater benefits for the lower classes, but within a traditional framework of order, hierarchy, corporatism, and authority.[47]

Brazil. Recent interpretations of Brazilian development have also emphasized its inherently corporative, elitist, and patrimonialist features. Building upon the earlier formulations of Faoro, for example, Riordan Roett has stressed the elitist nature of the Brazilian system historically, its low levels of social mobilization, its bureaucratic nature, and its clientelist, patrimonialist, and corporative features. These structures were institutionalized during some three centuries of colonial rule and were perpetuated on into the independence period when Brazil, alone among the Latin American nations, retained the monarchical form of government and the traditional moderating power of the crown. When Brazil became a republic in 1889, the constitutional forms were changed, but the basic structure of society and polity was retained and the army stepped in to play the moderating role formerly reserved for the

---

[47] All these themes need to be greatly elaborated, though it should be said that those who have examined the Caetano reforms in terms of its supposed "liberalizing" tendencies may be misunderstanding the Portuguese system. The workings of the Portuguese corporative system are analyzed in Wiarda "The Portuguese Corporative System"; and in Wiarda, *The Other Great 'Ism': Corporatism and Development in Modern Portugal* (forthcoming).

king. Despite the republican facade, politics remained in the hands of the elites who rotated in power periodically so that the benefits accruing with control of the patrimonialist state apparatus could be shared more broadly. The franchise remained limited, and *coronelismo* served for Brazil what *caciquismo* served for Portugal, as a local means for delivering electoral support and loyalty in return for favors and patronage. These institutions were related to the agrarian, rural, semifeudal society that Brazil remained.[48]

The 1930's marked a key turning point or structural reorganization in Brazil, as in Portugal. Already the new men of industrial and commercial wealth and much of the rising middle class had been and were being assimilated into the prevailing structure; now it also became the turn of the trade unions. Although Vargas was more a pragmatic politician and never the corporative ideologue that Salazar was, he and his key advisers were also influenced strongly by the Catholic-corporative ideas then current. Vargas' *Estado Novo* constitution never went into effect, but the strategy of dealing with the "social question" through the erection of official syndicates and labor tribunals and through the incorporation of this new social force into the prevailing corporative system under the control and direction of the state was remarkably similar.[49]

The Vargas system of officially sanctioned labor structures and trade union activities survived the restoration of republican government in 1945. Indeed, Roett demonstrates that the entire republican structure in the postwar period was not nearly so liberal and democratic as it is often portrayed, and that the basic structures of the corporative-patrimonialist state remained intact. In terms of the moderating role of the army, the patronage role of the parties, the perpetuation of *coronelismo* in the countryside, the power of traditional vested interests, the all-encompassing regulatory role of a now even more centralized and bureaucratic state apparatus, it is the continuities that are important as much as the changes. However, as the change process accelerated, as social mobilization went forward, as labor began to seek genuine autonomy and inde-

---

[48] *Op. cit.*

[49] Neuma Aguiar Walker, "Corporativismo y Clase Trabajadora," *Desarrollo Económico,* VIII (July-Dec., 1968) 313-48; Kenneth P. Erickson, "Labor in the Political Process in Brazil: Corporatism in a Modernizing Nation" (Ph.D. diss., Columbia University, 1970); and Howard J. Wiarda, "The Brazilian Catholic Labor Movement: Corporatism, Paternalism, Populism, and Change" in H. Jon Rosenbaum and William G. Tyler, eds., *Contemporary Brazil* (New York, 1972), pp. 323-47.

pendent bargaining power, and as a government came to power sympathetic to labor's goals and willing to turn over the traditional patronage and control mechanisms to labor itself, the traditional elites rebelled, determined to reinstall a regime capable of managing and controlling the change process in the historic, orderly manner.[50]

Roett's analysis is especially useful in showing the perpetuation over centuries and despite changes of regimes and constitutional systems of a sociopolitical structure dominated by a powerful patrimonial state and controlled by the elite. In emphasizing the present-day continuities with an earlier tradition, he shows that Brazilian corporatism and patrimonialism cannot be understood in terms of either the pluralist or the totalitarian models but must be looked at in terms of a distinct tradition and body of literature. Roett also indicates the varieties of forms that the corporative-patrimonialist system may take in Brazil: the "preservatory" form of President Dutra in the late 1940's, the left-syndicalist form of Goulart in the early 1960's, and the military-developmentalism form of the post-1964 period. What Roett does not deal with fully, however, is the present-day blending and overlap of the traditional elitist and corporative currents with the newer strains of liberalism, socialism, and mass mobilization; the fusions and frequently patchwork compromises and accommodations between them; the associational and institutional mixes, the disjointed dissentient polities that exist; and the ever-present possibility for national disintegration and breakdown. Fortunately, in Kenneth Erickson and Philippe Schmitter's work, we have considerable interview, archival, and other data to show the blends and cross-currents present, their relative strengths and dynamics, and some of the implications for Brazil's development for continuing to operate within the corporative-patrimonialist mold.[51]

Peru. Peruvian corporatism is treated elsewhere in this volume, and it is not my intention to repeat that material here. What calls our attention to Peru, however, is the effort by the military elite to fashion a *revolutionary* corporative model for the 1970's, in contrast to the more static and conservative (models 1 and 2, according to the Schmitter categorization) types of Brazil and Portugal. Peru represents an updated and restructured corporative model,

---

[50] Erickson, "Labor in Brazil."
[51] Erickson, "Labor in Brazil"; and Schmitter, *Interest Conflict.*

participatory at least in theory and now extended to the rural as well as the urban poor, but still (unabashedly and unashamedly, in the new climate of the 1970's) tutelary, corporatist, and patrimonialist in form.

The Peruvian regime proclaims itself nationalist and has taken considerable pains to fashion an ideology of corporatist development which it proudly presents as being uniquely Peruvian rather than derived from the outside. It has promised and moved partially to implement a broad range of social and structural reforms. It proclaims itself revolutionary and in fact has eliminated certain elites from a dominant voice in national affairs. At the same time, its ideology stresses popular participation for the Peruvian masses in the system, and freedom within a context of social democracy.[52]

The Peruvian regime clearly represents a leftist variant on the corporative model, although the degree of its revolutionary fervor is open to much debate. Julio Cotler has referred to the regime as one of "military populism," while Carlos Astiz has written of its technocratic and bureaucratic way of managing change.[53] In perhaps the most complete analysis so far available David Scott Palmer has pointed to the inherent conflict between the military goals of internal security and full participation for the masses. He shows that to date the government's tendency has been to emphasize the tutelary and control mechanisms rather than the participatory and potentially revolutionary ones, to use the corporative framework and ideology as a way of co-opting, institutionalizing, and hence defusing revolutionary pressures within an orderly and carefully regulated structure. The military has sought to preempt

---

[52] Among others see Carlos Astiz, "The Armed Forces as a Political Elite: Can They Develop a New Developmental Model?" (Paper presented at the 1969 Round Table of the International Political Science Association, Rio de Janeiro, October 27-31, 1969); Luigi Einaudi, "Revolution from Within? Military Rule in Peru Since 1968" (Paper presented at the Annual Meeting of the American Political Science Association, Chicago, September 7-11, 1971); Richard Lee Clinton, "The Modernizing Military: The Case of Peru," *Inter-American Economic Affairs*, 24 (Spring, 1971) 43-66; and Elizabeth Hyman, "Soldiers in Politics: New Insights on the Latin American Armed Forces," and her "Fire in the Firehouse? (Trends in the Latin American Armed Forces in the Seventies)" (Unpublished, 1970).

[53] Julio Cotler, "El Populismo Militar como Modelo de Desarrollo Nacional: El Caso Peruano" (Paper presented at the 1969 Round Table of the International Political Science Association, Rio de Janeiro, October 27-31, 1969); and Astiz, "Bureaucracy, Technocracy, and Democracy: The Peruvian Military in Power" (Paper presented at the Annual Meeting of the Northeastern Political Science Association, November 8-10, 1973).

the leftist and nationalist positions, but to do so within the confines of the older statist and corporatist lines. Meanwhile, where the corporative mechanisms have remained closed or too tightly regulated, the tendency for local forces has been to seek out other channels and means of influence, forcibly bypassing the corporative framework.[54] "The masses in Latin America are starting to stampede," as one Peruvian colonel said. "We the military [along with the mechanisms of the corporative system, one might add] are the only ones who are capable of leading them—and us—onto safe ground." This change can take place, however, only within a controlled and regulated framework, for which the corporative model has long been ideally suited. Meanwhile, the processes of social modernization, of conflicting group pressure, and of the capacity ultimately to go outside the system for recourse remain.[55]

An Assessment

There can be no doubt that corporatist models and experiments are resurgent in the present-day Iberic-Latin world. In addition to the systems described here, Mexico, Spain, Argentina, Ecuador, Bolivia, the Dominican Republic, Chile, and others are all experimenting with one or another form of corporative theory and organization. Although some analysts have seen in the new wave of corporatist experimentation a retrogression to earlier political forms and a reemergence of fascism, another quite different interpretation of corporatism's resurgence, as the present analysis suggests, is also possible. One can see in this resurgence an effort by the Iberic-Latin systems now for the first time in several decades to come to grips with their own indigenous realities and historical traditions, to devise new developmental ideologies and forms of organization suited to their own political culture and social structure rather than the older imitation of United States and European models, a nationalistic response and attempt to rediscover what is unique and distinctive in their own tradition and to update and fuse that model with the requisites of modern twentieth-century life. There is a direct and sustaining continuity, regardless of the con-

---

[54] Palmer, *"Revolution from Above"*; also Palmer and Kevin Jay Middlebrook, "Corporatist Participation under Military Rule in Peru" (unpublished).

[55] A fuller discussion is in Howard J. Wiarda, "The Latin American Development Process and the New Development Alternatives: Military 'Nasserism' and 'Dictatorship with Popular Support,'" *Western Political Quarterly*, XXV (September, 1972) 464-90.

stitutional forms and labels used, between the older, historic tradition of corporatism on which the Iberic-Latin systems were originally erected, and its more contemporary manifestations.

Corporatism thus seen represents an effort by the Iberic-Latin nations to rediscover their own "third way," to evolve their own particular "world of development," distinctive from either the socialist or the capitalist one. The corporatist resurgence also reflects, one suspects, the declining influence of the United States in the area and of the United States model of development, a spurning of the false alternatives (United States-style liberalism or socialism Soviet-style) imposed on the Iberic-Latin nations by the United States in its cold war considerations, and a rejection of that era, the 1960's particularly, of such immense United States influence and interference in Latin American affairs. That era has ended or is ending throughout the hemisphere, and in the present period of United States "benign neglect" toward Latin America, new indigenous developmental solutions are sprouting. Many will find that a welcome and healthy development. And though the corporatist label may still be an unfortunate one, conjuring up unpleasant, hateful connotations of nazi atrocities, we must begin to recognize that the mainstreams of corporatism in the Iberic-Latin world were always fundamentally different from and opposed to the nazi and fascist models and that the nations of the Iberic-Latin culture area are now nowhere served or accurately described by resort to the fascist or neofascist brands.

But, a word of caution. Corporatism and corporatist models have achieved a certain "in-ness" of late which needs to be kept in perspective. The corporatist model is useful as an explanatory tool in examining the Iberic-Latin development tradition, but it must be remembered that it is merely a heuristic device, helpful up to a point, and providing answers only to certain questions. We must recognize that other models and approaches must be employed to provide answers to other questions. In the minds of most observers, for example, the relative weights to be assigned to a corporatist political-cultural approach as determining Iberic-Latin political behavior, as opposed to a structural or class-based approach, have not been fully sorted out or finally decided.[56] The "delayed development" and "dependency" (at least through the

---

[56] A useful effort in this direction is William P. Glade, "The State and Economic Development in Mediterranean Politics" (Paper presented at the

1960's) theses as advanced by Schmitter, for instance, are also reasonable and useful.[57] Obviously we must be eclectic in our approach, recognizing the complex multicausality of historical events, using different models to explain different aspects of political behavior, and seeking to gauge in different times and circumstances the explanatory power of each. The corporative model cannot explain all Iberic-Latin political phenomena, since these nations are at best only partially and incompletely corporative systems, since the real centers of power and influence (even in Portugal, perhaps the most completely rationalized, in a formal-legal sense, of the corporative systems) often lie outside the corporate structures and institutions, and since the recourse to revolution or to political action beyond the boundaries of the corporative legal order are always possible. Indeed it would seem that some of the most exciting areas of research lie precisely in that murky area where our models overlap, where corporatist attitudes and organizations are mixed and jumbled together with liberal and/or socialist ones, where the traditional institutions are modernizing and the modernizing ones employing traditional techniques of spoils, patronage and the like. In all of this, both the scholarly dispute as to how best to interpret these events, as well as the political dynamics of change and conflict, will go on.

Corporatist theory and institutions can clearly take a great variety of forms and range from Left to Right on the political spectrum. Given this apparently dominant political culture, much useful research can be done on its national variations, the structural reasons why the Brazilian military took a rightist corporatist direction and the Peruvians a leftist one, the dynamics of modernization and development both within and outside of the corporative framework. The question as to why corporatist solutions are reemerging at precisely the time of declining United States influence throughout the hemisphere is also an intriguing one. Perhaps part of the answer lies in the growing recognition that while the United States cannot be the policeman to the world, it cannot be its philosopher either. Surely United States social scientists, long imbued with their own ethnocentric and culturally biased models of development, must also begin to recognize that fact.

1973 Annual Meeting of the American Political Science Association, New Orleans, September 4-8); but see also his *Latin American Economies* (New York: American, 1969).

[57] See Schmitter, "Paths to Political Development."

Natural Corporatism and the Passing of Populism in Spanish America

Ronald C. Newton

In the aftermath of the military revolt that overthrew the Popular Unity government of Dr. Salvador Allende in September 1973, reports began to seep out of Chile that the junta was supervising revision of the constitution in a "corporativist" sense. The structural alterations contemplated are designed, in the first instance, to ensure permanent military representation in the councils of government. However, General Augusto Pinochet Ugarte, head of the military junta, has made it known that the new constitution will also give a prominent place to industrial, commercial, agrobusiness, mining, and professional associations, which he terms "the authentic representatives of the people."[1] Such employers' and trade associations—known collectively as "gremios patronales," to distinguish them from trade unions or "gremios de obreros"—have been in existence for many years, but a number of them experienced a sharp upsurge of political militancy in the late 1960's in reaction to what their leaders perceived as the leftward drift of the then-ruling Christian Democratic Party. Their role, under the direction of the Confederation of Production and Commerce, in arousing resistance to the Popular Unity government elected in 1970 and, ultimately, in paralyzing it before its final downfall is widely known, at least in outline.[2]

The "gremialist" movement has found its theoretician in Jaime Guzmán, a professor of constitutional law at the Catholic University and a member of the junta's Constitutional Commission. In Guzmán's view, gremialist representation has a dual function: social mobilization to "counteract the excesses of political power" (that is, the allegedly divisive behavior of those conventional political parties that the junta may in future permit to reopen), and a "consultative, technical function" (Guzmán is explicit on the desirability of incorporating "technocratic elites" into decision-

---

[1] New York *Times,* October 23, 1973.

[2] NACLA (North American Congress on Latin America), *Latin America and Empire Report,* VIII, 8 (October, 1973), 3-5. The NACLA brings a "New Left" interpretation, frequently combined with extensive research, to the Latin American scene.

making and/or administrative structures). The *gremios*, according to Guzmán, are to be "autonomous"—autonomous, that is, of political parties.[3] Whether they are to remain autonomous of the authoritarian regime that is likely to prevail in Chile for the foreseeable future is unclear.

These are early days yet to attempt an analysis; it will be interesting, above all, to learn what function, if any, Chile's large and cohesive trade union movement will be assigned in the new structure. What is reasonably apparent, however, is that the Chilean right has resurrected a variant of the corporate state.

Most observers must find themselves bemused at this, for in the experience of the Atlantic world the corporate state is an anachronism, and a faintly tawdry one at that. I propose to argue, however, that in the larger Latin American context the Chilean episode is merely the first *overt* manifestation of a "natural corporativism"[4] that has been evolving obscurely behind the epiphenomena of *movimientos* and insurrections, electoral campaigns and *golpes*, since the depression of the 1930's and, more markedly, since the late 1940's. This essay will define the concept of natural corporatism, and mark the limits of its usefulness. Beyond that, in an attempt to discover leads to answers to questions that the concept raises but of its nature cannot cope with satisfactorily, I will consider some historical and situational factors that suggest reasons why natural corporatism should have arisen at a particular place and time. This in turn necessitates examination of the relation between natural corporatism and the political mood of "populism"; I shall propose that the two are not only roughly coeval, but that in natural corporatism are found the typical structures and processes of populism. Finally, it seems appropriate to touch briefly upon the function of natural corporatism in the contemporary transition in the more advanced states of Spanish America to more comprehensive forms of autocratic rule—the "new militarism" that has become a major preoccupation of Latin Americanist scholars since the Brazilian coup of 1964.[5]

---

[3] New York *Times,* October 23, 1973.

[4] Adapted from Philippe C. Schmitter, *Interest Conflict and Political Change in Brazil* (Stanford, 1971), 383 and *passim.* I have earlier objected to the use of "corporativism" to describe these phenomena; the objection is withdrawn. See Ronald C. Newton, "On 'Functional Groups,' 'Fragmentation,' and 'Pluralism' in Spanish American Political Society," *The Hispanic American Historical Review,* L (1970), 1-29.

[5] Brazil will be alluded to in passing, but the main concern of this essay is

The corporate state, idea and praxis, has not fared well at the hands of historians and political sociologists, certainly not those of the erstwhile Allied nations of World War II. The modern idea of corporatism has been around for a long time. Its origins go back to the conservative reaction against the Enlightenment and the French Revolution, to the "organic" sense of society in Burke, de Bonald, in some aspects de Maistre, and a major line of German theorists from Herder through Hegel and Savigny to Gierke. But toward the latter part of the nineteenth century, the accelerating processes of industrialization and urbanization, with their attendant phenomena of disruption of traditional class and status relationships, dissolution of long-standing social solidarities (which in extreme form would become "alienation" and/or "anomie"), proletarianization and gathering class conflict—all these made more urgent, by reaction, the quest for organic concepts of society, or organic "solutions." These were compelling modes of thought for writers who, with diverse rationales, rejected both the postulates of liberal bourgeois capitalism and the liberal state (with its mechanistic social relationships determined by the marketplace), and the Marxian dialectic (whose implacable unfolding also implied change of unknown magnitude). The "organic-mechanistic" antithesis was assimilated to formal sociology by, among others, Ferdinand Tönnies, who reformulated it as *Gemeinschaft-Gesellschaft*, an organizing concept whose ramifications would preoccupy sociologists for generations. The like concern of many writers with "primary" groups and solidarities led them to a reexamination of family, clan, commune, and occupational group, and generated in turn a revival of scholarship into the guilds and corporations of medieval Europe. Neo-medievalism was clear in the Catholic social thought of such ideologues as La Tour du Pin and Pope Leo XIII, but is equally evident in the somewhat later work of the secular humanitarians of the English circle of Guild Socialists. And derivations from the same loose idea system are clear enough in the evolving doctrines of revolutionary syndicalism that found their most fertile ground in pre-1914 Latin Europe.

Thus in the first decades of the twentieth century there was no single coherent corporatist doctrine, nor any dominant corporatist doctrinaire. Corporatism was, rather, an untidy intellectual kitchen

---

with the states of Spanish America and with a specifically Hispanic politico-legal tradition. For detailed treatment of Brazil see Schmitter, *Interest Conflict and Political Change in Brazil*.

midden comprised of brilliant social insights as well as the effluvia
from some badly cracked pots, strategies of working-class resistance
to the capitalist order and proposals for the reconstitution of a
harmonious and hierarchical Christian society, limited projects for
political and administrative reform through functional representation and the garbled verbalizations of the insecurities of individuals
—artisans, intellectuals, aristocrats—threatened by marginalization
in the onrushing change of industrializing Europe. But at the end
of World War I the very incoherence of corporatism facilitated its
assimilation, or fragments thereof, to the ideological reaction, first,
to the immediate threat of the spread of the Bolshevik Revolution,
and secondly, to the protracted crisis of liberal democracy and
liberal capitalism that had been exposed by the war and deepened
by postwar economic depressions. In a limited pragmatic response
to the collapse of 1929-30, the devices of corporatism, in the form
of industrial self-government through preexisting cartels, trade
associations, and chambers, were applied briefly by nonfascist
capitalist systems, including the United States of the New Deal
era (the NRA) and Nazi German.[6] But elsewhere, most particularly in Latin and Catholic Europe, corporatism was heralded forth
as a multipurpose nostrum in the context of authoritarianism and
(often largely rhetorical) nationalism. In industrial relations, the
creation, with the participation of state functionaries, of functional
corporations grouping together owners, managers, and workers,
and the public arbitration of disputes, offered surcease from conflict between capital and organized labor (and among capitalists);
but unlike the Bolshevik solution corporatism promised to leave
property rights, religion, the family, and hierarchical social status
virtually untouched. Its political corollary, functional representation through corporate chambers, offered a seemingly rational alternative to the disarray and ineffectuality of parliamentary systems, or
to the class bias and latent (if somewhat tarnished) internationalism
of the socialist movement, or to the despotism of a Leninist van-
guard. Indeed, it offered a means to the depoliticization of society,
hence to a renewal of ordered performance of functions in the body
politic, hence also to the enlightened rule of technical and administrative expertise. The nation-state thus came to be the reason for

---

[6] As pointed out recently by John A. Garraty in "The New Deal, National
Socialism, and the Great Depression," *American Historical Review*, LXXVIII
(1973), 914-15.

being of corporatist structures. In view of the libertarianism and emphasis upon the autonomy of social solidarities that had formed important though not dominant strands of pre-1914 corporatist thought, there is abundant irony in this.

Although the Italian Corporate State was not legislated into existence until 1934, and led at best a shadowy half-life thereafter, the international notoriety that the fascist regime had enjoyed for more than a decade caused Italy to serve as the best-known paradigm of corporatism. There, before the end of the 1930's, the disparities between rhetoric and praxis suggested to many that the Corporate State (and its predecessor, the Syndicalist State) had served mainly as a façade behind which the regime had destroyed the autonomy of the Italian trade union movement and reduced the living levels of Italian workingmen.[7] Marxists asserted at the time that "social peace" was but a code word for the obliteration of socialism within the working class, and "economic coordination" but a sanction for the monopolies, oligopolies, and cartels demanded by a faltering capitalist order; and subsequent historians have described the Italian Corporate State in such uncommonly blunt terms as "wind" and "a confidence trick."[8] But in the deepening international crisis of the late 1930's and the descent again into war, corporatism was much more generally discredited in the Western democracies by its frequent appearance in the ideologies, action programs, and (less commonly) institutional structures of the movements and regimes in alliance or sympathy with the Rome-Berlin Axis. The states in which it achieved some semblance of implementation—pre-*Anschluss* Austria, Vichy France, Mussolini's Italy— were in their turn absorbed by Nazi Germany and perished with it. Save for vestiges in the Iberian dictatorships that survived at the margin, corporatism as a formal doctrine has lain buried amidst much other trumpery paraphernalia of the European catastrophe for more than a quarter of a century.

In interwar Europe, corporatism was an explicit if not altogether coherent doctrine advocated by political movements seeking power, and an organizational principle imposed by regimes *in*

---

[7] S. Lombardini, "Italian Fascism and the Economy," in S. J. Woolf, ed., *The Nature of Fascism* (New York, 1968), pp. 156-162.

[8] H. Stuart Hughes, *The United States and Italy* (Cambridge, 1953), p. 88, cited by N. Kogan in Woolf, *The Nature of Fascism*, p. 17; anonymous reviewer in the *Times* (London) *Literary Supplement*, March 2, 1973, pp. 225-27.

power, often in the wake of substantial socio-political turbulence or violence. Until the very recent events in Chile, this has nowhere been the case in postwar Latin America. On the contrary, *natural* corporatism, as the adjective implies, has evolved slowly, unacknowledged, within or parallel to the conventional and more or less constitutional processes of electoral politics, civic paralysis, *golpes,* caretaker administrations, *pactos, convenios, acuerdos,* and more electoral politics. Where European-derived corporatism has figured at all in the doctrinal writings and programs of political activists, it has been the property of isolated sects and sectarians of the extreme right with few prospects of immediate access to power.[9] What is under discussion here, rather, is an *organizing hypothesis,* a mental construct developed by scholars with which to examine and explain socio-political phenomena which have not, generally, proven responsive to explication in terms of the postulates and categories of conventional liberal-developmental scholarship on Latin America.[10] Although one may feel—with no elation whatever—that the recent turn of events in Chile confirms some of the insights of this line of scholarship, the concept itself, as the diversity of approaches and conclusions in the present collection suggests, needs much further work.

The starting point, I suspect, has been the commonsense assumption that, despite the notorious frailty of Latin American party systems and legislatures and the frequent and apparently ruinous breaks in executive continuity, the essential business of politics—the transmutation of claims, demands, and grievances into legislation and dispensation, *input* into *output*—continues, after a fashion, to get done. And to examine how this occurs the scholars in question[11] have focused their attention upon the following: (a) secondary occupational or functional groups, normally urban-based—their emergence and growth as functions of indus-

---

[9] The most significant of these, perhaps, was the old Chilean *Falange Nacional,* which became the Christian Democratic Party in the late 1950's. With the transition the emphasis on corporatism was much diminished.

[10] To my knowledge, none of the writers associated with the "New Left" have utilized the corporatist approach. The *concept,* however, is not inherently anti-Marxist, nor an "alternative to Marxism," as the *ideology* has of course been.

[11] Most are represented in the present collection and citations thereto. I should, however, like to acknowledge my own intellectual debt to a number of authors—Gino Germani, L. N. McAlister, Richard Morse, K. H. Silvert—who are not.

trialization and/or urbanization, their legal status, social composition, the recruitment of their leadership, their efficacy as social solidarities and as vehicles for achievement of political ends; (b) the processes whereby they articulate their political demands and transmit them to the formal apparatus of government for dispensation; and (c) the relationships first, among such groups, the attempts to achieve functional monopoly, social interpenetration or "cross-cutting solidarities"; second, among the leadership cadres or functional elites of the several secondary groups within a system; and third, between functional and political elites.[12]

Let me attempt to outline the historical emergence of natural corporatism and summarize its salient characteristics.[13] It is first of all a function of the increase in complexity of social and economic organization attributable to urbanization and industrialization. Its beginnings in Latin America, therefore, are located in the limited import-substitution industrialization of the 1930's, and its further evolution in the patterns of rural-urban migration, expansion of urban white-collar and working-class aggregates, and spasmodic industrialization, since the World War II period. The phenomenon is consequently identified with Latin American states at "advanced" levels of socio-economic evolution; it is not found in the small peripheral states that have not experienced significant development of both urbanization and industrialization.[14] Apace with this evolution, there has emerged a new congeries of urban secondary groups based upon occupation or function; these comple-

---

[12] It is also likely that some scholars first became aware of the possibilities of the corporatist approach through examination of the PRI (Partido Revolucionario Institucional)-dominated post-Cárdenas Mexican system, which Robert Scott has long since identified as and described in terms of "corporative centralism" (*Mexican Government in Transition* [Urbana, 1959], pp. 162-176). Though not conspicuous for popular participation nor adherence to the conventions of representative democracy, the Mexican system, by the criterion of effectiveness, is clearly a success. The PRI's party and national executives have been able to contain the divisive importunities of the organized interests represented through the "sectors"; prolonged stability has permitted the regime to pursue its long-term developmental goals. But the present-day Mexican socio-political structure is the precipitate of the processes of the Revolution, and has no analogue elsewhere in Latin America.

[13] For a fuller treatment see my 1970 essay cited in note 4.

[14] In my earlier essay, I suggested that natural corporatism was also limited by a second set of factors: the existence of durable and viable structures of interest aggregation, the party system and legislature. As examples, I offered in 1970 Uruguay and Chile. In 1973 this no longer applies. Of the major states, only Venezuela and Colombia retain any vestiges of conventional systems.

ment, though, rarely supersede, the older primary solidarities of kinship, ethnicity, locality, and work place, and the intricate obligations of friendship and *relaciones*. These secondary groups have rapidly achieved formal organization and, in virtually all cases, legal recognition. They span a great range in terms of their attributes of social solidarity: from purely mechanical or contrived solidarities (trade associations, public bureaucracies staffed by place hunters), through professional organizations or paternalistic small and medium enterprises (in which the web of personal interaction grows denser), to those rooted in a shared way of life not yet seriously disrupted by change (landowning cliques, older skilled-trade unions, the military, the Church, until lately the university). Many toward the latter end of the scale have been effective in providing creature satisfactions, material and psychological; in doing so they have become partially closed social environments affording individuals a single source of authority and a single focus of allegiance: the group's leadership or functional elite or *patrón*. These are, to a degree, "inclusive" social solidarities, and correspondingly isolated from other such solidarities—the characteristics of a more traditional, preindustrial order of secondary-group structure.[15] Or to put it another way, in comparison with the unlimited pluralism of, for example, industrializing Great Britain or the United States, the number of secondary groups in contemporary urban Latin America is small (by virtue of lesser and later industrialization, and the hostility of the authoritarian state to the creation of voluntary groups, noted below), and the multiple affiliations or cross-cutting solidarities possible to or demanded of individuals are few. "The habit of voluntary association," in de Tocqueville's phrase, is not strong.

This pattern is reinforced by the controlling concepts and institutions of a traditional politico-legal culture, the Hispano-Roman, which is throughout antagonistic to the autonomous existence of secondary groups, but which conduces to the institutionalization—including, by legal or quasi-legal means, the bestowal of economic or social monopoly—of dependent, *non*autonomous secondary groups. In the classic situation of natural corporatism, however, the

---

[15] The failure to see that in industrialized society *most* secondary structures are of necessity "mechanical" and bureaucratized, are not and cannot be social solidarities, is, it seems to me, a chief weakness of the conservative theorists who sought to recreate harmonious, "integral" societies on what they took to be the preindustrial model.

latter are not completely subordinated and articulated to the structure of government. Rather, in the mode of what Juan Linz describes as the "limited pluralism" of Hispanic authoritarianism,[16] they possess the ability to mobilize men and influence, legal legitimacy and *fueros*, and, as *intereses creados*, the sanction of tradition to support their claims of respect for customary privilege. Indeed, this equilibrium between the state's authority to grant life to intermediary bodies, and the extensive defenses of the latter behind which to perpetuate their existence unmolested, is, it seems to me, a key to any understanding of the long-term immobility of the forms of Hispanic statecraft.[17]

Such a relationship implies continuing one-to-one interaction between functional elites and political elites, which means, where little or no permanent bureaucracy exists, the executive and his ministers and advisors. The vertical nature of these relationships provides channels of political flow that circumvent those of the constitutionally envisioned electoral and legislative processes. As the former prove ever more effective for the articulation of political demands—whether behind closed doors or through street *manifestaciones* or strikes, or some combination thereof—and for their satisfaction, the conventional structures can only decline further in prestige and legitimacy. The constant febrile effort, in an atmosphere of struggle necessary to keep the system in some sort of balance conduces to in-group solidarity, exacerbates the differences among groups, and strengthens the configuration of multiple lines of vertical interaction converging within the apparatus of government.

Nevertheless, in its earlier stages the system—which is rather too elegant a term—of natural corporatism was tolerably effective. It has ceased to be so because socio-economic change has altered the preconditions that once made it viable. One of these is, obviously, that the number of *intereses* to be satisfied be relatively small. This was true in the beginnings of urbanization and industrialization; it is true no longer. Similarly, increasing socio-economic complexity and shifts in the locus of power have undermined the ability of elites to manipulate the informal arrangements of corporatist politics and make them work. Traditional elites, not far removed from the classic complementary nineteenth-century triad

---

[16] "An Authoritarian Regime: Spain," in E. Allardt and Y. Littunen, eds., *Cleavages, Ideologies, and Party Systems* (Helsinki, 1964), pp. 291-341.

[17] See Newton, *The Hispanic American Historical Review, op. cit.,* esp. 22-28.

of landowners, ecclesiastics, and soldiers, were—even when they were fighting among themselves—relatively homogeneous; shared status and values bound functional and political leadership together (indeed, at times they were indistinguishable), informal channels of communication linked them together. Their social distance from the commonality, the relatively low levels of participation, the buffer provided by the melodrama of party politics, all contributed to the atmosphere of tranquility in which competing demands could be balanced off more or less rationally, crises managed more or less imperturbably. But older agrarian and extractive interests have had to cede place to newer and ever more ramified commercial and industrial interests. This has not, of course, spelled the wholesale eclipse and demise of older elite families. But the diversification of elite structures and the co-optation of the newly successful *have* meant a degree of fragmentation, more tenuous communications, and in turn far greater difficulties in the management of politics. This has been compounded, further, by the greater accessibility and visibility of elites. It may be that the economic gap separating functional elites from their constituencies has not appreciably lessened in the past two generations, but social distance certainly has. Status is less fully ascriptive; performance is more susceptible to scrutiny by an occasionally obstreperous press and a rather more exigent public.

The consequences can be schematized in structural-functional terms. Organized secondary groups are clearly serviceable vehicles of interest *articulation*. But as the sheer number of groups availing themselves of these procedures grows, in function both of economic diversity and the increasing intrusion of urban (and occasionally, rural) underclass aggregates into the circle of organized interests permitted to participate, the problem of interest *aggregation*—the compromises, operationalization and translation into legislation, adjustment of political demands to majority or national priorities— becomes ever more acute. It is hypothesized that in the earlier stages of this process the aggregating function was performed primarily through the informal horizontal solidarities of elite structures, and secondarily through the formal horizontal solidarities of parties and legislatures, or some combination thereof. But the formal processes have fallen into an advanced state of decrepitude through the success of the informal ones; the latter in turn, for very different reasons, have more lately also lost their capacity to aggregate effectively. Thus for a conventional regime forced to maneuver in the exquisitely narrow space between the "populistic" priorities of distribution and the "developmental" demands of production, a sequence of unprocessed and uncompromising demands is in all likelihood catastrophic, whether all the demands be satisfied or not; and the military authoritarian solution has proven all too obvious. It should be added that in the Mexican and Cuban systems the crucial slippage between formal polity and secondary groups, and their respective elites, has been diminished or eliminated through the interpenetration of elites and the subordination of functional leadership to men—party members and/or permanent bureaucrats—who are bearers of a more or less homogeneous national ideology and program; this process is best described by the Hitlerian term *Gleichschaltung*. In the more recent "modern" military regimes, those in which liberal rules and procedures have been definitively abandoned and "development" accepted as an overriding goal, military officers, especially those trained in managerial techniques beyond the requirements of narrow military expertise, and their civilian technocratic associates constitute an analogous horizontal solidarity, with the same aggregating capacity.

Although many subtleties remain to be introduced and ramifications traced out, the concept of natural corporatism *per se* cannot carry us much beyond the present point. If its potential uses are obvious, so also are its limitations. As a method of *static* analysis, it directs a searching light upon a fairly narrow range of phenomena—secondary (or "functional" or "intermediary") groups, and their relation to formal and informal government. To a degree it illuminates closely related areas, but leaves much of *total* sociopolitical systems in darkness. In structural-functional terms—and the derivation of the concept from structural-functional theory is evident enough—natural corporatism relies heavily upon analysis of *input* functions—interest articulation and interest aggregation—but can tell us little about *output,* except to make clear that the functions under the latter head must needs be performed with the minimum either of continuity or of rationality. Natural corporatism is not of much help in approaching the classic question, *who gets what?*, although it certainly suggests a means of finding out *how.*

As a means of discovering and analyzing the *dynamics* of sociopolitical change over time, the concept offers a schematic model, which is again useful though limited. As sketched above, the phenomenon of natural corporatism is restricted to a particular time period, roughly the four decades from 1930 to 1970. This is the phase of Latin American socio-political history that is coming to be called "populist." The descriptive label "populism," it seems to me, lumps together causes, informing assumptions, and processes: the incorporation of ever-greater sectors of populations into political society, attempts to create cross-class coalitions (either under the aegis of quasi-revolutionary *movimientos* such as the Bolivian MNR [Movimiento Nacionalista Revolucionario] or Peronism in its first and second incarnations, or through electoral arrangements such as those associated with Peru's APRA [Alianza Popular Revolucionaria Americana] and its daughter parties), emphasis on (and bitter competition over) *distribution* of the social product, and a peculiar style which one associates with enhanced and strident mobilization, the mass *manifestaciones* of assorted *sindicatos, ligas, gremios, comisiones, federaciones,* and so on. Natural corporatism, it has been argued, arose as a function of urbanization and industrialization, the consequent emergence, growth, and proliferation of organized secondary groups, and the incapacity of traditional liberal constitutional procedures (which have not, however, been explicitly repudiated) to articulate their wants, much less to satisfy them. The two concepts, in other words, are congruent; the latter is, one hopes, a fairly precise model of the mechanics of the former. But it goes further: though effective at first, natural corporatism's inherent inability to afford *orderly* methods in a *national* context for the containment of the competing demands of production and distribution has caused it to break down. Under pressure, natural corporatism, itself the offspring of the traditional Hispanic mode of authoritarianism, has developed easily into regimes more modern and thoroughgoing in their use of command and coercion. But it is clear that although the dynamic schema can lead to a more accurate understanding of *what* has happened, the underlying reasons *why* these particular kinds of change have occurred in this particular place and time remain elusive.[18]

---

[18] Only time, of course, will prove or disprove the assumption that populism and natural corporatism are drawing to a close. One may be fairly certain, however, that national systems now growing sufficiently "advanced" to experience these phenomena will not in fact do so to any great extent. We are a long way from the crudities of a "stages" thesis, *à la* Rostow, which would demand that each system recapitulate, with perhaps a bit of telescoping, the entire trajectory of more "developed" systems. Within Latin America, the demonstration effect is close enough at hand to obviate this. I suspect also that, on the South American continent, at least, mingled admiration for and fear of

The fact that the concept of natural corporatism is restricted by place and time in its applicability is significant. After all, the industrialization process everywhere has been accompanied by growing social complexity, the proliferation of secondary groups, changes in elite structure and composition, and expansion in the ambit of political participation. In the Atlantic world, many societies, including the United States, have been plagued by the conflict between the sanctioned procedures of electoral politics and the more covert workings of interest group politics. Yet except for affinities to the interwar experiences of the states of Latin Europe, most markedly those that eventuated in the status quo corporatist dictatorships of Salazar and Franco, the natural corporatism of Spanish America appears to be unique in its configuration and in its historical trajectory of rise, dysfunctionality, and transformation into more comprehensive forms of authoritarianism. Thus the obvious next step is some consideration—exploratory at best, in the present state of scholarship—of historical and situational factors.

I have proposed elsewhere[19] that in the sixteenth and early seventeenth centuries the structure of Spanish political society congealed into a stasis from which it has yet fully to extricate itself: an equilibrium between an autocratic central state which could not tolerate the legal or constitutional autonomy of intermediary bodies; and those intermediary bodies, which succeeded in clothing themselves in legal charters, *fueros*, and customary privilege, and which achieved, especially under weak monarchies, a near-parity of de facto power with the Crown. The first element was created by the centralizing efforts of Ferdinand and Isabella and their successors of the House of Austria through Phillip II (and their bureaucracies), who suppressed in turn the autonomy of the towns, the Church and military orders, great noble houses, and functional corporations such as the *Mesta*. In the process, however, the internal authority and customary privileges of these latter were altered only in small degree; they were, rather, yoked to the fortunes of the Crown as coordinate arms of administration. The second element of the stasis was a function of the psychologically ruinous and financially catastrophic failure of Spain's imperial mission in the seventeenth century, demographic decline, and the concurrent con-

the Brazilian model will accelerate present trends toward military authoritarianism.

[19] See note 17.

traction and impoverishment of the nation's internal economy. The Crown's expedients for revenue in a failing cause increased its dependence upon and concessions to intermediary bodies; disillusionment and gross economic recession stimulated in the latter, one might argue, an overriding concern to consolidate past gains. In this stasis, the decay into almost total irrelevancy of the several *cortes* halted the formation of horizontal political solidarities and strengthened the pattern of multiple vertical flows of political interaction.

The weight of historical tradition is also a historian's customary escape hatch, and I do not wish to labor it here. Other states of early modern Europe experienced, and in time evolved away from, centralized autocracy and corporatist socio-legal structures; they have also long since fashioned, often from unpromising beginnings, systems of political representation. The *economic* factor, however, appears to be more suggestive for our purposes—the factor, to be more precise, of the reality or perception or fear of economic collapse and long-term stagnation, which must be taken in conjunction with its implications—legal, administrative, customary, intellectual —for the evolution of secondary-group solidarities. One does not, after all, find enduring corporatist structures in societies, or sectors of societies, characterized by headlong economic growth and its attendant social flux and optimistic view of the future—a point apparent enough to the liberal assailants of corporate privilege of the late eighteenth and nineteenth centuries.

This factor, I suggest, has had ample opportunity to recur, in differing contexts, in the Hispanic lands. Karl Marx's observations at a much later date, for example, echo what has been proposed above:

> We have not here to state the circumstances, political or economical, which destroyed Spanish commerce, industry, navigation, and agriculture. For the present purpose it is sufficient to simply recall the fact. As the commercial and industrial life of the towns declined, internal exchanges became rare, the mingling of the inhabitants of different provinces less frequent, the means of communication neglected, and the great roads gradually deserted. Thus the local life of Spain, the independence of its provinces and communes, the diversified state of society originally based on the physical configuration of the country, and historically developed by the detached manner in which the several provinces emancipated themselves from the Moors, and formed little independent commonwealths — was now finally strengthened and confirmed by the

economical revolution which dried up the sources of national activity. And while the absolute monarchy found in Spain material in its very nature repulsive to centralization, it did all in its power to prevent the growth of common interests arising out of a national division of labor and the multiplicity of internal exchanges — the very basis on which alone a uniform system of administration and the rule of general laws can be created.[20]

Spain was not, in the mid-nineteenth century — nor in the seventeenth, for that matter — a "primitive" society flirting with the beginnings of "development." The point of Marx's observation is, rather, the corrosive effect of prolonged economic depression, exacerbated at the time by loss of much of the income from a colonial empire, upon an elaborately developed social system with centuries of complex evolution behind it — one in which, however, the dynamic of capitalist economic development had gone sluggish at an early stage.

In twentieth-century Spanish America, it is not difficult to place this factor in relation to the asymmetries or socio-political evolution that have often been commented upon. The starting point is the growing urbanization since the turn of the century — necessarily, since urbanism is the context and *sine qua non* of the social differentiation and secondary-group development under discussion. Included in this process were the restoration of the city (the primate city, normally) to preponderance in national economic, political, and administrative life, the expansion of urban white-collar population groups, and, in some regions, the beginnings of trade unionism. All were functions, of course, not of indigenous industrialization (except for primary processing) but of the more effective articulation of the Latin American primary-product economies, in subordinate situations, to the European- and North American-dominated world trading system. This meant, among other things, that ever-larger (and more vocal) population segments were exposed more nakedly to the vagaries of world business cycles culminating in the depression of the 1930's. It would be an exaggeration, it seems to me, to regard the depression era as the "crisis of liberalism," except insofar as "liberalism" was equated narrowly with the uninhibited flow of commodities and capital. Otherwise, however, one must be skeptical of the extent to which

---

[20] Karl Marx and Friedrich Engels, *Revolution in Spain* (New York, 1939), pp. 25-26. Originally published in the New York *Daily Tribune,* 1854.

the postulates either of liberal democracy or free-enterprise capitalism had been absorbed in the first place. By the same token, the corporatist projects of a José Uriburu in Argentina or a Getulio Vargas in Brazil are perfectly comprehensible, if premature, in terms both of their challenge to majority political rhetoric and to important export-oriented sectors; nor was social mobilization sufficiently advanced.

By now it is generally accepted, however, that the limited import-substitution industrialization of the 1930's and 1940's set events in train that would culminate in the crisis of the bourgeoisie. For much of the latter had established itself in the occupations of the preindustrial city — bureaucracy, the professions, commerce, "service" — and participated but little in the industrialization process, such as it was, in competition with immigrant entrepreneurs, foreign branch plants, and state and foreign sources of capital. Industrialization, in any event, proved an inconstant lure, both during World War II when the profitability of primary products diverted capital again into traditional extractive production, and in the late 1940's when the industrial nations were once more able to flood Latin America with consumer goods. The urban middle classes, whose apparent emergence to political self-consciousness was signalized by the wave of democratic reformist regimes of the immediate postwar period, had in fact entered upon modernization very belatedly, and were thus condemned in the main to white-collar functions not directly related to technologically and organizationally advanced manufacturing processes. Moreover, hard on their heels emerged not only a more demanding and politically potent organized working class, but also a rapidly increasing underclass of rural origins, whose potential for turbulence was perceived at the time as incalculably menacing. In the more advanced societies, the nether millstone was set firmly in place by the early 1950's.

The politics of populism and the unacknowledged evolution of what has been described earlier in these pages as natural corporatism expanded from this period onward, in repeated cycles of standpat military regimes, overthrow, reformist projects, multiclass coalitions, stalemate, and military restoration of the situation. The raw increase in population save in a few areas, the even greater demand for social services it provoked, the growing capability of organized interests representing ever larger population aggregates to articulate their demands, resulted in increasingly bitter competition for the proportion of the social product that could be distributed, and a concern to protect what had been so gotten. For even with foreign borrowings for current expenses, the social product did not keep pace. The provenance of this upper millstone has been a matter of dispute for a decade and more. The shortcomings of Latin American capitalism have been attributed by respectable scholarly opinion, especially in the United States, to the hopelessly preindustrial "attitudes" and "values" of what should be the bourgeois cutting edge of industrialism; given the asymmetries noted above one must concede some substance to this view, despite its all too comfortable congruence with the intellectual needs of United States policymakers. But of course there is here a nice question of an interrelated chain of causes and effects over an extended period of time. It makes more sense to examine, in the first instance, the pressures of industrial trading partners to expand and rationalize production at the expense of indigenous industrialization, the long-term decline in the world prices of those commodities as against the rise in the cost of manufactures, the gradual transfer of foreign investment from the primary to the secondary and tertiary sectors and the expansion of foreign-controlled branch-plant enclaves, and the drainage of capital in the form of remitted profits and payments in service of debt. In any case, the functional and political elites of the populist phase — the "national bourgeoisie" in current Marxist terminology — have proven unequal to either the developmental or the aggregative tasks; the "new military," who are among other things counter-elites, are now proposing to make good these failures.

In summary: it may be that in the hands of the Chilean right and possibly elsewhere corporatism will be revived as a working ideology — or, properly speaking, an element of an ideology. The Chilean case could prove instructive, for it is not certain that the military have been trained to assume manifold administrative and technical positions as their brother officers in Brazil and Peru have been; nor indeed is it certain that they are prepared to make the decisive break with their upper-status civilian compeers that would enable them to pursue roughshod the lure of development. In such a situation, the uses of corporatist structures as means to depoliticization and social demobilization are apparent; and we may in fact see a true Corporate State, a regime with strong affinities to the past — post-Civil-War Spain, for example — as well as to the present of the "new military."

I must emphasize again, however, that for the time being natural corporatism is an analytical construct, a scholar's tool, and nothing else. Even for those in the tricky business of operationalizing scholarship into policy or rationalizations for policy, it must be obvious that the concept of natural corporatism is not the stuff of which policy recommendations are made.

Authoritarianism, Corporatism and Mobilization in Peru *

James M. Malloy

In recent years there has been a renewed interest among social scientists in authoritarianism, both as a type of regime and as a specific political approach to the problems of economic development and modernization.[1] This revival of interest has been spurred in part by the proliferation of authoritarian regimes in the less developed countries and by the fact that many of these regimes are doing a more than creditable job in stimulating and managing the process of development and modernization.

The "Revolutionary Government of the Armed Forces," which seized power in Peru in October of 1968, is one of the more interesting current examples of a development-oriented authoritarian regime. The new government, headed by General Juan Velasco Alvarado, has veered sharply from the stereotyped image of Latin American military regimes. It has initiated a number of structural reforms that are profoundly altering Peruvian society. While one might count the Peruvian regime as more benevolent than that in Brazil, the fact remains that both are authoritarian in political form and share the common goal of promoting the rapid economic development of their respective societies. These are characteristics that both share with a number of other military and mixed civil-military regimes throughout the world. Whatever its unique characteristics, it would, therefore, be of at least heuristic value to view the Peruvian regime as a case of the more general phenomenon of "nontraditional," or perhaps, "modernizing" authoritarianism.

Approaching the Peruvian regime from this perspective, it is

* This work was supported by an International Affairs Fellowship of the Council on Foreign Relations and by funds from the University Center for International Studies of the University of Pittsburgh. Helpful comments were made by the members of the "Peru Seminar" organized by Abraham Lowenthal and held at the Center for Inter-American Relations, New York. I would also like to thank my colleagues, Charles Jones, Murdo McLeod, Roland Paulston and Reid Reading, for valuable criticisms. I am particularly grateful to Paul Allen Beck for his unflagging willingness to read and criticize various drafts of the paper. I also owe an intellectual debt to the work of Julio Cotler and Aníbal Quijano. I am of course responsible for the paper's shortcomings.

[1] For a discussion of the new trend, see Susan Kaufman Purcel, "Authoritarianism," *Comparative Politics* (January, 1973), pp. 301-312.

useful to take as a starting point the definition of authoritarianism formulated by Juan Linz:

> Authoritarian regimes are political systems with limited, not responsible political pluralism: without elaborate and guiding ideology (but with distinctive mentalities); without intensive or extensive political mobilization (except some points in their development); and in which a leader (or occasionally a small group) exercises power within formally ill-defined limits but actually quite predictable ones.[2]

Linz's definition is of necessity rather general and explicitly leaves open the question of delineating subtypes of authoritarian regimes. A central argument of this paper is that the new Peruvian regime has shown a marked tendency, at the level of both ideas and organizational principles, toward the creation of a corporate-state structure, and therefore illustrates a potentially important variant of authoritarianism evident in many Latin American countries and other cultural areas as well.

Owing to its association in many minds with fascism, corporatism as both an ideology and an analytical perspective has long been discredited and swept under the intellectual rug. It is by no means coincidental, however, that the recent interest in authoritarianism has been accompanied by a revived concern with the theory and practice of corporatism. This has been true particularly among Latin Americanists who have begun to employ the concept in a number of intellectually stimulating ways.

The concept has been used at three distinct but not unrelated levels of analysis in discussing Latin American politics: the analysis of institutional and cultural principles derived from the Hispanic tradition that persist in contemporary Latin America and have important effects on the political process;[3] the analysis of a de facto mode of group formation and interest articulation that persists in Latin America alongside and impinging upon other modes of group conflict and which is inadequately grasped by the usual liberal or Marxist group theories of politics;[4] the analysis of particular mode

---

[2] Juan Linz, "An Authoritarian Regime: Spain" in Erik Allardt and Stein Rokkan, eds., *Mass Politics* (New York, 1970), p. 255.

[3] See, for example, Howard J. Wiarda, "Toward a Framework for the Study of Political Change in the Iberic-Latin Tradition: The Corporative Model," *World Politics*, XXV (January, 1973), 206-236.

[4] Ronald C. Newton, "On Functional Groups, Fragmentation, and Plural-

of formally organizing and integrating a political system, for example, a regime type that exists in Mexico and is developing in Peru.[5] All these studies point out that whatever its ideological aspirations, corporatism is based upon an empirically useful group theory of politics.

Thus, while formal ideals of government are seldom realized in practice, corporatism does give us a different perspective to approach the politics of countries such as Mexico and Peru, and other Latin states as well, whose political processes may come closer to the corporate model of group dynamics than either the liberal-interest group or Marxian models. The key to the longevity of the postrevolutionary Mexican system may be that it has to a large degree formalized and institutionalized corporatist modes of activity long alive in Mexico, but largely ignored by other political schemes. In Peru, we may be witnessing an even more elaborate formalization of basic corporatist group dynamics common to all Latin American societies.

Theories of the corporate state have an ancient lineage, but in the late nineteenth and early twentieth centuries corporatism was advanced in many contexts, particularly in Catholic social doctrine, as a specific alternative to either capitalism or socialism to grapple with the problems of economic development and modernization in an essentially "humanistic" way. As an "ideology of development," corporatism has been intellectually diffuse, embracing a variety of positions which in corporatist terms could be arranged on a right-left continuum. However, one can extract from this diversity a number of basic themes common to all corporatist thinking.[6] Among the more salient of these themes are the following:

> Corporatism assumes that a harmonious process of development and modernization can be achieved if society is correctly organized and based upon an adequate notion of distributive but not necessarily egalitarian justice.

> The state is charged with overseeing the process by maintaining

ism in Spanish American Political Society," *The Hispanic American Historical Review*, L (February, 1970), 1-29.

[5] Julio Cotler, "Bases Del Corporativismo en el Perú," *Sociedad y Política*, I (October, 1972), 3-12.

[6] For a review of the corporatist thinking, see Ralph H. Bowen, *German Theories of the Corporate State* (New York, 1947); Matthew H. Elbow, *French Corporative Theory, 1789-1948* (New York, 1966); Richard L. Camp, *The Papal Ideology of Social Reform* (Leiden, 1969).

correct organization and regulating intergroup relations: the state intervenes in the society and economy but does not absorb them; thus the state is regulative but limited.

Corporatism rejects liberal individualism and Marxist class analysis in that both proceed from the belief that conflict is inevitable and to a certain extent legitimate. In corporatism conflict is not seen as inevitable and is therefore illegitimate. Corporatism seeks to eliminate conflict by basing social integration around functional and vocation groupings seen to be the "natural" basis of society.

Corporatism rejects the liberal politics of citizen constituencies, political parties, and votes for representation in a legislative assembly based on territorial divisions.

Corporatism is antisecular and stresses the moral dimensions of social life which it equates with natural groups and the organic social whole as opposed to "classes for themselves" or utility-maximizing individuals.

From the perspective of organizational structure, corporate groups are a form of what Max Weber calls imperative coordination.[7] As such, they are not ad hoc, transitional, or oriented to the pursuit of a single instrumental goal; corporate groups constitute a form of closed social relationship endowed with the authority to maintain an order, that is, a legally recognized and enforceable code that gives the group a formal identity and a permanence beyond the life of its members. As Philippe Schmitter has pointed out, groups of this type could be "natural" in the sense of recognizing groups already there or "artificial" in the sense of government-created groups.[8]

This discussion of corporatist organizational principles brings us back to an important element in Linz's analytical scheme, pluralism. Linz say authoritarianism is characterized by "limited pluralism," as opposed to democracy's open pluralism. This is difficult theoretical terrain, vaguely mapped. But viewing corporatism as a subtype of authoritarianism enables us to surmount this problem at least partially. Corporatism is a form of limited pluralism, but it is also considerably more: it is a coherent and operationally definable group theory of politics that is opposed to other group

---

[7] Max Weber, *The Theory of Social and Economic Organization* (New York, 1964), p. 145.

[8] Philippe C. Schmitter, *Interest Conflict and Political Change in Brazil* (Stanford, 1971), p. 112.

theories. We can grasp the corporatist group theory most readily by contrasting it with the prevailing group theory in American political science, "interest group liberalism."[9]

Interest group liberalism has a lineage traceable to English social contract theory. In this scheme the basis of the state is its individual members who participate in the state (become citizens) because it is in their interest to do so; compared to the state of nature, the formal state provides an arena in which, although all of one's interests cannot be met, each citizen stands a better chance of maximizing gains and minimizing losses. In any event, the state exists to regulate the intercourse of such utility-maximizing individuals so as to redound to at least the partial satisfaction of all.

Modern interest group theory implicitly retains this atomistic model but notes at least three problems that have led to the elaboration of a more sophisticated model. In modern society the distance between the state and the individual is such that individuals acting on their own have little chance of influencing policy. Moreover, government cannot cope with all the potential interests in society and therefore there must exist some intermediary structures which articulate broad categories of interests and aggregate them into manageable packages, thus, interest groups and political parties. Also, governmental stability demands a base of legitimacy, rooted not only in calculated advantage, but also in shared values regarding the "rules of the game." Modern democratic process, then, is based on a plurality of groups that emerge spontaneously and voluntarily out of a multiplicity of discrete instrumental interests. As individual perceptions of interests and relevant groups to articulate them can change (groups can come in and out of existence and at any point in time), there are actual interest groups and potential interest groups. These groups compete with one another within a commonly accepted set of rules and function to check one another, thereby making governmental power both limited and responsible.

The individual citizen is integrated into the system through the group infrastructure; conversely, if the intermediary structure fails to develop or breaks down, a situation of massification and instability results.[10] The citizen can belong to a number of such

[9] For an overview of the American pluralist perspective, see Henry S. Kariel, ed., *Frontiers of Democratic Theory* (New York, 1970), part two.

[10] This position is argued in W. Kornhauser, *The Politics of Mass Society* (London, 1960).

instrumental groups and therefore has a multiplicity of crosscutting group loyalties. Hence, the individual has no primordial attachment to any one group and can give his terminal loyalty to the larger state and national community. Indeed, for most United States theorists of modernization, this movement from loyalty to lower primordial attachment groups to the larger state, and the concomitant development of an infrastructure of voluntary instrumental groups rather than consummatory groups is a hallmark of modernity and a prerequisite to further modernization and economic development.[11] Although it is beyond the scope of this paper, one should note that this group model of politics has been the subject of much recent criticism both as a theory of modernization and an adequate description of political dynamics in modern states such as the United States.[12]

Corporatism in turn is predicated on the assumption that in any society there exists a limited number of primary or natural interests based mainly on occupation and vocation. Since one's occupation is the major component of his adult life, this is the individual's major area of concern. Thus, one's work not only represents interests but also orders and regulates a large part of his individual life. For him, it is more than a group; it is a community with consummatory as well as instrumental dimensions. These groups, not atomized individuals, constitute the base of society. The individual gains a sociopolitical identity and a range of rights and privileges from corporate group membership.

For the classic liberal, liberty is a product of the absence of restraint and while social living demands some restraint, one seeks to organize the state to minimize constraints on utility-maximizing individuals. For a corporatist such as Durkheim, however, "genuine liberty is a product of regulation" which is based on the principle that "human passions stop only before a moral power they respect."[13] This "moral power" is in the first instance the corporate group.

---

[11] For example, see Marion J. Levy, Jr., *Modernization and the Structure of Societies* (Princeton, 1969).

[12] See Ronald Rogowski and Lois Wasserspring, "Does Political Development Exist? Corporatism in Old and New Societies," *Sage Comparative Politics Series,* 01-024, II (1971) and Alejandro Portes, "Modernity and Development: A Critique," *Studies in Comparative International Development,* in press. For a critique of the model as applied to the United States, see Theodore J. Lowi, *The End of Liberalism* (New York, 1969).

[13] Emil Durkheim, *The Division of Labor in Society,* preface to the second edition (Toronto, 1966), p. 3.

A corporate system is a regulated system, but regulation exists at two levels. In terms of the bulk of primary social and economic activities, regulation is the function of the corporate group which is endowed with the legal and moral authority to maintain an order in its sphere; it is a form of imperative coordination with semi-sovereign characteristics. The state, in turn, is charged with the function of maintaining the "general health of the social body" by regulating intercorporate group relations. The state, in theory at least, is limited to this sphere and is, therefore, regulative but not interventionist. Thus, a full-blown corporate state is a partic-ular kind of "limited pluralism" in which plurality is formalized and legalized by the state, either by recognizing already existing groups or creating a number of new types of groupings or both.

This point is again relevant to the authoritarian scheme of Linz, for he stresses the existence of "groups not created by or dependent on the state which influence the political process in one way or another."[14] This dimension of pluralism in authoritarian regimes becomes rather fuzzy in his article, however, because he goes on to talk of legal plurality, institutionalized plurality, auton-omous groups, and so on. The real issue may be the question of effective autonomy no matter how difficult that is to define. In the corporatist scheme the principle is that groups are to be relatively autonomous in intragroup decisions but the groups exist by virtue of recognition and to that extent are dependent on the state. If they have semisovereign qualities in their spheres, it is because the state confers them upon them and then assumes the role of regulat-ing intergroup relations. In formal terms, a corporate state is a lim-ited and, in a real sense, constitutional state. A corporate state in principle could, therefore, be either democratic or authoritarian or various mixes of the two. It could, for example, be democratic in terms of intragroup decisions and authoritarian at the level of intergroup decisions.

The remainder of this paper will be divided into three sections. In the first, the orientation, or to use Linz's term, "mentality," of Peru's present leaders will be examined in an attempt to show that the ideas, concepts and rhetoric of the regime show a marked similarity to the corporatist ideological principles discussed above. In the second section, the analysis will focus on some of the regime's rather innovative attempts to reorganize Peruvian society and solid-

---

14 Linz, p. 255.

ify its control over it. In particular, we will focus on the government's recent attempt to systematically mobilize mass support through a new state organization known as *Sistema Nacional de Apoyo a la Movilización Social* (National System in Support of Social Mobilization), or SINAMOS. Again, the purpose will be to show that the operational and organizational principles being implemented by SINAMOS conform closely to organizational principles of corporatist group theory.

In the final section Peru will be viewed as adopting a corporatist structure as a specific political model of achieving rapid economic development. In this section it will be argued that any approach to development must grapple with certain political and economic problems (to be discussed below) common to all underdeveloped environments. It is obviously too early to assess the specific implications of the Peruvian process. However, we do have enough material to engage in informed speculation. In this regard it will be argued that, while a corporate state in principle need not be authoritarian, and while the Peruvian military leadership has a declared intention to create a democratic and participationist society, the environmental constraints in relation to its other goal of rapid economic development will push the regime, in the foreseeable future, to emphasize central control over broad participation and thereby maintain at all levels a decidedly authoritarian decision-making style. Thus, the paper will project the emergence in Peru of a corporate subtype of modernizing authoritarianism and close by analyzing the probable implications of the corporate approach in terms of a likely system of political economy.

Orientation of the Peruvian Regime

Since the coup d'etat of 1968, Peru's military leaders have rather self-consciously avoided the elaboration of a systematic ideological line; likewise, they have not identified themselves with any standard ideologies and have resisted all attempts to pin ideological labels on the Peruvian process. Regime spokesmen have, however, expended considerable effort to explain and justify the regime's actions to the Peruvian people and foreign observers. As a result, there does exist a large body of public statements from which a number of recurrent themes can be drawn. Thus, as the Linz scheme would lead us to expect, this regime, while not advancing a specific ideology, is characterized by a distinctive "mentality."[15]

This distinctive characteristic of authoritarian regimes arises in part from the fact that such regimes rest upon a plurality (albeit limited) of relatively autonomous groups and institutions which gives rise to the existence of a plural elite structure. This is true in Peru where, although the military is dominant, autonomous power groupings (the church, business associations, professional groups, some unions, etc.) continue to exist and interact effectively with governmental decision-makers. This elite diversity militates against the adoption of a specific ideology; what binds the elite together is a store of assumptions, common goals and concepts that form a core orientation which provides a set of standards for intraelite debate over specific programs and policies. Such an orientation can be delineated in the Peruvian regime.

More often than not, the regime defines itself in negative terms, the usual expression being that the system that is being constructed is neither communist nor capitalist. When more positive concepts are used, the government usually describes itself as being revolutionary, nationalist and popular: revolutionary because its reforms are significantly altering the country's traditional power structure; nationalist because it is dedicated to the solution of Peru's specific problems in a uniquely Peruvian way, and popular because it seeks to promote social justice for those excluded by the previous scheme of things. The popular groups include the middle class, workers, peasants and other marginal sectors; that is, the vast bulk of the population which, according to the regime, shares a common set of interests against the oligarchy and the foreign imperial interests it served. The primary goals of the regime's reforms thus far have been to break the power of the so-called oligarchy, and to sever the bonds of Peru's dependence on the industrial capitalist powers. The purposes of these actions are the nation's economic independence, the promotion of rapid economic development by means of industrialization, and the sowing of the fruits of development among the masses. An interesting aspect of the populist dimension of the regime's thinking is the belief that, given the commonality of interests among those exploited by the oligarchy, society can be so organized that development can be achieved without the traditional forms of intergroup or class conflict. An integrated or "inte-

---

[15] An excellent compendium of speeches is *Velasco la VOZ de la Revolución* (Lima, 1971).

gral" harmonious social whole is therefore another regime goal.

At the moment, at least, the regime's formal thinking about agencies such as SINAMOS denies any inclination toward totalitarianism and, in fact, rejects any notion of its having an authoritarian control function. In launching SINAMOS, the government has sought to justify it and define its role by elaborating a bit more specifically (although still very vaguely) the type of society it plans to create.

The key concept in the latest elaboration of the regime's formal thinking is that of a society which will be a "democracy with full participation" (*una democracia de participación plena*). What is most interesting from the viewpoint of a foreign observer of the Peruvian experiment is the fact that, as yet, the concept of participation has not been defined in any formal political terms, such as legislative bodies, parties, interest groups, etc. Rather, the regime has restricted its discussions of participation exclusively to the economic sphere. The logic appears to be that the oligarchy dominated Peru because of its economic power; hence, the major aim of the reforms is to undercut the economic power of the oligarchy and restructure the economy so that previously excluded groups can effectively control the decisions that directly affect their destiny. The clear implication of the regime's pronouncements is that the most important decisions that affect a person's life are economic decisions and the primary place for participation is the work place.

Concomitant with the advancement of the concept of full participation, therefore, has been a more specific projection of how the Peruvian economy will be eventually structured. The regime projects an economy based on three sectors defined in terms of ownership; a state sector, a reformed private sector, and a sector of "social interest" or social property.* The private sector will be reformed by the establishment of worker communities which will

---

* The "social interest" sector as conceived by the Peruvian military regime bears considerable similarity to the "communitarian society" (*sociedad comunitaria*) that various Chilean Christian Democratic ideologists hoped to bring into being. The "communitarian society," within which the distinction between capital and labor would be eliminated as the two functions came to be embodied in the same men through profit-sharing programs that would eventually bring ownership over the means of production into the hands of workers' associations, was in turn highly derivative. It revealed a striking parallel to the "national syndicalism" of the early revolutionary Spanish Falange, the Falange before it was tamed and transformed into a component of a nonrevolutionary system by Francisco Franco.—Ed.

gain an increasing role in management. Similar communities will
be established in the state sector. Thus, in these two sectors there
will be private and public ownership with worker participation.
The concept of property in the social sector is still somewhat vague
and confusing. In the social sector firms will be completely worker
managed, but the property will not belong directly to the workers
of the firm either individually or collectively, but to all the workers
of all the social property firms. According to projections, the reformed private sector will contract until it becomes smallest, the
state sector (which will monopolize basic industry) will expand
but stop short of dominating the economy, while the social property
sector will expand until it becomes the largest and, therefore, major
economic sector.

In the new scheme of things, the economy will, in the main,
be organized horizontally in terms of co-ops and communities
rather than vertically in terms of owners and workers or managers
and workers. From this projection is derived another critical concept advanced by the regime—*auto-gestión* or self-direction. In
the future, economic life will be primarily the result of the decisions
of all these self-directed economic units. In sum, the aim is to
create:

> an economy fundamentally self-directed, in which the means of
> production will be predominantly social property, under the direct
> control of those who through their work generate the wealth.[16]

The state and more specifically "the president of the republic
and his council of ministers" are charged with the task of promoting the realization of the new economic system and in particular of facilitating the process by which the vast majority of the
populace will participate in the new organizations—this in fact is
what social mobilization is all about. All components of the public
administrative apparatus share in this responsibility. However,
such a vast and complex process demands a "common focus, orientation, and methodology" and this can be achieved only by "organizing certain functions in one state organism that is charged with
the coordination of sectorial actions and the organization of the
population as well as the direct execution of tasks designed to

---

[16] *¿ A Donde Vamos?* a publication of SINAMOS (Lima, 1972), p. 7.

achieve effective popular participation through autonomous base organizations."[17] That agency is SINAMOS.

Before turning to a description of the formal organization of SINAMOS, it would be well to probe some of the less formalized aspects of the thinking going into the organization. An organization that is just in the process of being built will no doubt be heavily influenced by the ideas and attitudes of its chief architects. An interesting aspect of SINAMOS is that, although it is the creature of a military government and is headed by a military man, a coterie of civilian intellectuals is playing the preponderant role in constructing the organization and defining its operational criteria. This group by no means overrides the military, but it is they who are giving organization and operational substance to the military government's concept. By far, the most important of the civilian chiefs of SINAMOS is Carlos Delgado.

Delgado has long enjoyed a reputation as an important social theorist. He was also a prominent member of Peru's longest lived and most powerful antioligarchical party—*Alianza Popular Revolucionaria Americana*—APRA, as well as the one-time private secretary to the party's perennial leader, Víctor Raúl Haya de la Torre. In the 1950's, however, disillusioned with the tactical line of APRA, Delgado broke with the party and assumed an independent revolutionary stance. Since the coup of 1968, Delgado has gradually emerged as one of the chief civilian advisers to President Velasco, defender of the regime's policies, and propounder of its ideas and concepts. Since its founding, Delgado has been the chief spokesman of SINAMOS.

Aside from reiterating many of the ideas outlined above, Delgado has prefaced most of his speeches, interviews and articles with an analysis of why and how the revolution of 1968 came about. A brief sketch of Delgado's analysis will provide an important indicator of the attitudes of many in SINAMOS and the regime toward important aspects of Peru's traditional political life.[18]

For Delgado, Peru's political crisis began in the 1930's when a number of groups emerged to try to unseat the oligarchy and drive imperialism from Peru. Formed in parties and labor unions, these

---

[17] *Ibid.*, p. 9.

[18] This analysis is based on a lecture given by Delgado at the Superior School of Public Administration (Lima, July 21, 1972) and on Carlos Delgado, "Significado político y social del proceso revolucionario peruano," *Libre*, No. 3 (1972), pp. 35-43.

groups developed a theoretical critique of the traditional system and offered a variety of images of a different and better Peru. Although they raised the needed standard of revolution, these groups for various reasons were unable to unseat the oligarchy. The Marxist parties and unions failed due to a mechanical attempt to apply Marxian class categories to Peru. They failed to grasp the fact that the problem in Peru was not class conflict but the oppression of all the popular sectors (middle class, workers, and peasants) by the oligarchy and imperialism. Moreover, as agents of Moscow, they never adopted a nationalist stance and, hence, remained an isolated sectarian group oriented to a working-class base that was too small to mount a revolution. The need was for a movement that would mobilize all of Peru's oppressed groups behind the banners of nationalism and populism.

With the emergence of APRA, it appeared that the need would be fulfilled. But, although APRA developed a viable position and thereby became the nation's major force for change, the party fell under the personalistic sway of Haya, who, over the years, led it away from its own principles. By the late 1950's, APRA had abandoned the left nationalist position and actually had become an agent of the very oligarchy it professed to hate. Thus, due to either ignorance or chicanery, the leftist parties failed in their mission.

The outstanding proof of failure and betrayal came in the 1960's when APRA allied itself with the forces of ex-dictator Manuel Odría (1948-1956) to control the legislature and block even the mildly reformist efforts of the Belaúnde regime. This legislative obstruction further revealed the weakness of Peru's political institutions. Peru had fallen into the twin evils of a political vacuum and an institutional crisis.

At the same time as this negative process was taking place, two institutions, the army and the church, formerly identified with the oligarchy, were going through a major change of orientation from the Right to the Left. Increasingly significant elements in both moved to a progressive nationalist and potentially revolutionary position.

As the political and institutional crisis of the 1960's worsened, it became increasingly evident that a way out had to be found and that the existing parties could not do the job. In the face of the civil impasse it became apparent that only institutionalized power could break the stalemate. Thus, the military, which had evolved a clear perception of Peru's needs, was forced to seize power because of the failure of civil politics. Peru demonstrates, Delgado argues, that not only can the military adopt the role of revolutionary, but no true nationalist revolution can take place without the active involvement of the military.

There are, I think, a number of themes in this analysis which are important to keep in mind when viewing SINAMOS, for Delgado is expressing deeply held views of many in SINAMOS and the military government it serves. First is the reiteration of the national populist theme of the commonality of interests among various sectors of the populace and by extension the belief that correct organization can eliminate class conflict. Of more profound significance is the view that traditional political organizations, such as parties and unions, as well as traditional political institutions, have been abysmal failures. Given the peculiar organizational thrust SINAMOS has taken thus far, one is tempted to speculate that Delgado and others have concluded that political life as such (as we have known it in the West) has failed in Peru. Their concept of democracy is restricted to some form of economic democracy with the larger classical political questions still wide open. I will return to this question below, but for the moment the relevant point is that the government clearly sees no place in Peru's political future for the traditional parties or unions or for traditional political institutions. SINAMOS, in fact, is the first step in a drive to supplant the parties and unions and to organize a new and fundamentally different state structure.

SINAMOS

The events in Peru since 1968 have often been characterized as "revolution from above" or most recently "revolution by fiat."[19] These characterizations call attention to the fact that the process of change in Peru was not preceded by a dramatic popular insurrection, but a well-executed bloodless coup d'etat. Indeed, many have argued that one of the reasons the Peruvian military seized power in the first place was to forestall the outbreak of such a popular uprising. According to this view (which I share), the fear

---

[19] Jane S. Paquette, "Revolution by Fiat: The Context of Policy Making in Peru," *The Western Political Quarterly,* XXV (December, 1972), 648-667.

of an unpredictable mass revolutionary process is an important motive behind the structural reforms the regime has implemented. Thus, while the Peruvian military is obviously committed to the significant restructuring of Peruvian society, the military is also committed to the proposition that reforms will be implemented in an orderly manner with themselves firmly in control of the process. The Peruvian revolution is being made in the name of the masses and popular justice, but its makers harbor considerable apprehension of those same masses acting on their own or at the behest of other leaders.[20]

During its first two and one half years in power, the Velasco regime was not particularly mobilization-minded; in the main the government sought to generate popular support through occasional mass rallies and a steady barrage of nationalistic and patriotic gestures and rhetoric. It did not seek to systematically organize a mass base and moved with alacrity to squash any attempts at spontaneous and autonomous popular organization.[21]

For a number of reasons which are beyond the scope of this essay, the Velasco government in June, 1971, made a dramatic about-face from this more "typical authoritarian approach" and is now moving vigorously to enlist in a systematic and organized manner the active involvement of almost the entire populace in support of its revolution.

In initiating this nation-wide process of "mobilization," the government has bypassed all of Peru's traditional political parties and most other extant forms of organization as well. Yet the regime has not sought to organize its own political party; rather, it has created a new, and in the regime's eyes, unique type of governmental agency, SINAMOS. The newest creation of the "revolution," SINAMOS is already one of the largest and best-funded administrative agencies in Peru. With an initial official budget of nine million dollars and a starting staff of 4,800, SINAMOS has

---

[20] This position has been argued by many. One of the basic statements is that of Víctor Villanueva, *El CAEM y la revolución de la Fuerza Armada* (Lima, 1972).

[21] The most dramatic manifestation of this took place in 1969 with the emergence in many parts of Peru of numerous local "Committees for the Defense of the Revolution." Some were organized spontaneously while others were organized by political groups such as the communists. At first the government sought to control these groups but then, obviously fearful of them, the government forced them to disband. For a discussion of the CDR's, see David Scott Palmer, "Revolution from Above: Military Government and Popular Participation in Peru," (Ph.D. diss., Cornell University, 1973), ch. 2.

absorbed eight previous state agencies as well as taken over many of the functions and personnel of established ministerial offices. As one might expect, the appearance of SINAMOS has set off a great deal of bureaucratic infighting and has generated a great deal of hostility among administrative agencies that have been hurt by it as well as those who perceive it as a potential threat. What the outcome of this battle for administrative existence will be is anyone's guess but, for the moment at least, SINAMOS is officially charged with the task of organizing the bulk of the populace and there are no formally defined limits to the range of functions it may ultimately perform.

The primary task of SINAMOS is to carry out a generalized process of social mobilization. However, it is not to be simply any kind of mobilization but a process of "responsible" and "constructive" mobilization. A central principle of SINAMOS is that "There is no mobilization possible without organization." This process of organized mobilization will lead to a social democracy of full participation which in turn will be based on the following principles: "A moral order of solidarity, *not* individualism; a basically self-directed economy in which the means of production will be mainly social property; a political order where the power of decision, far from being the monopoly of a political or economic oligarchy, will be diffuse and located essentially in social and political institutions conducted without intermediaries or a minimum of them by the men and women who form the organization."[22] The aim is for a true self-directed and self-controlled set of participating organizations.

But "if social mobilization represents a process, it would be illusory to think that the men and women of Peru *immediately* can exercise their power of decision over *all* the problems that affect their daily lives as members of society. Our people, who never before had real power of decision, will have to responsibly prepare and train themselves in order to assume this new role" (emphasis mine).[23] This is a rather important caveat to which we will return below.

The specific functions of SINAMOS are defined in relationship to these operating principles and further definitions of what "social mobilization" will entail in Peru. Following from the

---

[22] *SINAMOS ¿ de Quién y Para Que?* publication of SINAMOS (Lima, 1972), p. 3.

[23] *Ibid.*, p. 7.

regime's populist orientation, social mobilization is perceived as a blend of "complex and diverse phenomena that have many expressions, operate on many levels, and manifest themselves in many manners." Whatever else it may be, "it would be a crass error to consider it as an institutionalized mechanism for *class* conflict" (emphasis mine). Many of the most critical problems regarding communities and work relations are in this view "not properly political, in the sense that word is generally used."[24] What they are is not defined except to reiterate the need for the people to train themselves for responsible participation which, along with structural reforms, will lead to the creation of a new "type of state."

It should be kept in mind, however, that social mobilization is in the first instance an integral part of the revolution and its primary base of support: "The people, organized and vigilant, will be the best defense against any attempt to detain or divert the revolution."[25] SINAMOS can be said then to have two primary tasks: in the long run, to facilitate the emergence of the new type of state; in the short run, to mobilize the populace to defend, support, the revolution. The new state remains undefined and, given the vagueness of definitions, the revolution can be understood concretely as simply the government and its policies at any point in time.

SINAMOS has another critical task which, along with the mobilization of support for the government, could become its main one; whatever its political goals, the Velasco regime is also dedicated to promoting the rapid economic development of Peru. As the achievement of economic independence and rapid economic development are often presented as the necessary foundation of other goals, development is in some sense the main immediate goal of the revolution. Thus, SINAMOS is charged with the task "of achieving the conscious and active participation of the national population in those activities essential to economic and social development."[26] It is of more than passing interest that this statement appears in the first article of decree law 18896 creating SINAMOS.

This rather significant shift in emphasis from the grandiose

---

[24] *Ibid.,* p. 8.
[25] *Ibid.,* p. 11.
[26] *Ibid.*

task of creating a democratic society of full participation to the more utilitarian ends of supporting the government and promoting development is reinforced by the definition of the organization's medium- and long-range goals. The medium-range objectives of SINAMOS are defined as: a) "to identify the popular sectors with the process of structural reforms"; b) "to amplify the social base of support for present and future reforms"; and c) "to promote the participation of the popular sectors in development planning." The long-range objective of SINAMOS is:

> to create a new society with the structural participation of the entire Peruvian population.[27]

To achieve these defined objectives, SINAMOS is to organize Peruvian society from the top to the bottom—"from the highest level of the revolutionary government it ought to descend to the local level, with the end of consolidating, promoting and articulating the base organization."[28] In elaborating its structure, SINAMOS will organize the populace along regional as well as functional lines.

At the top level, SINAMOS is the principal agency in charge of social mobilization. As such it is charged with regulating the entire public administrative apparatus in terms of its relationships with the populace. It is charged with the duty of seeing to it that the public administration conforms with the interests and aspirations of the people. In this regard, SINAMOS will have to carry out a true reform of the public administration. This will entail not only changes in procedures and methods, but, even more important, SINAMOS will develop means to change the mentality, attitude and values of Peru's archaic bureaucracy. If these particular provisions are enforced (it remains a big "if"), SINAMOS could emerge as, among other things, the watchdog of the entire public administrative apparatus.

With regard to the articulation of an organized connection between the government and the populace, SINAMOS' activities will fall in five functional categories: a) diffusion; b) capacitation; c) support of intrastructure; d) financial support, and e) juridical administrative support. The concept of capacitation is often also referred to as "conscientization" and springs from the assumption

---

[27] *Ibid.,* pp. 13-14.
[28] *Ibid.,* p. 22.

noted above that the popular masses are not yet ready to assume all of the responsibilities implied in self-direction and participation. Hence, even as SINAMOS must act to change the mentality of the bureaucracy, it must also change the mentality of the populace at large; it must develop the means to raise the level of consciousness of the masses as well as develop their capacity for self-government.[29]

As currently set up, there are no defined limits to the areas of Peruvian life that SINAMOS may penetrate. Lacking such explicit limits, the organization could potentially penetrate all groups and activities. But, for the moment, its functional activities are specifically targeted at six broad population groupings it will immediately seek to organize: a) neighborhood organizations—mainly in the squatter settlements, now known by the benign term "young towns"; b) youth organizations; c) formation of worker organizations; d) cooperative and self-directed organizations; e) rural organizations, and f) professional and cultural organizations.[30] Not all of society, but quite a large chunk.

On paper SINAMOS has a clearly delineated organization chart that coordinates office functioning at the national, regional, provincial and local levels. The highest organization is the national office—*Oficina Nacional de Apoyo a la Movilización Social*, ONAMS. This office is the centerpiece of the system and charged with implementing the system. The ONAMS is defined as being essentially a normative office that will formulate the general mobilization policies. But the ONAMS has the complementary function of regulating the regional offices to see to it that they follow and implement nationally defined policies.

Below ONAMS are thirteen regional offices—*Oficinas Regionales de Apoyo a la Movilización Social*, ORAMS. If the ONAMS is the center of the system, the ORAMS are the critical points linking the national and local levels. They will be the chief planning and administrative offices of the system, operating on the principle of maximum decentralization and delegation of power. The ORAMS will formulate the regional plans by rendering compatible plans coming from the local level with those developed at the national level. They will then formulate specific programs and the budgets to support them, as well as be responsible for implement-

---

[29] *Ibid.*, p. 25.
[30] *Ibid.*, p. 26.

ing the programs. The ORAMS are clearly the critical operational offices.

To avoid duplication of efforts, there are at present no plans to establish provincial offices. One goes directly from the regional to the local level, where a series of zonal offices will be established— *Oficinas Zonales de Apoyo a la Movilización Social*, OZAMS. These offices will be the direct link between SINAMOS and the populace. Here planning will no longer be the activity of technocrats, but begin to be the work of the ordinary citizen. Here the populace "will detect problems that affect their communities, in the planning of the actions designed to resolve such problems—but *within a previous evaluation to establish priorities*—and, finally, back the projects with popular support" (emphasis mine).[31]

The OZAMS are defined as the critical link in the system that will open the direct participation of the "organized populace in the development of thousands of projects and activities." These zonal offices will link up with the localities by means of an undetermined number of promoters (*promotores*) who will act in accord with the needs of the communities in which they work.

The entire system is to be constructed in phases beginning with ONAMS and working down; the target date for completion is 1973-74. SINAMOS is unmistakably beginning its life from the top down; but according to the government, it will grow and mature into an organization that will live its life from the bottom.

Summary

In the last two sections I attempted to show that in one form or another the basic themes of corporatist ideology appear in the Peruvian government's rhetoric and in the operational principles of SINAMOS. Since 1968 the public sector has expanded rapidly (aside from a proliferation of public corporations, the government percentage of total investment jumped from 17.9 percent in 1967 to 41.1 percent in 1972) and the state has adopted a regulatory role; but the regime promises that the state will not dominate all other spheres. As we saw, SINAMOS seeks a "moral order of solidarity not individualism," and rejects class conflict. The regime's disdain for Peru's traditional politicians, parties and insti-

---

[31] *Ibid.*, p. 36.

tutions is evident and SINAMOS is presented as an *apolitical* phenomenon.

Whatever its official designation, it seems fairly clear that a primary purpose of SINAMOS, in fact, is to undercut the infrastructure of the pre-1968 political system. Through SINAMOS, the regime is attempting to modify vertical divisions by organizing economic activity into primary communities in which all will have a stake. The creation of such communitarian interests is designed to diminish class consciousness and develop a sense of loyalty to the community which will diminish loyalty to the traditional unions and thereby curtail support for preexistent parties such as APRA and the communists.[32] At its base Peru will be compartmentally divided into a series of parallel and, in the main, functionally defined communities.

Central to all of this, in my view, is a general governmental effort to depoliticize Peruvian society in at least two ways. First is a redefinition of politics in essentially corporatist terms by denigrating the former political apparatus, claiming that SINAMOS is nonpolitical, and by a notable failure to define how intergroup relations will be regulated and national goals defined. Implicitly at least, politics is reduced to some kind of primary functional communitarian democracy; concomitantly political space is contracted to the narrow spheres of such communities, which in the main means the work place. The bulk of the populace will be organized within work-based communities and the bulk of their participatory activities restricted to that narrow sphere. The regime appears to be saying that these spheres constitute not only the areas of primary and, hence, legitimate concern of the masses, but also define the limits of their competence to participate. Moreover, the expressed belief that the populace in the main is not yet ready to participate and, hence, must be "capacitated" calls into question the competence of the masses even at this narrow level. As it stands presently, questions regarding intergroup relations and national goals are by default left to the "authorities."

In Peru both "natural" and "artificial" corporate groups exist —the regime has officially recognized various preexistent organiza-

---

[32] The issue of the government versus the preexistent unions came to the fore in late 1972 when SINAMOS launched its own "Confederation of Revolutionary Workers." This action sparked considerable bitterness on all sides but especially from the communist-led General Confederation of Workers which saw many important unions bolt its ranks for the government confederation.

tions—but the bulk of the organizations envisaged by SINAMOS fall into the latter category. In any event, Peru is presently being organized around a series of base organizations that meet the corporate-group criteria used here. A large part of economic life will be compartmentalized into Indian communities, various types of co-ops, the various economic communities (industrial, fishing, mining, etc.). Each such organization is a separate functional entity with its own government-drafted organic law (*ley orgánica*) and juridical personality recognized by and ultimately dependent on the state.

Corporatism and the Future

No one can predict with any certitude what lies ahead for SINAMOS and Peru's revolution. Nonetheless, there are a number of paradoxes and potential contradictions in the present situation that allow one to speculate on some possible trends. One definite possibility (one might say probability) is that, despite claims to be organizing the populace for self-directed mobilization and participation, SINAMOS will, in fact, increasingly become an instrument of central control—organizing and mobilizing the populace primarily for regime-defined goals.

This anticipation arises first from the paradox alluded to above —that, while the regime speaks in the name of the masses, it has evidenced considerable suspicion of the masses and definite fear of any spontaneous mobilization on their part. If one assumes, as I do, that Peru's military rulers are determined not to let the revolutionary process get out of hand, and that any process of true self-mobilization and participation of such diverse social groupings as exist in Peru of necessity would be somewhat disorderly and unpredictable, how much real self-mobilization and participation can one legitimately expect? Can a regime dedicated to a process of controlled and orderly change bring itself to tolerate the Pandora's box of self-directed mobilization? Is not the concept of an orderly, organized process of self-mobilization something of a contradiction in itself? Is not the concept even more contradictory when the organization is launched by an authoritarian government?

Perhaps we are merely quibbling over words and creating verbal contradictions where in practice none exist. Yet it does seem significant that the mobilization process was not allowed to be

initiated from below. SINAMOS is not starting by allowing local
communities and groups to organize themselves and present demands to the government but rather with a centrally organized
structure that will eventually sponsor local organizations. In their
official documents, the leaders of SINAMOS speak incessantly of
self-controlled participation, but at the same time declare that
because of their backward condition, the bulk of the people are
"not ready" to assume that responsibility. This obviously elitist
attitude is reinforced by allusions to the need for "responsible" and
"constructive" mobilization and participation. Such elitist attitudes
are hardly new to modern revolutions, but there are factors in the
Peruvian content which reinforce the attitude even further. Depending upon how one calculates the figure, somewhere around 50
percent of the Peruvian population consists of rural Indians who
are both racially and culturally distinct from the rest of the populace. Another significant group are the urban migrants often referred to as *cholos* who, while no longer culturally Indian, are
identifiably different in racial and cultural characteristics from the
westernized mestizo and white middle and upper classes. Antagonism, mutual misunderstanding and racial conflict have long marked
the relations among these groups; since the nation's inception,
mestizo and white Hispanicized culture has systematically suppressed and exploited *cholo* and Indian culture. The revolutionary
government has committed itself to the abolition of this sorry situation, but the fact remains that the military officers who govern and
the civilian intellectuals and technocrats who staff the chief decision-making posts in SINAMOS are overwhelmingly mestizo and
white products of the urbanized and modernized cultural minority.
Despite the good intentions, SINAMOS has all the potential of
being another case of a manifestation of white and mestizo Hispanicized culture (albeit progressive in orientation) acting upon
cholo and Indian culture.

A question that has long plagued governments is, who knows
the interests of the people best, the people themselves or those who
for one reason or another govern them? This question becomes
even more complicated in a society like Peru that is divided racially
and culturally, as well as developmentally, between a highly urbanized and modernized "advanced" sector and a much larger provincial and rural "backward" sector.

The assumption that the people (through no fault of their own) are not ready for the responsibilities of full participation, and that mobilization must be "reponsible" and "constructive," is the basis of SINAMOS' immediate task, the development of the capacities and consciousness of the masses. Leaving aside the manipulative possibilities of such "capacitizing" activities, one feels compelled to ask, who will define what constitutes "responsible" and "constructive" mobilization? Who will determine when the people have the capacity and the consciousness to assume the full responsibilities of participation? We have enough historical experience to know that, whatever their original ends, elaborate bureaucracies once founded tend to develop purposes of their own, often quite contradictory to the ends of those they were designed to serve, and that bureaucratic elites tend to become primarily concerned with organizing their constituencies to serve organizational goals rather than vice versa.

Peru can quite easily be seen as a case of a military organization seizing power in an attempt to resolve the myriad problems of what Huntington has called a praetorian society. In Huntington's view, a military government that wishes to stabilize its rule and create a new order out of a praetorian situation must mobilize a broad social base and build effective political institutions. However, "the problem is military opposition to politics" and the fact that "military leaders can easily envision themselves in a guardian role; they can also picture themselves as the far-seeing impartial promoters of social and economic reform in their societies. But with rare exceptions they shrink from assuming the role of political organizer."[33] At first the Peruvian military showed opposition to politics, and they still do in the sense of opposition to Peru's traditional parties and institutions, but with the creation of SINAMOS the Peruvian regime is clearly seeking to mobilize and institutionalize a broad base of support and thereby become one of Huntington's "rare exceptions."

The question of mobilization, however, raises some interesting questions in relation to Linz's scheme of authoritarianism. In his analysis of authoritarianism, Linz focuses on three factors: limited pluralism, ideology versus mentality, and apathy versus mobilization. Of the three, apathy versus mobilization appears to be the most important in that it has causal significance for the other two.

---

[33] Samuel P. Huntington, *Political Order in Changing Societies* (New Haven, 1969), p. 243.

A critical, if not the most critical, feature of a stable authoritarian regime is that it is "characterized by a lack of extensive and intensive political mobilization of the population." He equates low or no mobilization with "depolitization" and argues that an increase in politicization over any significant period of time would cause changes in the other factors and therefore a transformation of regime type.

"We would like to argue that this participation is not likely to be maintained over a long period of time, unless the regime moves into a totalitarian or a more formally democratic direction."[34] However, he also argues that "degrees of mobilization might be the most useful criteria on which to distinguish subtypes of authoritarian regimes."

It would seem then that mobilization versus apathy is not a dichotomy, but a polar opposite continuum along which one can make qualitative distinctions between regime types and within that regime subtypes. Whichever, it is clear that mobilization versus apathy is a most important causal variable in Linz's scheme. One obvious, but most understandable, problem with the scheme is that it provides no criteria of measurement to distinguish among regime types or subtypes. Until such criteria are defined, however, one could still make plausible and suggestive arguments for more or less rough distinctions. A more serious problem is the lack of clear definitions of apathy and mobilization. Linz equates mobilization with a variety of phenomena: enthusiasm, politicization, participation, governmental manipulation. His underlying view appears to be that too much mobilization in the direction of autonomous participation would lead to formal democracy, while too much mobilization in the sense of government-controlled participation would lead to totalitarianism. There are outer limits to both types of mobilization which cause regime-type changes away from authoritarianism but within those limits a variety of subtypes of authoritarianism are possible. However, *stable* authoritarianism seeks to limit mobilization in all senses and root itself in public apathy.[35]

Any attempt to speculate on mobilization and its effects must first put the question into its specific Peruvian context. In this case

---

[34] Linz, p. 259.
[35] *Ibid.,* p. 260.

we have raised the possibility of Peru's adopting corporatism as a political model to achieve the self-declared goals of rapid economic development by means of a policy of industrialization. SINAMOS, in turn, is charged with the immediate task of mobilizing support for the regime and its development goal.

As I argued previously, any approach to the process of development must grapple with certain fundamental problems and ideals, and, notwithstanding, the manner in which those problems are resolved will determine the concrete implications of any specific approach. A root dilemma is that between investment and consumption. Given the situation of scarcity prevalent in Latin America, the goal of economic development demands that an investable surplus be generated by means of internal economies, such as restricting consumption. Thus, in countries like Peru, there is a conflict (in the short run at least) between the reformers' goals of social justice and economic development. This conflict is heightened by the fact that in order to govern reformist regimes must generate popular support, usually by meeting the concrete economic demands of various social sectors. Thus, there is also a conflict between the political goal of gaining support and the economic goal of development. Self-styled popular or populist regimes, such as the Peruvian, face an even more aggravated situation because they claim to be generating support from and offering social justice to all sectors of the society except the oligarchy, that is, at the minimum to the middle classes, workers and peasants.

The turbulent history of Bolivia since its populist revolution of 1952 illustrates a number of inescapable facts that are quite relevant to an understanding of the politics of development in Peru and elsewhere in Latin America. At the risk of oversimplification, those facts are: 1) a relatively backward country cannot follow a simultaneous policy of economic development and popular consumption; 2) any process of restructuring for development demands that some social groups pay the "costs" of the new course; and 3) the populist premise of a community of interests among the middle classes, workers and peasants is illusory. Any consistent approach to development, whatever its label, requires that the government be in a position to restrict consumption in the name of development and that it choose which social groups, including its original supporters, will gain and which lose. A model of development entails fundamentally the formation of a coalition powerful enough to resolve these problems and impose the solution it favors on the rest of society.[36]

It will not be long before SINAMOS comes up against these situational dilemmas. If SINAMOS consistently follows its stated goal of broad self-directed mass participation, the inevitable result will be an enormous increase in the quantity and quality of demands pressed on the government. Given the marginal economic position of the bulk of the populace, the vast proportion of these new demands will be for an improvement in living standards. To meet these demands and try to develop at the same time would entail a dramatic increase in consumption levels which would weigh heavily on the nation's limited economic base, curtail the amount of capital available for investment, and most probably set off an inflationary spiral similar to that which plagued the Bolivian revolutionary government between 1952 and 1958, and which undermined the Allende government in Chile and helped prepare the way for the military takeover in September of 1973. Such a policy of demand satisfaction might in the short run win support for the government but its negative economic effects would in the long run undercut that support.

It seems most unrealistic to expect that the Peruvian regime will set aside its developmental goals. Thus, given the experience of numerous other revolutionary governments, it seems realistic to expect that SINAMOS will not be used to stimulate an across-the-board increase in demands. It seems more likely that while the demands of some powerful groups will be processed and at least in part fulfilled by the agency, its primary function will be to carry out a centrally controlled process of mobilization while restraining the populace's demands on the government by manipulative and coercive means. Rather than a mechanism through which the populace makes demands on the government, SINAMOS will most likely become a mechanism through which the government, in the name of development and a future better society, makes demands on the populace.*

The situational constraints of Peru are such that as it goes into operation, SINAMOS will become less and less concerned with its

---

[36] This argument is elaborated on in my *Bolivia: The Uncompleted Revolution* (Pittsburgh, 1972).

* Strikingly similar approaches seem to have been embodied into the *justicialista* program of Argentine dictator Juan Domingo Perón (1946-1955). —Ed.

long-range goal of a democratic society of full participation and become more and more concerned with its medium-range goals of generating support for the government and its policies, and spurring rapid economic development. When one adds to this the authoritarian cast of the regime, its distrust and fear of spontaneous mass action, the regime's belief that the people are not ready to act in their own behalf, and the tendency of bureaucratic organizations toward rigidity and elitism, the prospects for SINAMOS to become a locally directed system of self-directed popular participation are dim. The more likely outcome is that Peru's revolutionary regime, like most other development-oriented revolutionary governments, will seek to realize its goals by increasing, not lessening, central control and coordination, and that it will fashion SINAMOS to that end.

As I argued above, one problem with the Linz scheme is that it fails to define terms such as mobilization and politicization, concepts which are used in many different ways in the literature of political science. In this paper politicization is defined as an increase in political participation in terms of the numbers participating and the levels of the system in which they can participate; mobilization refers to the attempt by a government to elicit in a systematic and organized manner the support of the populace for a regime and the goals it defines for society. A fundamental problem of development-oriented regimes is to generate support in the broadest sense (aside from political conformity, willingness to work, etc.), while containing demands to manageable proportions given collective resources, which the regime seeks to accumulate, control and allocate in a productive manner. In the short run, the regime needs to extract more resources from at least some sectors in the society than it gives back. Given these factors it seems reasonable to expect that SINAMOS will develop a thrust to depoliticize at least part of Peru—by restricting participation and demands—even as it attempts to increase levels of mobilization.

In the Linz scheme mobilization and participation are causal variables that can transform regime types and/or subtypes; too much participation in our sense will result in a democracy, while too much mobilization will lead to a totalitarian or, to use Apter's term, a "mobilization system."[37] However, I would argue against Linz's view that stable authoritarian regimes persist because of

---

[37] David Apter, *The Politics of Modernization* (Chicago, 1966).

broad popular apathy. It is inaccurate at least as far as development-oriented authoritarian regimes are concerned.* A regime
that seeks only to maintain a given status quo may tend toward
apathy, but a regime such as Peru's, which seeks to conduct structural reforms and pursue rapid development in a relatively underdeveloped environment, must establish a more dynamic relationship
with the populace around the problem of extracting resources while
controlling demands. For regimes such as Peru's, the problem is to
find an effective mix of participation and mobilization and then to
stabilize by means of institutionalization. Corporatism can be
viewed as a subtype of development-oriented or modernizing
authoritarianism based upon a mix of limited participation and
limited mobilization (the mix can, of course, vary) institutionalized
around the organizational principles discussed above.

There is another problem with the use of the Linz scheme
(Huntington's as well) to analyze development-oriented authoritarian regimes such as Peru's; namely, it defines authoritarianism
in purely formal political categories when the real issue is one of
political economy. Whatever their political structure, models of
development are also systems of distribution; they address the
question—who gets what, when and how? In looking at Peru as a
budding form of corporate authoritarianism it would be well to
keep Latin America's three previous revolutionary experiences in
mind, Mexico, Bolivia and Cuba.

Two critical economic factors stand out in this regard: sectoral
emphasis in the development scheme, and the role of the private
sector. The Peruvian regime has clearly defined its intention to
develop rapidly by emphasizing industrialization but it has yet to
adopt a clear position on the role of the private sector. The confused signals from the regime regarding the private sector have led
to a precipitous decline in private investment from both local and
international sources. Hence, the development achieved up to now
has been due mainly to a significant increase in government spending. Along with an increase in government investment, there has
been an increase in consumption demands and subsequent building
up of inflationary pressures. This situation is being compounded
by balance-of-payment problems and a growing governmental

---

* The lessons of *peronismo* in Argentina and perhaps also, although much
less clearly, of the Getulio Vargas dictatorship in Brazil (1930-1945) seem to
confirm the author's interpretation.—Ed.

deficit. Hence, while the regime has been able to be somewhat flexible thus far and pursue often contradictory goals, at least one observer has built a convincing case that the government is rapidly running out of maneuvering room and, if it intends to promote rapid development, must soon face the difficult questions of "trade-offs."[38]

While it is no doubt oversimplified, we can project two scenarios of political economy revolving around the question of the role of the private sector. The first would be similar to the Cuban model while the second resembles the model followed successfully by Mexico and thus far unsuccessfully by Bolivia. If the regime reduces to insignificance the role of the private sector, it will have to move increasingly toward a command economy and the state will assume a broadly interventionistic role. Assuming that such a move will curtail foreign private investment even further, Peru will be forced to rely more and more on its own resources. This in turn would increase the need to contain internal consumption demands and to significantly increase levels of mobilization. The costs of the process would fall first on established upper- and middle-sector groups; but as the case of Cuba, not to mention other "socialist" revolutions, indicates, even if such groups are stripped, there will still not be enough surplus to underwrite rapid development. Hence, at some point the remaining social groups will have to shoulder the burden and if they do not choose to do so voluntarily —a fair assumption is that many, if not most, will not so choose— then the government will have to find other means, including force, to make them do so.[39] To be sure, the government may, as

[38] The percentage growth of GNP in 1972 was approximately 7 percent with government investment running about 41 percent of total investment. The consumer price index was rising at the rate of 6.8 percent, the money supply increased by 25 percent and expenditures for personal consumption rose 9.0 percent. The budget deficit for 1972 was about 12 percent of expenditures. The balance of trade has dropped from a +425.6 million dollars in 1970 to a projected +47 million in 1972. Data drawn from: *Economic Indicators,* U.S. Embassy (Lima, 1972); *Anexo Estadístico,* Instituto Nacional de Planificación (June, 1972); Ministerio de Economía y Finanzas, Exposición 21 XXII CDN del CAEM, (May 15, 1972); "The Economic Situation of Peru: Fourth Quarter, 1972," *Peruvian Times* (February 8, 1973), pp. 7-9. For an overall projection of Peru's potential economic problems, see Robert E. Klitgaard, "Observations on the Peruvian National Plan for Development 1971-1975," *Inter-American Economic Affairs,* XXIII (Winter, 1971), 3-32.

[39] For an elaboration of this analysis of Cuba, see my "Generation of Political Support and Allocation of Costs" in Carmelo Mesa-Lago, ed., *Revolutionary Change in Cuba* (Pittsburgh, 1971).

in Cuba, establish a floor of basic necessities shared by all, but the burdens would still be onerous. Moreover, if the government continues to emphasize industrialization, the great mass of Indian peasants would probably bear a disproportionate share of the burden. Hence, in my view, the nature of a command (i.e., centrally planned) system, the problem of costs and the necessity of maintaining mobilization in an environment of scarcity would create a marked tendency to create a total control structure. In short, if the Peruvian regime seeks to promote rapid development without a private sector or an insignificant one, this would lead to a need to increase mobilization and sustain it to such a degree that the regime would be transformed into a totalitarian or "mobilization" system.

If, on the other hand, the thrust is toward industrialization with a significant private sector, another scenario can be projected. A mixed economy based on a relative balance between the public and private sectors would emerge. In Peru, components of the "social sector" might also become significant, but in all cases modern efficient enterprises (public, private, mixed and cooperative) will be favored over small-scale traditional operations.[40] International and local private capital will play a significant role within a limited market where the state seeks to define "the rules of the game" in such a way as to benefit national development. Costs will be allocated through public policy, reflecting in part the ability to bargain in the market which in turn will depend on the ability to deploy organized political and economic power. The bulk of the costs will tend to fall on the peasant mass,[41] urban marginals and the less well organized workers. As in the case of Mexico, organized workers in strategic industries may form a labor aristocracy. In Peru then, workers in some enterprises such as mining, fishing and the coastal agro-industry may be relative beneficiaries although the regime, as in Mexico, will by various means, including co-optation of leaders, seek to keep their demands down. Indeed, the case of Mexico seems particularly relevant in contemplating Peru's future

[40] For an analysis of Bolivia in terms of this model, see Melvin Burke and James Malloy, "Del Populismo Nacional al Corporativismo Nacional: El Caso de Bolivia 1952-1970," *Aportes* (October, 1972), pp. 66-97.

[41] Either development scenario, by emphasizing industrialization, would entail a heavy allocation of costs on the peasant mass. For a theoretical justification of this prediction, see W. F. Owen, "The Double Developmental Squeeze on Agriculture," *American Economic Review*, LVI (March, 1966), 43-70.

not as a model or carbon copy but as a theme which can be elaborated on and modified.

We can expect the emergence of a plural elite of public and private entrepreneurs, technocrats, bureaucrats and some labor leaders coordinated through recognized corporate groups and mechanisms like SINAMOS. There will, therefore, be some pluralized participation, but it will be limited especially as regards groups bearing costs. Because it will not be a command system and because certain types of mobilization could be perceived as threats by components of the elite, there will be a tendency to limit the level of mobilization as well. The regime will probably try to stabilize both participation and mobilization at some intermediate to lower level; again the mix can vary with time and circumstance but in the first stages one might expect more mobilization than participation. Control will be elaborated through institutions such as SINAMOS (its full role, however, is still in doubt) and based upon selective demand satisfaction, symbolic rewards, clientelism, co-optation and selective repression.

Of the two scenarios the latter seems the more probable outcome. First, because the generals have carefully stated that they view themselves to be a product of a "humanistic Christian tradition" which rejects state socialism as well as unfettered capitalism. Hence, while they have gored such capitalist oxen as International Petroleum Company and opened relations with socialist states, they have assiduously sought to maintain ties with the industrial West. Moreover, the ability of Cuba to break out of the United States orbit and establish a state socialist model was due in no small part to the willingness of the Soviet Union to underwrite the Castro regime politically, militarily and economically. Given the cautious approach the Russians assumed toward Allende's government in Chile, it seems reasonable to argue that they have neither the will nor ability to give such blanket support to another Latin American regime.

Conclusion

In this paper we have approached Peru since 1968 as an important case of a development-oriented authoritarian regime and analyzed it in part in terms of the model of authoritarianism advanced by Juan Linz. More particularly we have argued that

Peru will tend to adopt a pluralized system of political economy which will be neither democratic nor totalitarian but a formalized subtype of developmental authoritarianism which we have termed corporatism. It has been noted that corporatism is not synonymous with fascism and that aside from its ideological aspirations corporatism is based on an analytically useful group theory of politics. Corporatism, therefore, can give an important perspective on certain de facto modes of group politics common to Latin America and perhaps elsewhere. It is the position of this paper that Peru, in confronting the complex problems of development, mobilization and participation is, through organizations such as SINAMOS, formalizing into a new state structure the basic corporatist group dynamics which were present in that society prior to 1968. Peru, therefore, is attempting to resolve its problems of political economy in a manner similar to that of Mexico. There is no guarantee that the Peruvian military will continue in the corporatist direction or that it will be successful in imposing a new system of political economy on Peru. Nonetheless, the Peruvian case illustrates the potential utility of revising and enlarging the concept of corporatism as a specific subtype of development-oriented authoritarianism.

Still the Century of Corporatism?*

Philippe C. Schmitter

The twentieth century will be the century of corporatism just
as the nineteenth was the century of liberalism . . .

Mihaïl Manoïlesco

Until recently, Manoïlesco's confident prediction could easily
be dismissed as yet another example of the ideological bias, wishful
thinking and overinflated rhetoric of the thirties, àn *événementielle*
response to a peculiar environment and period.[1] With the subsequent defeat of fascism and National Socialism, the spectre of
corporatism no longer seemed to haunt the European scene so fatal-
istically. For a while, the concept itself was virtually retired from
the active lexicon of politics, although it was left on behavioral
exhibit, so to speak, in such museums of atavistic political practice
as Portugal and Spain.

Lately, however, the spectre is back amongst us—verbally at
least—haunting the concerns of contemporary social scientists with
increasing frequency and in multiple guises. Almost forty years to
the day when Manoïlesco declared that "the ineluctable course of
fate involves the transformation of all the social and political institutions of our times in a corporatist direction,"[2] perhaps we
should again take his prediction seriously and inquire whether we
might still be in the century of corporatism—but only just becoming aware of it.

The purposes of this essay are to explore various usages of the
concept of corporatism, to suggest an operational definition of it
as a distinctive, modern system of interest representation, to discuss
the utility of distinguishing subtypes of corporatist development and
practice and, finally, to set forth some general hypotheses "explaining" the probable context of its emergence and persistence.

* An International Affairs Fellowship from the Council on Foreign Relations (New York) for the academic year 1973-74 and the generous infrastruc-
tural support of the European Center of the Carnegie Endowment for International Peace have made this research possible. Specifically I would like to
thank Ms. Barbara Bishop of the European Center for having deciphered my
handwriting and prepared a legible manuscript.

[1] Mihaïl Manoïlesco, *Le Siècle du Corporatisme,* rev. ed. (Paris, 1936).
The original edition was published in 1934.

[2] *Ibid.,* p. 7.

I

The first step, I propose, is to rescue the concept of corporatism from various usages of it which have crept into the literature and which seem (to me) to do more to dissipate or to disguise than to enhance its utility. On the one hand, it has become such a vaguely bounded phenomenon that, like clientelism, it can be found everywhere and, hence, is nowhere very distinctive; on the other hand, it has been so narrowly attached to a single political culture, regime-type or macrosocietal configuration that it becomes, at best, uniquely descriptive rather than comparatively analytic.

Undoubtedly, the most difficult task is to strip the concept of its pejorative tone and implication. This is made all the more difficult by the fact that—unlike the thirties—there are very few regimes today who overtly and proudly advertise themselves as corporatist. It, therefore, becomes a tempting game to unveil and denounce as corporatist practices which regimes are condoning or promoting under other labels, such as "participation," "collaborative planning," "mixed representation," and "permanent consultation." On the other hand, if corporatism is left to mean simply "interest-group behavior or systems I do not like" and/or used synonymously with such epithets as "fascist" and "repressive," then it can become of little or no utility for purposes of systematic comparison. This is not to say that those who use the concept must somehow be enjoined from uttering evaluative statements or even from expressing strong normative reactions to its role or consequences. I have now studied several corporatist systems and come openly to quite firm personal judgments about each of them. But, I hope that those who disagree on its desirability can at least arrive at some common prior agreement as to the empirical referents which identify its basic structure and behavior. They then can dispute the costs and benefits and the intrinsic "goods" and "bads" it produces.

In my work I have found it useful to consider corporatism as a system of interest and/or attitude representation, a particular modal or ideal-typical institutional arrangement for linking the associationally organized interests of civil society with the decisional structures of the state. As such it is one of several possible *modern* configurations of interest representation, of which pluralism is perhaps the best-known and most frequently acknowledged alternative —but more about that below.

Restricting the concept, so to speak, to refer only to a specific concrete set of institutional practices or structures involving the representation (or misrepresentation) of empirically observable group interests has a number of important implications. These sharply differentiate my preferred usage from those of several others who have recently employed the same conceptual label.

First, by defining corporatism in terms of its praxis, the concept is liberated from its employment in any particular ideology or system of ideas.[3] While, as will become manifest in later sections of this essay, I am quite interested in the arguments put forth by particular proponents of modern or neocorporatism, my reading of its use in the recent history of ideas suggests that an extraordinary variety of theorists, ideologues and activists have advocated it for widely divergent motives, interests and reasons.

These range from such romantic, organic theorists of the state as Friedrich Schlegel, Adam von Müller, G. W. Friedrich Hegel and Rudolf Kjellen; to the pre-Marxist, protosocialists Sismondi, Saint-Simon and Proudhon; to the Social Christian, ethically traditionalist thought of Wilhelm von Ketteler, Karl von Vogelsang, the Marquis de la Tour de Pin, Albert de Mun and, of course, Popes Leo XIII and Pius XI; to the fascist authoritarianism of Giuseppe Bottai, Guido Bortolotto, Giuseppe Papi and Francesco Vito; to the secular modernizing nationalism of a Mihaïl Manoïlesco; to the radical (in the French sense) bourgeois solidarism of Léon Duguit, Joseph-Paul Boncour, Georges Renard and Emile Durkheim; to the mystical universalism of an Ottmar Spann; to the internationalist functionalism of Giuseppe de Michelis and David Mitrany; to the reactionary, pseudo-Catholic integralism of Charles Maurras, Oliveira Salazar, Marcello Caetano and Jean Brèthe de la Gressaye; to the technocratic, procapitalist reformism of Walter Rathenau, Lord Keynes and A. A. Berle, Jr.; to the anticapitalist syndicalism of Georges Sorel, Sergio Panunzio, Ugo Spirito, Edmondo Rossoni, Enrico Corradini and Gregor Strasser; to the guild socialism of G.D.H. Cole, the early Harold Laski, S. G. Hobson and Ramiro de Maeztu; to the communitarianism

---

[3] For an example of such a definition by ideology, see James Malloy, "Authoritarianism, Corporatism and Mobilization in Peru," elsewhere in this volume. Also Howard Wiarda, "The Portuguese Corporative System: Basic Structures and Current Functions" (Paper prepared for the Conference Group on Modern Portugal, Durham, N.H., Oct. 10-14, 1973). In both cases the authors were heavily, if not exclusively, influenced by "Social Christian" versions of corporatist thought.

or bourgeois socialism of a François Perroux or an Henri de Man—not to mention such contemporary advocates as Bernard Crick, W. H. Ferry, Pierre Mendes-France and David Apter.

All of these—and the list is by no means complete nor are the above groupings by any means sharply distinctive[4]—have converged upon the advocacy of an institutional relationship between the systems of authoritative decision-making and interest representation which can be considered as generically corporatist by my praxiological definition (and frequently defined as such by the authors themselves), although they conceived of this arrangement as involving radically different structures of power and influence, as benefiting quite distinct social classes, and as promoting diametrically opposite public policies.

A French student of corporatism described the situation quite well when he said:

> The army of corporatists is so disparate that one is led to think that the word, corporation, itself is like a label placed on a whole batch of bottles which are then distributed among diverse producers each of whom fills them with the drink of his choice. The consumer has to look carefully.[5]

The situation is even further confused by the fact that many contemporary theorists, ideologues and activists are peddling the same drink under yet other labels.

Not only is corporatism defined as an ideology (or worse as a weltanschauung) difficult to pin down to a central set of values or beliefs and even more difficult to associate with the aspirations or interests of a specific social group, but virtually all detailed empirical inquiries of corporatist praxis have shown its performance and behavior to be at considerable variance—if not diametrically opposed—to the beliefs manifestly advanced by its verbal defenders. As another French scholar of the forties (himself an advocate of corporatism *à sa manière*) observed, "The reality of existing corporatisms is, without a doubt, infinitely less seductive than the doctrine."[6] Contemporary conceptualizations of corporatism based

---

[4] To this article I have appendixed a working bibliography of some 100 titles which seem important to an understanding of the ideological and praxiological bases of corporatism up to and including the interwar period.

[5] Louis Baudin, *Le Corporatisme. Italie, Portugal, Allemagne, Espagne, France* (Paris, 1942), pp. 4-5.

[6] Auguste Murat, *Le Corporatisme* (Paris: Les Publications Techniques, 1944), p. 206. For excellent critical treatments of corporatist practice in the

exclusively on the stated motives and goals of actors or their apologists tend only to obfuscate this "less than seductive" reality in praxis.

In short, I find there is simply too much normative variety and behavioral hypocrisy in the use of the corporatist *ideological* label to make it a useful operational instrument for comparative analysis.

Nor do I find it very productive to consider corporatism to be an exclusive part or a distinctive product of a particular political culture, especially one linked to some geographically circumscribed area such as the Iberian Peninsula[7] or the Mediterranean.[8] This approach to corporatism not only runs up against the usual (and in my view, well-founded) criticisms raised against most, if not all, political-cultural "explanations"[9]—especially against those based on impressionistic evidence and circular reasoning[10]—but also fails

1930's, see Roland Pré, *L'Organisation des rapports économiques et sociaux dans les pays à régime corporatif* (Paris, 1936); Louis Rosenstock-Franck, *L'Economie corporative fasciste en doctrine et en fait* (Paris, 1934; and François Perroux, *Capitalisme et Communauté de Travail* (Paris, 1937), pp. 27-178.

[7] For a subtle, institutionally sensitive presentation of this argument, see Ronald Newton "On 'Functional Groups,' 'Fragmentation' and 'Pluralism' in Spanish American Political Society," *Hispanic American Historical Review* L, no. 1 (February, 1970), 1-29. For an approach which relies essentially on an ill-defined, Catholic weltanschauunglich argument, see Howard Wiarda, "Toward a Framework for the Study of Political Change in the Iberic-Latin Tradition," *World Politics* XXV, no. 2 (January, 1973), 206-235.

[8] See especially the argument by Kalman Silvert, "The Costs of Anti-Nationalism: Argentina," in K. Silvert, ed., *Expectant Peoples* (New York, 1967) pp. 358-61. Also his *Man's Power* (New York, 1970), pp. 59-64, 136-8; "National Values, Development, and Leaders and Followers," *International Social Science Journal* XV (1964), 560-70; "The Politics of Economic and Social Change in Latin America," *The Sociological Review* Monograph XI (1967), 47-58.

[9] As Max Weber scornfully put it to earlier advocates of political cultural explanations, "the appeal to national character is generally a mere confession of ignorance." *The Protestant Ethic and the Spirit of Capitalism,* p. 88, as cited in Reinhard Bendix, *Max Weber: An Intellectual Portrait* [New York, 1962] p. 63, fn. 29).

[10] Such reasoning has been particularly prevalent among Anglo-Saxon students of Latin America where, from the start, these area specialists seem to have drawn the following syllogism: "Latin Americans behave differently from North Americans; Latin America was colonized by Spain and Portugal; North America by Great Britain; Latin Americans are Catholics, North Americans are predominantly Protestant; *ergo,* Latin Americans behave differently from North Americans because of their Catholic-Iberian heritage!"

The few systematically comparative studies of attitudes which have included both Latin and North American samples have generally concluded that once one controls for education, class, center-periphery residence, age, etc., residual differences that could be assigned specifically to culture are statistically

completely to explain why similar configurations and behavior in interest politics have emerged and persist in a great variety of cultural settings, stretching from Northern Europe, across the Mediterranean to such exotic places as Turkey, Iran, Thailand, Indonesia and Taiwan, to name but a few. This form of pseudoexplanation also cannot contribute much to answering the question of why, even within the presumed homeland of such an ethos, that is, the Iberian Peninsula and its "fragments," corporatism has waxed and waned during different historical periods. Are we to believe that political culture is a sort of "spigot variable" which gets turned on every once in a while to produce a different system of functional representation? Also we might ask, why do societies supposedly sharing the same general ethos exhibit such wide diversity in interest-group values, practices and consequences? By all empirically available standards, Spain is more Catholic than Portugal, Colombia more so than Brazil, yet in each case it is the latter which has by far the more corporatist system. At best, then, culturalist arguments must be heavily supplemented to account for such embarrassing deviations in outcome.

Finally, since those who have advanced such an explanation also tend to place a great deal of emphasis on ideology (occasionally even accepting word for fact), we might wonder why the major ideologues of corporatism have *not* come from this part of the world. A quick glance at the admittedly incomplete bibliography attached to this essay will show that the intellectual origins of corporatism are predominately German, Belgian, French and Austrian and, secondarily and belatedly, English, Italian and Rumanian. Those who advocated corporatism in the Iberian and Latin American areas unabashedly and unashamedly imported their ideas from abroad. Modern, nonmedieval, corporatism was diffused to the Iberian-Mediterranean area, not created within it.[11]

---

insignificant. See especially Joseph Kahl, *The Measurement of Modernity* (Austin, Texas, 1968).

[11] It is also worth mentioning that many, if not most, of the theorists of modern corporatism have not been Catholics. Many were in fact militantly secular. Even those who most publicly claimed to be inspired by "Social Christian" ideals, such as Salazar and Dollfuss, followed a much more bureaucratic, statist and authoritarian praxis. Also worth stressing is that among "Social Christians" or more broadly, progressive Catholics, not all by any means advocated corporatism. Such prominent figures as Jacques Maritain and Emmanuel Mounier opposed it. See Henri Guitton, *Le Catholicisme Social* (Paris, 1945).

Also worth mentioning is that corporatism has been considered quite

Another tendency which has cropped up in recent discussions of corporatism is to define or, better, submerge it into some wider political configuration such as "the organic state" or "the authoritarian regime."[12] The "organic state" concept runs up against many of the criticisms of definitional vagueness, lack of potential empirical specificity and circularity of argument leveled above at the political cultural approach. More importantly, it fails to take into account the historical fact that many "organically conceived" states were not composed of corporatist subunits, but built upon a great variety of "organs" ranging from the *curies* and *phratries* of Fustel de Coulange's ancient city,[13] to the "metallic" orders of moral excellence in Plato's ideal polity,[14] to the three to five estate systems of various anciens régimes,[15] to the phalanges of Fourier,[16] to the *régions* of Robert LaFont,[17] even to the autonomous, plural communities of Percival and Paul Goodman or Gar Alperovitz.[18] If one accepts that a special characteristic of modern corporatism (this in both ideology and practice) concerns the role of *functional* interest associations, then it is but one of many possible structural units, for example, familial, territorial-communitarian, moral, religious, "productionist," etc., which may go into the establishment of an "organic state." Emphasizing that macrocharacteristic does little to specify concrete relations of authority, influence and representation, except to differentiate them from equally vague notions of the "mechanical state."

---

compatible with many non-Catholic, non-Iberian cultures. See, for example, Samuel H. Beer, *British Politics in the Collectivist Age* (New York, 1969) and Thomas Anton, "Policy-Making and Political Culture in Sweden," *Scandinavian Political Studies* IV (Oslo, 1969), 88-102.

[12] See the concept of "limited pluralism" in Juan Linz, "An Authoritarian Regime: Spain," in E. Allardt and S. Rokkan, eds., *Mass Politics* (New York, 1970), pp. 251-83, 374-81.

In subsequent conversations with this author, Linz has advanced and defended the idea of an "organic state model" as the appropriate framework for the discussion of corporatism. See also the essay cited above (fn. 3) by James Malloy in this volume.

[13] Fustel de Coulange, *La Cité Antique,* 4th ed. (Paris, 1872).

[14] Plato, *Laws* 5-6.

[15] Emile Lousse, *Organização e representação corporativas* (Lisbon, 1952), a translation of his *La Société d'Ancien Régime* (Bruxelles, 1943).

[16] F. Charles Fourier, *Théories de l'Unité Unité Universelle* (1822) and *Le Nouveau Monde industriel et sociétaire* (1829).

[17] Robert LaFont, *La Revolution Regionaliste* (Paris, 1967).

[18] Percival and Paul Goodman, *Communitas* (Chicago, 1947) and Gar Alperovitz, "Notes toward a Pluralist Commonwealth," *Warner Modular Publications,* Reprint No. 52 (1973).

The relation of corporatism in interest politics to a specific global type of political regime is a much more complicated (and, in my view, interesting) issue. For reasons which will, I hope, become apparent in the course of this essay I have found it more useful to define it as a concrete, observable general system of interest representation which is "compatible" with several different regime-types, i.e., with different party systems, varieties of ruling ideology, levels of political mobilization, varying scopes of public policy, etc. Then I will endeavor to specify distinct *subtypes* of corporatist representation which seem to have at least an elective affinity for, if not to be essential defining elements of, specific regime-types during specific periods of their development.[19]

Yet another tendency in the revived discussion of corporatism which differs from that proposed here is that which submerges the concept, not in some wider concept of regional political culture, state form or regime-type, but in some marcosocietal characteristic such as the presence of visual stigmata,[20] or the existence of religiously, ideologically or linguistically determined *zuilen lager,* or *familles spirituelles*.[21] Here the problem is simply that stigmatized or pillared societies exhibit quite different degrees of corporatism in the sense used herein and that, vice versa, many heavily corporatized systems of interest representation exist in societies which have no marked visual stigmatization or pillared social and cultural structures. Sweden is no less corporatized because it lacks both

---

[19] In earlier works, I tended to define corporatism exclusively in relation to authoritarian rule. See the concluding chapter of my *Interest Conflict and Political Change in Brazil* (Stanford, 1971); also, "Paths to Political Development in Latin America," *Proceedings of the American Academy* XXX, no. 4 (1972), 83-108 and "The Portugalization of Brazil?" in A. Stepan III, ed., *Authoritarian Brazil* (New Haven, 1973).

[20] Ronald Rogowski and Lois Wasserspring, *Does Political Development Exist? Corporatism in Old and New Societies* (Beverly Hills, Sage Professional Papers, II, no. 01-024, 1971).

[21] For example, Arend Lijphart, *The Politics of Accommodation* (Berkeley, 1968)—where in all fairness the concept of corporatism itself does not appear. In a forthcoming essay by Martin Heisler, however, these "pillared" notions are expressly linked to a corporatist model of European politics: "Patterns of European Politics: The 'European Polity' Model," in M. O. Heisler et al., *Politics in Europe: Structures and Processes* (New York, forthcoming).

Also relevant are Arend Lijphart "Consociational Democracy," *World Politics* XXI, no. 2 (January, 1969), pp. 207-25; Val R. Lorwin "Segmented Pluralism: Ideological Cleavages and Political Cohesion in the Smaller European Democracies," *Comparative Politics* III, no. 2 (January, 1971), 14-75; Gehard Lembruch, *Proporzdemokratie: Politisches System und politische Kultur in der Schweiz und in Österreich* (Tübingen, 1967).

dimensions;[22] Belgium no more so because it suffers from both.[23] These are interesting and salient dimensions of societies, in and by themselves, but they do not seem to bear any close association with the phenomenon upon which I recommend we focus our attention with the concept of corporatism.

In the present state of nominalistic anarchy prevailing in the discipline, it is absurd to pretend that scholars will somehow "rally" to a particular conceptualization, spurn alternative uses of the term, and, henceforth, agree to disagree on the basis of a common lexical definition. About all one can expect from an introductory discussion such as this may be to gain a few recruits for a more specific and bounded use of the concept of corporatism, and to warn the reader that a great deal of what has recently been written about corporatism and of what will subsequently be discussed in this essay may be of no mutual relevance at all.

II

Having rejected a series of alternative usages of the concept of corporatism and expressed a preference for a more empirically bounded specification which focuses on a set of relatively directly observable, institutionally distinctive traits involving the actual practice of interest representation, it is now incumbent upon me to produce such a conceptual specification:

> Corporatism can be defined as a system of interest representation in which the constituent units are organized into a limited number of singular, compulsory, noncompetitive, hierarchically ordered and functionally differentiated categories, recognized or licensed (if not created) by the state and granted a deliberate representa-

---

[22] Roland Huntford, for example, argues that is is precisely social and economic homogenization which contributes to the thoroughness of Swedish corporatism; see *The New Totalitarians* (New York, 1972), pp. 86-87ff. Also Olaf Ruin, "Participation, Corporativization and Politicization Trends in Present-day Sweden" (Paper presented at Sixty-second Annual Meeting of the Society for the Advancement of Scandinavian Study, New York, May 5-6, 1972).

[23] On the contrary, a recent analysis of Belgium's associational structure argues persuasively that multipillared conflicts in that polity serve to sustain a more pluralist (i.e., nonmonopolistic, competitive, overlapping) system of interest representation; see A. Van Den Brande, "Voluntary Associations in the Belgian Political System 1954-1968," *Res Publica*, no. 2 (1973), pp. 329-356.

tional monopoly within their respective categories in exchange for observing certain controls on their selection of leaders and articulation of demands and supports.[24]

Obviously, such an elaborate definition is an ideal-type description,[25] a heuristic and logicoanalytical construct composed of a considerable variety of theoretically or hypothetically interrelated components. No empirically extant system of interest representation may perfectly reproduce all these dimensions, although two which I have studied in some detail (Brazil and Portugal) come rather close.[26] While the whole gestalt or syndrome is not directly

---

[24] At this point it is perhaps worth repeating that this constructed definition does not correspond to any of the ones advanced by specifically corporatist theorists. Moreover, it ignores a number of institutional and behavioral dimensions they tended to stress. For example, it does not specify the existence of singular associations (corporations) grouping both employers and workers. (These rarely exist and where they have been formally established—Portugal, Spain and Italy—they do not function as units.) Nor does it say anything about the presence of a higher council or parliament composed of functional or professional representatives. (Many polities which are not otherwise very corporatist, France or Weimar Germany, have such a *Conseil Economique et Social* or *Wirtschaftsrat;* many heavily corporatist countries which do have them, e.g., Portugal, do not grant them decisional authority.) Nor does the definition suggest that corporatist associations will be the only constituent units of the polity—completely displacing territorial entities, parties and movements. (In all existing corporatist systems, parties and territorial subdivisions continue to exist and various youth and religious movements may not only be tolerated but encouraged.) These institutional aspects as well as the more important behavioral issues of how and who would form the unique and hierarchical associations, what would be their degree of autonomy from state control and whether the whole scheme really could bring about class harmony and constitute a *tertium genus* between communism and capitalism were the subject of extensive debate and considerable fragmentation among corporatist ideologues.
The ideological definition closest to my analytical one is Mihaïl Manoïlesco's: "The corporation is a collective and public organization composed of the totality of persons (physical or juridical) fulfilling together the same national function and having as its goal that of assuring the exercise of that function by rules of law imposed at least upon its members" (*Le Siècle du Corporatisme,* p. 176).
[25] Actually, the concept is more "a constructed type" than an ideal type. The former has been defined as: "a purposive, combination, and (sometimes) accentuation of a set of criteria with empirical referents that serves as a basis for comparison of empirical cases" (John C. McKinnes, *Constructive Typology and Social Theory* [New York, 1966], p. 3).
[26] See my *Interest Conflict and Political Change in Brazil* (fn. 19) and "Corporatist Interest Representation and Public Policy-Making in Portugal" (Paper presented at the Conference Group on Modern Portugal, Durham, N.H., October 10-14, 1973). Also "The Portugalization of Brazil?" (fn. 19).

accessible to measurement, its postulated components can be easily assessed, if not immediately quantified. Such detailed inquiry into the extent to which a given system of representation is limited in number of component units, compulsory in membership, noncompetitive between compartmentalized sectors, hierarchically ordered in internal structure, recognized or certified in some de jure or de facto way by the state, successful in exercising a representational monopoly within functionally determined categories and subject to formal or informal controls on leadership selection and interest articulation will not only enable us to distinguish what type of interest system it belongs to, but may help us gauge the extent to which these multiple dimensions are empirically as well as logically interrelated. It is, of course, quite conceivable at this early stage in research into these matters that what I have found to be a set of interrelated institutional practices coalescing into a distinctive, highly covariant and resistant modern system of interest representation may be quite limited in its scope of applicability, for example, only to Iberian authoritarian regimes, or restricted to only one subtype of corporatism, such as ones "artificially" established from above by the state.

One purpose in developing this elaborate general model, beyond that of describing the behavior of a certain number of political systems which have interested me, is to offer to the political analyst an explicit alternative to the paradigm of interest politics which has heretofore completely dominated the discipline of the North American political science: *pluralism*. While a considerable number and wide variety of scholars have discovered that pluralism (and with it, the closely associated liberal democratic regime-type) may be of little utility in describing the likely structure and behavior of interest-group systems in contemporary developing polities, and while some have even gone so far as to suggest that it may no longer be of much utility when applied to the practices of advanced industrial polities, few if any of these scholars have proposed an alternative or contrasting model of modern representative association-state relations. Most of them merely mourn the passing or degeneration of pluralism and either advocate its return,[27] its replacement with some more formalistic, authoritative (if not authoritarian) "jurid-

---

[27] For example, Henry Kariel (ed.), *Frontiers of Democratic Theory* (New York, 1970), and his, *The Decline of American Pluralism* (Stanford, 1961); also Grant McConnell, *Private Power and American Democracy* (New York, 1966).

ical democracy,"[28] or its periodic *bouleversement* by spontaneous social movements.[29]

Pluralism and corporatism share a number of basic assumptions, as would almost any realistic model of modern interest politics: (1) the growing importance of formal associational units of representation; (2) the persistence and expansion of functionally differentiated and potentially conflicting interests; (3) the burgeoning role of permanent administrative staffs, of specialized information, of technical expertise and, consequently, of entrenched oligarchy; (4) the decline in the importance of territorial and partisan representation; and (5) the secular trend toward expansion in the scope of public policy and interpenetration of private and public decision arenas. Nevertheless, despite this wide area of mutual agreement, pluralism differs markedly from corporatism as an ideal-typical response to these facts of modern political life.

> Pluralism can be defined as a system of interest representation in which the constituent units are organized into an unspecified number of multiple, voluntary, competitive, nonhierarchically ordered and self-determined (as to type or scope of interest) categories which are not specially licensed, recognized, subsidized, created or otherwise controlled in leadership selection or interest articulation by the state and which do not exercise a monopoly of representational activity within their respective categories.

Practitioners of corporatism and of pluralism would heartily agree with James Madison that "among the numerous advantages promised by a well-constructed union, none deserves to be more accurately developed than its tendency *to break and control* (my emphasis) the violence of faction." They would also agree that "giving to every citizen the same opinions, the same passions and the same interests . . . is as impracticable as [suppressing them altogether — PCS] would be unwise." Where the two practitioners would begin to diverge is with Madison's further assertion that "it is in vain to say that enlightened statesmen will be able to adjust these clashing interests and render them all subservient to the public good." Corporatists, basing their faith either on the superior wisdom of an authoritarian leader or the enlightened foresight of technocratic planners, believe that such a public unity can be found

---

[28] Theodore Lowi, *The End of Liberalism: Ideology, Policy and the Crisis of Public Authority* (New York, 1969).

[29] Theodore Lowi, *The Politics of Disorder* (New York, 1971).

and kept. Their "scheme of representation," to use Madison's felicitous phrase, instead of extending the "number of citizens" and the "sphere of interests" would compress them into a fixed set of verticalized categories each representing the interdependent functions of an organic whole. Madison's metaphor was more mechanistic, and more dynamic. Hence, he was less sanguine about limiting and ordering the sources of faction—whether from above by imposition or from below by elimination. Corporatists of whatever stripe express confidence that an "enlightened statesman" (or an "enlightened state") can co-opt, control or coordinate not only those "most frivolous and fanciful distinctions [which] have been sufficient to kindle unfriendly passions and excite their most violent conflicts," but also that "most common and durable source of faction . . . the various and unequal distribution of property."[30]

In short, both pluralists and corporatists recognize, accept and attempt to cope with the growing structural differentiation and interest diversity of the modern polity, but they offer opposing political remedies and divergent images of the institutional form that such a modern system of interest representation will take. The former suggest spontaneous formation, numerical proliferation, horizontal extension and competitive interaction; the latter advocate controlled emergence, quantitative limitation, vertical stratification and complementary interdependence. Pluralists place their faith in the shifting balance of mechanically intersecting forces; corporatists appeal to the functional adjustment of an organically interdependent whole.

While time and space limitations prevent me from developing the idea further, I suspect that these two contrasting but not diametrically opposed syndromes do not by any means exhaust the possible alternative system-types of modern interest representation.

For example, the Soviet experience suggests the existence of a "monist" model which could be defined as

a system of interest representation in which the constituent units are organized into a fixed number of singular, ideologically selective, noncompetitive, functionally differentiated and hierarchically ordered categories, created, subsidized and licensed by a single party and granted a representational role within that party and vis-à-vis the state in exchange for observing certain controls on their selection of leaders, articulation of demands and mobilization of support.

[30] The quotations are all from *The Federalist Papers,* no. 10.

Much more difficult to specify in terms of the component dimensions we have been using for the other three because of its radical and utopian nature is the syndicalist alternative. Barely sketched in by a number of theorists (several of whom subsequently became corporatists), this projected model seems to reject or to seek to transform substantially many of the given characteristics of the modern political process—more or less accepted or even encouraged by the other three syndromes. Nevertheless, a brief description of its characteristics will be offered below, partly because it has emerged with increasing frequency (if not specificity) in recent discussions of participation and representation,[31] and partly because it seems to round out in logical terms the combinatorial possibilities of the variables used to define the other three types.

> Syndicalism could be defined as a system of interest aggregation (more than representation) in which the constituent units are an unlimited number of singular, voluntary, noncompetitive (or better hived-off) categories, not hierarchically ordered or functionally specialized, neither recognized, created nor licensed by state or party, nor controlled in their leadership selection or interest articulation by state or party, not exercising a representational monopoly but resolving their conflicts and "authoritatively allocating their values" autonomously without the interference of the state.

With this last definition-model we have moved some distance from our stated limited concern with specifying the characteristics of corporatism as a distinctive and self-sustaining system of interest representation, and not confusing it with a whole system of political domination. Nevertheless, this excursion has served to remind us that the process of capturing, organizing and articulating the demands of civil society as well as those of receiving, interpreting and even applying the "imperative coordinations" of the state is only part of the political process, and hence only intelligible in purpose and consequence when considered in relation to other political subsystems and whole regime configurations. This wider set of concerns, ironically, leads us to a consideration of possible subtypes of corporatism.

---

[31] See especially the article by Gar Alperovitz and works cited therein '(fn. 18), even though the author associates his proposals with the tradition of pluralism, rather than that of syndicalism. Also Jaroslav Vanek, *The Participatory Economy* (Ithaca, 1971).

III

To illustrate that the skeletonal connotation of corporatism offered above accurately describes the system of interest representation of a large number of countries, including many whose global political systems differ markedly, would not be difficult—even at the existing lamentable state of our empirical knowledge. Hence, it has been argued and rather convincingly shown that Sweden,[32] Switzerland,[33] the Netherlands,[34] Norway,[35] Denmark,[36] Austria,[37] Spain,[38] Portugal,[39] Brazil,[40] Chile,[41] Peru,[42] Greece,[43] Mexico[44] and Yugoslavia[45] have, by and large, singular, noncom-

[32] Nils Elvander, *Interesse-organisationer i Dagens Sverige* (Lund, 1966); Thomas J. Anton (fn. 11), Olaf Ruin (fn. 22) and Roland Huntford (fn. 22). Also Hans Meijer "Bureaucracy and Policy Formulation in Sweden," *Scandinavian Political Studies,* no. 4 (Oslo, 1969), pp. 103-16.

[33] Hans Huber, "Swiss Democracy" in H. W. Ehrmann, ed., *Democracy in a Changing Society* (New York, 1964), esp. p. 106.

[34] P. E. Kraemer, *The Societal State* (Meppel, 1966). Also John P. Windmuller, *Labour Relations in the Netherlands* (Ithaca, 1969).

[35] Stein Rokkan, "Norway: Numerical Democracy and Corporate Pluralism" in R. Dahl, ed., *Political Opposition in Western Democracies* (New Haven, 1966), pp. 105-106ff.

[36] Kenneth E. Keller, *Government and Politics in Denmark* (Boston, 1968), esp. pp. 169-70ff.

[37] Alfred Diamant, *Austrian Catholics and the First Republic. Democracy, Capitalism and the Social Order 1918-1934* (Princeton, 1960). Also, Gehard Lembruch (fn. 21) and Frederick C. Engelmann, "Haggling for the Equilibrium: the Renegotiation of the Austrian Coalition, 1959," *American Political Science Review* LVI, 3 (September, 1962), 651-620.

[38] In addition to Juan Linz, "An Authoritarian Regime: Spain" (fn. 12), see Juan Linz and Armando de Miguel, *Los Empresarios ante el Poder Público* (Madrid, 1966); Juan Linz, "From Falange to Movimiento-Organizacion: The Spanish Single Party and the Franco Regime, 1936-1968" in S. P. Huntington and C. H. Moore, eds., *Authoritarian Politics in Modern Society* (New York, 1970), esp. pp. 146-183. Also Fred Witney, *Labor Policy and Practices in Spain* (New York, 1964).

[39] Schmitter, "Corporatist Interest Representation and Public Policy-Making in Portugal" (fn. 26).

[40] Schmitter, *Interest Conflict and Political Change in Brazil* and "The Portugalization of Brazil?" (fn. 26).

[41] Constantine Menges, "Public Policy and Organized Business in Chile," *Journal of International Affairs* XX (1966), 343-65. Also James Petras, *Politics and Social Forces in Chilean Development* (Berkeley, 1969), pp. 199-203, 209-19.

[42] Julio Cotler, "Bases del corporativismo en el Peru," *Sociedad y Política,* I, no. 2 (October, 1972), 3-12; also James Malloy (fn. 3).

[43] Keith Legg, *Politics in Modern Greece* (Stanford, 1969).

[44] Robert E. Scott, *Mexican Government in Transition* (Urbana, Illinois, 1959), esp. chapters 5 and 6.

[45] International Labour Office, *Workers' Management in Yugoslavia*

petitive, hierarchically ordered, sectorally compartmentalized, interest associations exercising representational monopolies and accepting (de jure or de facto) governmentally imposed or negotiated limitations on the type of leaders they elect and on the scope and intensity of demands they routinely make upon the state.[46] As a result, such associations have attained "a quasi-legal status and a prescriptive right to speak for their segments of the population. They influence the process of government directly, bypassing the [parliament]. They are agents of authority. They deputize for the state in whole sectors of public life, and they have duties delegated to them that properly belong to the civil service."[47] The summary above applies specifically to Sweden, but it is broadly descriptive of the countries cited above—and undoubtedly of many others yet to be investigated.

Such a demonstration of broad structural identity does have the virtue of debunking, if not divesting, some of these polities of the pluralist labels they have acquired—a prestigious title usually bestowed upon them for no better reason than the mere existence of a multitude of organized interests. It may also serve to call into question the relevance of many supposed properties associated with pluralism and assumed, therefore, to apply to these polities: competitiveness within sectors and, hence, accountability to members; cross-pressures and overlap and, hence, vacillation and moderation in demands; open competitiveness between interest sectors and, hence, incremental, split-the-difference solutions; penetration and

(Geneva, 1962). Also Dusan Sidjanski, "La Représentation des intérêts et la décision politique" in L. Moulin (ed.), *L'Europe de Demain et ses Responsables* (Bruges, 1967). Something approaching the corporatist model has been implicitly but not explicitly advanced in describing certain "degenerate" varieties of totalitarian ("partialitarian") rule in other Eastern European polities: Poland, Czechoslovakia, Hungary and Rumania, even the U.S.S.R. itself. For an intelligent survey and critique of this literature's misuse of the pluralist paradigm, see Andrew Janos, "Group Politics in Communist Society: A Second Look at the Pluralistic Model" in S. P. Huntington and C. H. Moore, eds. (fn. 38), pp. 537-50.

[46] In an even wider range of polities, authors have suggested that parts, if not substantial portions, of the interest group universe can be described as "corporatized"; e.g., the United States: Grant McConnell (fn. 27); Theodore Lowi, *The End of Liberalism* (fn. 28), pp. 59-100; Great Britain: Samuel Beer (fn. 11); Western Germany: Ralf Dahrendorf, *Society and Democracy in Germany* (London, 1968); Canada: Robert Presthus, *Elite Accommodation in Canadian Politics* (New York, 1973); France: Suzanne Berger, "Corporative Organization: The Case of a French Rural Association" in J. Pennock and J. Chapman (eds.), *Voluntary Associations* (New York, 1969), pp. 263-84.

[47] R. Huntford (fn. 22), p. 86.

subordination of political parties and, hence, broad aggregative party goals, low party discipline and absence of strong partisan ideologies; absence of stable hierarchies of organizational influence and, hence, irrelevance of class or ruling elite as political categories; low barriers of entry into the policy process and, hence, key roles assigned to "potential groups" and absence of systematic bias or exclusion; major importance attached to lobbying and, hence, concentration of attention upon parliament; assumption that policy initiatives are produced by group activity "from below" and, hence, passive roles assumed on the part of state executive and administrative bureaucracies; wide dispersion of political resources and, hence, neither omnipotent veto groups nor powerless marginal elements; and, finally, sheer multiplicity of interest and free associability ensuring spontaneous emergence of countervailing forces and, hence, a general tendency toward homeostasis or shifting equilibria.[48] Corporatist systems may manage to acquire and sustain similar outcomes of demand moderation, negotiated solutions, leader accountability, "deideologization," inclusive participation, countervalence of power and homeostatic balance, but they do *not* do so through the processes which theorists and analysts of pluralism have emphasized. For example, in the studies I have conducted of one type of corporatism, I have found that such process features as preemption of issues; co-optation of leaders; vertical or sectoral policy compartmentalization; permanent institutionalization of access; "juridization" or legalization of group conflicts through labor and administrative courts; state technocratic planning and resource allocation; extensive development of functionally specialized, parastate agencies; political culture stressing formalism, consensus and continuous bargaining; symbiotic relation with clientelist and patrimonialist practices in certain issue areas and regime levels; deliberate narrowing and encapsulation of "relevant publics"; periodic but systematic use of physical repression and anticipatory intimidation and, finally, the establishment of what Dahrendorf called a "cartel of anxiety" among restricted elites representing the apexes of the differentiated hierarchic "orders" or "corporations"[49] contributed to the persistence and viability of those systems—even over protracted periods of economic and social change and when faced

---

[48] These hypotheses about the functioning of pluralist systems are developed further and contrasted with corporatist ones in my "Inventory of Analytical Pluralist Propositions," unpublished MS, University of Chicago, 1971.

[49] See the sources cited in fns. 19 & 26.

with acute, externally induced political crises. While comparisons of institutional longevity are difficult to make, there is no evidence I can see that corporatist systems of whatever type are less stable or shorter lived than pluralist ones. There is, however, very strong evidence that they function quite differently—if often to produce generally similar outcomes.

This delineation of an equally elaborate, alternative model to pluralism may seem to some to be in and by itself sufficient justification for this exercise, but most readers must be feeling some vague sense of incompleteness if not of acute discomfort. After all, Sweden is not Portugal and Switzerland is not Greece; and yet, there they are—ignominiously grouped together under the same rubric.

The reason for this latent (or in some cases already manifest) sense of dissatisfaction lies, no doubt, in the stretch of the conceptual distinction I have made between corporatism and pluralism. While this may be an indispensable preliminary step in classifying interest systems, especially given the ubiquity and prestige of the pluralist label, it is still one which, to use Sartori's expression, "does not travel well," or better, "travels too far too easily." If our research objective is not to make universalizing suprahistorical comparisons, but to explore middle-range hypotheses which are explicitly qualified as to cultural, historical and even geographical space, then we must proceed further, *per genus et differentiam,* in our taxonomic trip. We must, in short, develop the notion of possible subtypes of corporatist interest politics (just as, of course, we should with pluralist ones, although that will not be attempted here).[50]

That most original and stimulating of corporatist theorists, Mihaïl Manoïlesco, provided the key distinction between two different subtypes. The one he called *corporatisme pur,* in which the legitimacy and functioning of the state were primarily or exclusively dependent on the activity of singular, noncompetitive, hierarchically ordered representative "corporations." The second in contrast he called *corporatisme subordonné,* in which similarly structured "corporations" were created by and kept as auxiliary and dependent organs of the state which founded its legitimacy and effective func-

---

[50] I am following here the advice (and occasionally the vocabulary) of Giovanni Sartori, "Concept Misformation in Comparative Politics," *American Political Science Review* LXIV, 4 (December, 1970), esp. pp. 1034-5.

tioning on other bases.[51] This radical distinction is one which, as we shall see, involves not only the nature of power and influence relations but also the developmental pattern by which corporatism emerges, has been reiterated, expanded upon and discussed at great length by Portuguese corporatist theorists where the two subtypes were labelled *corporativismo de associação* and *corporativismo de Estado*.[52] For our purposes we could label the former, autonomous and penetrative, as *societal corporatism;* and the second, dependent and penetrated, as *state corporatism.*

Some clues to the structural and behavioral elements which differentiate these two subtypes of corporatism can be found in our initial global connotation, or more specifically in what was deliberately *not* included in that definition.

(1) *Limited number*: does not indicate whether established by processes of interassociational arrangement, by "political cartels" designed by existing participants to exclude newcomers, or by deliberate government restriction.

(2) *Singular*: does not indicate whether the outcome of spontaneous co-optation or competitive elimination is by surviving associations, or by state-imposed eradication of multiple or parallel associations.

(3) *Compulsory*: does not specify whether de facto through social pressure, contractual dues checkoff, provision of essential services and/or acquisition of private licensing capacity, or de jure through labor code or other officially decreed, exclusively conceded authority.

(4) *Noncompetitive*: does not state whether the product of internal oligarchic tendencies or external, treaty-like, voluntary agreements among associations, or of the continuous interposition of state mediation, arbitration and repression.

(5) *Hierarchically ordered*: does not indicate whether the outcome of intrinsic processes of bureaucratic extension and/or consolidation, or of state-decreed centralization and administrative dependence.

---

[51] *Le Siècle du Corporatisme,* p. 92. Manoïlesco also noted the existence of "mixed corporatism" combining the two ideal-types.

[52] João Manuel Cortez Pinto, *A Corporação,* vol. I (Coimbra, 1955); also José Pires Cardoso, *Questões Corporativas* (Lisbon, 1958).

A somewhat similar distinction, but one which placed primary emphasis on its role in furthering class collaboration by different means, is François Perroux's between *corporatisme lato sensu* and *corporatisme stricto sensu* in *Capitalisme et Communauté de Travail* (fn. 6), pp. 7-19.

(6) *Functionally differentiated*: does not specify whether arrived at through voluntaristic agreements on respective "turfs" and nonraiding provisions, or by state-established *enquadramento* (framing) of occupational-vocational categories.

(7) *Recognition by state*: does not differentiate between recognition granted as a matter of political necessity imposed from below upon public officials and that granted from above by the state as a condition for association formation and continuous operation.

(8) *Representational monopoly*: similar to above, does not distinguish between that which is independently conquered and that which is dependently conceded.

(9) *Controls on leadership selection and interest articulation*: does not suggest whether this is the product of a reciprocal consensus on procedure and/or goals, or of an asymmetric imposition by the "organized monopolists of legitimate violence."

Through this exercise in intention—the further elaboration of properties which combine to form a global concept—we have constructed two quite distinctive subtypes. The first, involving all or most of the initial elements in the either/or dichotomies made above, corresponds ideally to what we have called societal corporatism. Empirically, it is best exemplified by the cases of Sweden, Switzerland, the Netherlands, Norway and Denmark, as well as by emergent properties which have been observed by scholars in such other, supposedly pluralist, systems as Great Britain, Western Germany, France, Canada, and the United States. The second type, described by the latter elements in each either/or distinction, coalesces into a subtype we have labelled state corporatist and this conforms historically to the cases of Portugal, Spain, Brazil, Chile, Peru, Mexico, and Greece—as well of course to the defunct experiences of Fascist Italy, Petainist France, National Socialist Germany[53] and Austria under Dollfuss.

When viewed statically, descriptively, institutionally, these two subtypes exhibit a basic structural similarity, one which sets them apart from pluralist, monist or syndicalist systems of interest representation. When viewed in motion, however, they are revealed as

---

[53] Actually, Nazi Germany is an ambiguous case. For an excellent analysis of the struggles involving competing conceptions of interest politics and the eventual demise of corporatist tendencies after 1936 in that polity, see Arthur Schweitzer, *Big Business in the Third Reich* (Bloomington, Indiana, 1964).

the products of very different political, social and economic processes, as the vehicles for very different power and influence relations, and as the purveyors of very different policy consequences. Societal corporatism is found imbedded in political systems with relatively autonomous, multilayered territorial units; open, competitive electoral processes and party systems; ideologically varied, coalitionally based executive authorities—even with highly "layered" or "pillared" political subcultures. State corporatism tends to be associated with political systems in which territorial subunits are tightly subordinated to central bureaucratic power; elections are nonexistent or plebiscitary; party systems are dominated or monopolized by a weak single party; executive authorities are ideologically exclusive and more narrowly recruited and are such that political subcultures based on class, ethnicity, language, or regionalism are repressed. Societal corporatism appears to be the concomitant, if not ineluctable, component of the postliberal, advanced capitalist, organized democratic welfare state; state corporatism seems to be a defining element of, if not structural necessity for, the antiliberal, delayed capitalist, authoritarian, neomercantilist state.

IV

Corporatism appears under two very different guises: the revolutionary and the evolutionary. It is either the product of a "new order" following from a fundamental overthrow of the political and economic institutions of a given country and created by force or special "collective spirit"; or the outcome of a natural evolution in economic and social ideas and events. In the latter case, corporatism then emerges as an aspect of a certain *idée-force* progressing along with the amplification and specification of the process of associational development, generating what one calls today in several democratic countries, "the corporative mystique."[54]

The Swiss author of these lines, himself rather caught up in "the corporative mystique" which swept his country in the 1930's, illustrates not only that theorists who contemplated the matter comparatively were well aware of the distinction between the two subtypes we have defined above, but were also quite conscious of the need for two essentially separate theories for explaining the emergence of modern corporatism. One of these would be more likely

---

[54] Jean Malherbe, *Le Corporatisme d'association en Suisse* (Lausanne, 1940), pp. 13-14.

to emphasize long-term trends and slow, incremental change, cultural and institutional continuity, gradual intellectual awareness and passive political acceptance; the other more likely would be forged out of immediate *conjoncture* and impending collapse, strong leadership and repressive action, architectonic vision and inflated rhetoric. In a nutshell, the origins of societal corporatism lie in the slow, almost imperceptible decay of advanced pluralism; the origins of state corporatism lie in the rapid, highly visible demise of nascent pluralism.

The task of constructing this set of dual theories is enormous given the apparently bewildering variety of contexts in which one type or the other of corporatism has emerged, and the frustrating absence of empirical studies on the historical dynamics of whatever type of interest group system. Complicating the task even further is the natural tendency to confuse this problem with the more general and clearly interrelated one of the causes of the erosion/collapse of liberal democracy and the advent/consolidation of authoritarian rule.[55] Even if we focus specifically and exclusively on those factors which hypothetically affect changes in the system of interest representation, we must admit from the start that the best we can do is to identify some probabilistically necessary but clearly insufficient conditions. We can only try post factum to strip historical cases of their idiosyncrasies of personality and culture, of their accidents of good and bad fortune, of their immediate but superficial catalysts and precipitants in order to reveal the underlying elements of structural conduciveness which led (and may lead in the future) to such similar and yet different outcomes as societal and state corporatism.[56] I hardly need to emphasize the preliminary and speculative nature of the following dual theories.

Nor should I have to stress that they may not contribute much to explaining specific occurrences or nonoccurrences. For example, why did the halting and tentative experiments in state corporatism by Sidónio Pais in Portugal (1917-18), Primo de Rivera in Spain (1923-30), Pangalos in Greece (1925) and José Uriburu in Argentina (1930-31) all fail to take hold when, ten to twelve years later,

---

[55] Although I do not have them with me in my current voluntary exile, I do not recall that any of the case studies to be published shortly under the editorship of Juan Linz on "The Breakdown of Democracy" specifically concentrates on interest associations.

[56] For the theoretical model underlying these distinctions between "structural conduciveness" and "precipitating factors," see Neil Smelser, *Theory of Collective Behavior* (New York, 1963).

corporatism flourished in each case? Why did Sweden, Denmark, Switzerland and the Netherlands adopt internal "social peace" treaties between peak associations of employers and workers in the 1930's and then move rapidly and incrementally toward generalized societal corporatism in the 1940's and 1950's, while other countries such as Finland, Norway and Belgium moved more hesitantly and fitfully, and still others such as France, Great Britain, Ireland and the United States have proven consistently more resistant to the blandishments of corporatism? I doubt whether the following speculations can answer such specific questions very satisfactorily.

Whatever reservations one may have about the degree of determination exercised by the structure and mode of production upon such political variables as individual attitudes, voting choice, party systems and ideological doctrines, inquiry into the origins of corporatism of either type leads one very quickly to the constraints, opportunities and contradictions placed upon political actors by the operation of the economic system. More specifically for the cases which have interested me, it leads to a consideration of the basic institutions of capitalism and the class structure of property and power engendered by it.[57] Perhaps it is the directness of the linkage between the system of interest representation and these institutions of concentration of production and inequality of distribution, but the resultant situation is particularly "naked."

As a macrohypothesis, I suggest that the corporatization of interest representation is related to certain basic imperatives or needs of capitalism to reproduce the conditions for its existence and continually to accumulate further resources. Differences in the specific nature of these imperatives or needs at different stages in the institutional development and international context of capitalism, especially as they affect the pattern of conflicting class interests, account for the difference in origins between the societal and state forms of corporatism.

Summarizing, again in a nutshell, the decay of pluralism and its gradual displacement by societal corporatism can be traced primarily to the imperative necessity for a stable, bourgeois-dominant regime, due to processes of concentration of ownership, competition

---

[57] Incompetence prevents me from even speculating about the tendencies toward corporatization which appears to exist among societies with a quite different system of economic exploitation, namely, bureaucratic-centralized socialism. For an initial treatment of these issues, see the excellent article by Janos (fn. 45) and the works discussed therein.

between national economies, expansion of the role of public policy
and rationalization of decision-making within the state to associate
or incorporate subordinate classes and status groups more closely
within the political process.

As for the abrupt demise of incipient pluralism and its dramatic
and forceful replacement by state corporatism, this seems closely
associated with the necessity to enforce "social peace," not by co-
opting and incorporating, but by repressing and excluding the autonomous articulation of subordinate class demands in a situation
where the bourgeoisie is too weak, internally divided, externally
dependent and/or short of resources to respond effectively and
legitimately to these demands within the framework of the liberal
democratic state.

Of course, to these general elements, one must add several other
"overdeterminative" factors which combine with the former, making corporatism an increasingly likely outcome: (1) secular trends
toward bureaucratization and oligarchy within interest associations;
(2) prior rates of political mobilization and participation; (3) diffusion of foreign ideologies and institutional practices; (4) impact
of international war and/or depression. Nevertheless, the core of
my speculation about structural conduciveness rests on the problems
generated by delayed, dependent capitalist development and non-
hegemonic class relations in the case of state corporatism, and advanced, monopoly or concentrated capitalist development and collaborative class relations in the case of societal corporatism.

Turning to an explication of the advanced capitalism-societal
corporatism relation, I shall be brief, partly because of my lesser
familiarity with this side, partly because there exists a series of
evocatively presented and excellently documented studies of the
subject.

The first major theorist to perceive certain emergent imperatives of capitalism and to link them explicitly with corporatism was
John Maynard (Lord) Keynes. In a startling essay published in
1926 entitled "The End of Laissez-Faire," Keynes first debunks
the orthodox claims of liberalism:

> It is *not* true that individuals possess a prescriptive "natural
> liberty" in their economic activities. There is *no* "compact" con-
> ferring perpetual rights on those who Have or those who Acquire.
> The world is *not* so governed from above that private and social

interest always coincide. It is *not* a correct deduction from the Principles of Economics that enlightened self-interest always operates in the public interest. Nor is it true that self-interest *is* enlightened; more often individuals acting separately to promote their own ends are too weak to attain even these. Experience does *not* show that individuals, when they make up a social unit, are always less clear-sighted than when they act separately.[58]

Given these negative results (and *sous-entendu* a growing awareness of them among wider and wider publics exercising the liberal voluntaristic rights accorded them by the open franchise and free associability), the *agenda* and *nonagenda* (as Keynes called it) of the state must be modified. Or, as he put it more bluntly in another essay, "In the future, the Government will have to take on many duties which it has avoided in the past."[59] The objective of this imperative policy expansion is to exercise "directive intelligence through some appropriate organ of action over the many intricacies of private business, yet . . . leave private initiative and enterprise unhindered." More specifically, he noted the need for (1) "deliberate control of the currency and of credit by a central institution," (2) "dissemination on a great scale of data relating to the business situations," (3) "coordinated act(s) of intelligent judgement . . . as to the scale on which it is desirable that the community as a whole should save, the scale on which these savings should go abroad . . . and whether the present organization of the investment market distributes savings along the most nationally productive channels" and, finally, (4) "a considered national policy about what size of Population . . . is most expedient."[60] For 1926, that was a prescient statement about the future role of the state in capitalist societies—even down to the itemized content and sequential ordering of the new policy agenda.

Despite the unorthodoxy of these suggestions for "improvements in the technique of modern capitalism," Keynes wisely observed that "there is nothing in them which is seriously incompatible with what seems to me to be the essential characteristic of capitalism, namely the dependence upon an intense appeal to the money-making and money-loving instincts of individuals as the main motive

---

[58] John Maynard Keynes, *Essays in Persuasion* (London, 1952), p. 312. This essay was initially published as a separate pamphlet in 1926.

[59] *Ibid.*, p. 331. The title of this essay, a speech delivered in 1925, is "Am I a Liberal?" Keynes's answer was, "Yes, *faute de mieux*."

[60] *Ibid.*, pp. 317-19.

force of the economic machine."[61] The reason for his confidence in their compatibility stems from the political instrumentality he advocated to bring about this policy revolution, namely, societal corporatism.

> I believe that in many cases the ideal size for the unit of control and organization lies somewhere between the individual and the modern state. I suggest, therefore, that progress lies in the growth and recognition of semi-autonomous bodies within the state—bodies whose criterion of action within their own field is solely *the public good as they understand it,* and from whose deliberations motives of private advantage are excluded, though some place it may still be necessary to leave, until the ambit of men's altruism grows wider, to the separate advantage of particular groups, classes, or faculties—bodies which in their ordinary course of affairs are mainly autonomous within their prescribed limitations, but are subject in the last resort to the sovereignty of democracy expressed through parliament. I propose a return, it may be said, towards medieval conceptions of separate autonomies.[62]

While there is no evidence (that I know of) that Keynes's slim pamphlet exerted a direct, blueprint-like, influence or even provoked a general intellectual awareness of the issues he raised, in or outside of Great Britain,[63] the subsequent course of policy development in most developed Western nations confirmed his prognosis. The fundamental paradox involved has been excellently put by a Dutch scholar:

> The more the private citizens succeed in organizing themselves into powerful combines and associations for the promoting of their manifold and often conflicting interests, the more they undermine the conditions that are essential to the actual functioning of the classical Liberalist concept of an automatically achieved equilibrium of freely competing societal forces. And the more this spontaneous harmonization proves to have little relation to reality, the more the government is impelled to interfere in order to secure a deliberately regulated and planned integration of interests.[64]

---

[61] *Ibid.,* p. 319.

[62] *Ibid.,* pp. 313-14 (my emphasis).

[63] The much later discussion of these issues in the United States was, as might be expected, even more privatistic and antistatist than that of Keynes. For a critical evaluation of this literature, see Hal Draper "Neo-corporatists and neo-reformers," *New Politics* (Fall, 1961), pp. 87-106.

[64] Kraemer (fn. 34), p. 83.

To this I would simply add another: the more the modern state comes to serve as the indispensable and authoritative guarantor of capitalism by expanding its regulative and integrative tasks, the more it finds that it needs the professional expertise, specialized information, prior aggregation of opinion, contractual capability and deferred participatory legitimacy which only singular, hierarchically ordered, consensually led representative monopolies can provide. To obtain these, the state will agree to devolve upon or share with these associations much of its newly acquired decisional authority, subject, as Keynes noted, "in the last resort to the sovereignty of democracy expressed through Parliament."

This osmotic process whereby the modern state and modern interest associations seek each other out leads, on the one hand, to even further extensions of public guarantees and equilibrations and, on the other, to even further concentration and hierarchic control within these private governments. The modalities are varied and range from direct government subsidies for associations, to official recognition of bona fide *interlocuteurs,* to devolved responsibilities for such public tasks as unemployment or accident insurance, to permanent membership in specialized advisory councils, to positions of control in joint public-private corporations, to informal, quasi-cabinet status, and finally to direct participation in authoritative decision-making through national economic and social councils. The sequence by which societal corporatism has crept into the polity probably varies considerably case by case,[65] but to the extent that the Dutch pattern is representative, it shows a peculiar circular trend. There it began with local and sectoral level, jointly managed social insurance schemes (1913); then moved to abortive attempts at establishing Conciliation Boards (1919, 1923); to sectoral consultative bodies (1933); to public extensions of cartel decisions (1935) and labor-management agreements (1937), obligatorily covering nonmembers and nonparticipants; to sectoral licensing boards on investment (1938); to the reestablishment of a nationally coordinated wage determination board (1945); to indicative national planning (1945); then back to the establishment of specialized Product and Industrial Boards, along with an overall co-

---

[65] A study which illustrates this particularly well in a nicely controlled cultural and developmental setting is Nils Evander, "Collective Bargaining and Incomes Policy in the Nordic Countries: A Comparative Analysis" (Paper prepared for delivery at the APSA Annual Meeting, New Orleans, Sept. 4-8, 1973).

ordinating agency, the Social and Economic Council (1950); then down to the establishment of consultative councils in each individual enterprise (1950) and, finally, to the creation of a national level, joint coordination council for social insurance (1959)—right back where they started in 1913.[66] The resultant pattern evolved pragmatically and unevenly, not by the unfolding of some concerted, grand corporatist design. It moved *up and down* from enterprise to local to national level; *back and forth* from a concern with specific goods and services (insurance, health, apprenticeship), with specialized vertical production areas (metallurgy, electronics, chemicals, retail commerce) and with broad horizontal sectors (industry, commerce, agriculture); and *sideways* from one issue area to another (wages, prices, investment, indicative planning). While the Netherlands' osmotic adaptation may be unique in many respects, I suspect that a sequential plotting of measures of creeping corporatism in other advanced capitalist societies would not be very different.[67]

Thanks to the effort of Andrew Shonfield, it hardly seems necessary to pursue these speculations much further. In his magisterial, *Modern Capitalism,* he has demonstrated in great detail how, in order to correct inherent defects linked to processes of internal concentration and external competition, the modern "positive" state finds itself simultaneously attempting to foster full employment, promote economic growth, prevent inflation, smooth out business cycles, regulate working conditions, cover individual economic and social risks and resolve labor conflicts. This drastic modification of the governmental agenda/nonagenda has in turn led to (and is in part the product of) a major change in the relationship between interest associations and the public bureaucracy, as advocated and predicted by Lord Keynes. Shonfield unhesitatingly labels this formula as corporatist: "The major interest groups are brought together and encouraged to conclude a series of bargains about their

---

[66] The work from which this primitive sequential account is drawn [Kraemer (fn. 34), pp. 54-65] leaves off in 1958. No doubt further private-public interpenetration has occurred since then.

[67] Not all treatments of the emergence of societal corporatism place as much emphasis as I do on the role of advanced capitalism and the imperative transformations it forces on the modern state. Huntford (fn. 22), pp. 87 ff., for example, places most of his explanatory emphasis on the traditional agricultural system of Sweden, the role of temperance societies and a particular type of industrial settlement (*bruk*). Thomas J. Anton bases his argument on a distinctive "Swedish policy-making style and elite culture" (fn. 11), pp. 92-99.

future behaviour, which will have the effect of moving economic events along the desired path. The plan indicates the general direction in which the interest groups, including the state in its various economic guises, have agreed that they want to go."[68]

In postwar Western Europe, Shonfield finds this approach competing or combining with two others: (1) intellectualized, technocratic "indicative" planning, and (2) reinforced, direct economic control and ownership by the state. In a series of thoroughly researched and well-constructed case studies, he explores the extent to which this societally corporative approach has crept differentially into European policy processes, alone or in combination with the other two. In specific instances, he emphasizes general historical-institutional-legal variables,[69] ideological residues,[70] prior levels of voluntary associational consolidation and decision-making style,[71] seriousness of demographic pressures and economic reconstruction,[72] well-entrenched conceptions of role on the part of organized interests,[73] as all providing a greater incentive for corporatization.

---

[68] Andrew Shonfield, *Modern Capitalism* (New York, 1965), p. 231. Shonfield goes on to remark: "It is curious how close this kind of thinking was to the corporatist theories of the earlier writers of Italian Fascism, who flourished in the 1920's. Corporatism got its bad name, which has stuck to it, essentially because of its association with the one-party state" (p. 233).

[69] "The corporatist form of organization seems to be almost second nature to the Austrians. It is not that they are undemocratic; they nearly all belong to their business and professional associations, their trade unions, their religious and other groups, indeed membership in some of them is compulsory. And the Government is in turn under legal compulsion to consult these organizations before it takes legislative or administrative action of certain specified kinds" (*Ibid*, pp. 193-94).

[70] "It is interesting to find the old corporatist ideal which was deeply embedded in Italian pre-war thinking—the ideal of a balanced and responsible economic group with quasi-sovereign powers administering itself—cropping up again in this new guise" (*Ibid.*, p. 192).

[71] "In Sweden there is a society in which interest groups are so strongly organized, their democratic basis so firm and their habit of bargaining with each one another independently of the government so well established . . . (yet) the Swedish Government still manages to act in a decisive fashion when circumstances require it . . . . It just happens that it is the Swedish way to treat the process of government as being in large part an extended dialogue between experts drawn from a variety of bodies, official and unofficial, whose views are expected to be merely tinged rather than finally shaped by those who pay their salaries" (*Ibid.*, pp. 199-200).

[72] "The remarkable willingness of the trade unions to collaborate actively in this policy of wage restraint is to be explained by their anxiety about the future supply of jobs for Dutchmen" (*Ibid.*, p. 212).

[73] "The general point is that German *Verbände* have traditionally seen themselves as performing an important public role, as guardians of the long-term interests of the nation's industries, and they continue to do so. The

Even more fascinating are his explanations of why certain European countries have resisted, or better, not so quickly or thoroughly succumbed to this approach. For France, he stresses the role of specialized training and corporate self-consciousness on the part of higher civil servants;[74] for the United Kingdom, he finds the answer in "the traditional British view of the proper relationship between public and private power (in which) the two . . . are thought of as utterly distinct from one another," as well as resistance by industrialists to compulsory membership and jurisdiction.[75] In a brilliant discussion of the American paradox—"the Americans who, in the 1930's, acted as the precursors of the new capitalism, seemed to stall in their course just when the system was coming to fruition in the Western world—showing its full powers to provide the great gifts of economic growth, full employment, and social welfare"—Shonfield searches for the causes of this abortive attempt to encourage corporatist forms of policy-making during the early New Deal (1933-35). He finds them in the internally competitive, overlapping jurisdictions of the federal and state bureaucracies, the preferred leadership style of Roosevelt ("his penchant for the role of bargainer-in-chief, his evident delight in the exercise of a kind of administrative athleticism"), in the active, intrusive role of Congress in the administrative process, the juridical and legalistic imprint imposed on the American state by the special role which lawyers have played within it, and in the absence of a more professionalized, self-confident elite of civil servants.[76] While Shonfield does carry his analysis into the mid-1960's, it is too bad that it stops before Lyndon Johnson and even more rapidly, Richard Nixon, who managed to transform this "arm's-length relationship with private enterprise" (as Shonfield describes it) into something more closely resembling the sort of "active huddle" which the NRA corporatists had advocated in the early thirties.[77]

Modern Capitalism provides us with a veritable gold mine of interesting general hypotheses concerning the emergence of societal

---

development one observes since the war is that the approach to problems of policy has become more consultative, with the emphasis on technical advice. Power and influence are still present; but the manner is different" (*Ibid.*, p. 245).

[74] *Ibid.*, pp. 122 ff.

[75] *Ibid.*, p. 99; also pp. 231-33 for a more explicit contrast with the French tradition.

[76] *Ibid.*, pp. 298-329.

[77] Mark Green and Peter Petkas, "Nixon's Industrial State," *The New Republic,* September 16, 1972, p. 18.

corporatism and specific, if somewhat *ad hoc,* subhypotheses explaining its differential role in contemporary Western polities and its emergent relations with other policy-mechanisms of advanced capitalist management. From my admittedly less knowledgeable vantage point, I would tend to emphasize a longer period of historical regress, for example, to include planning, rationing, mobilization and reconstruction measures taken during and following World War I and their impact upon subsequent "public policy paradigms."[78] Add to these a more explicit discussion of certain political variables, such as degree of prior class consciousness and intensity of class antagonism, extent of prior party-interest association interpenetration (*lager*-type structures), ideological diffusion and international climate, plus prior rates of political mobilization and participation. Nevertheless, in our understanding of societal corporatism we are off to an impressive, if still speculative, start.

We are not so fortunately endowed at either the theoretico-deductive or the empirico-inductive level with respect to state corporatism. Of course, one reason is that there exists no companion volume to *Modern Capitalism* entitled *Dependent* or *Derived Capitalism*—not yet. But this lack of detailed comparative case studies or even good single country monographs is only part of the difficulty.

Theorists-apologists for state corporatism are usually not very helpful. This, not so much because they tended to be less perceptive and personally objective than, say, Lord Keynes, but because they were caught in a built-in contradiction between their subjective speculative task and the objective political function they were indirectly called upon to perform.

So, for example, there is scarcely a single state-corporatist theorist who does not proclaim his opposition to statism, his com-

---

[78] Shonfield concentrates almost exclusively on the post-World War II period. Only in the case of the United States does he systematically probe further back. Is it just a coincidence that those European countries which were neutral in World War I moved more rapidly and thoroughly towards corporization (except Austria), than the belligerents? Also worth exploring in greater detail are the diverse policy responses to the Great Depression—as our rapid sketch of the Netherlands illustrated.

For the concept of "dominant paradigm of public choice" and its effect in reducing alternative courses of action, see Charles W. Anderson, "Public Policy, Pluralism and the Further Evolution of Advanced Industrial Society" (Paper prepared for delivery at the APSA Annual Meeting, New Orleans, 1973).

mitment to decisional decentralization and his desire for eventual associational autonomy.[79] Nevertheless, our theorist is aware that given the fragmented, ideologically charged and class-divided nature of the political system he is operating within, singular, non-conflictive, hierarchically ordered and functionally compartmentalized associations are not likely to be spontaneously forthcoming. He therefore advocates the temporary use of state authority to establish these compulsory structures—and to remove voluntaristic, competing ones—all, of course, in the name of national and/or public interest. Other than some vaguely specified reference to the eventual emergence of a "corporatist consciousness" (his equivalent to the New Soviet Man), our theorist conveniently forgets to specify the political mechanism by which the state's authoritarian presence can be made to "fade out," leaving those imagined self-governing agents of decentralized decision-making behind. Perhaps the most obvious case of this praxiological hypocrisy has been Portugal, if only because Oliveira Salazar so repeatedly and (apparently) sincerely expressed his fervent opposition to statism or even to any form of governmental economic intervention, while presiding over the creation of one of the most overbureaucratized, minutely regulated, centralized state apparatuses ever observed.

If such theorists can hardly be trusted with regard to the state, then neither can one expect them to be entirely candid about corporatism's relation to capitalism and specific class interests. One of their favorite themes—admittedly one which is today somewhat less loudly proclaimed—is that corporatism from above constitutes some sort of *tertium genus* between and distinct from either capitalism or socialism-communism. Hence, while they are often capable of decrying, in lurid and quite convincing terms, the inequitable and rachitic performance of existing capitalist institutions (and of conjuring up terrible visions of life under godless socialism), they are obviously not very concerned with revealing how the forceful implantation of corporatism acts as an instrument for rescuing and consolidating capitalism rather than replacing it. Given the unan-

---

[79] A partial exception would have to be entered for the Fascists: Bottai, Bortolotto, Papi and Vito but not, for example, for Ugo Spirito who even went so far as to suggest that *corporazione* should replace both private individuals and the state as the basis for property and decision-making, thereby causing a minor scandal at the 1932 Ferrara Congress on Corporatism. *Capitalismo 'e Corporatismo,* 3rd ed. (Florence, 1934). Interestingly, Spirito's works have been recently reedited.

imous emphasis they place on functional interdependence and group harmony, we should hardly expect them to delve too deeply into the elements of class conflict, status antagonism and center-periphery tension that such an imposed system of interest representation is designed to suppress, if not overcome.

In short, as we attempt to put together speculatively some hypotheses as to the contexts in which this state corporatist response emerges and the possible range of variation and sequences of implantation it may encompass, we are not likely to get much help from its manifest theorists-apologists, as we did in the case of societal corporatism.

There is, fortunately, one interesting exception: Mihaïl Manoïlesco. Manoïlesco was a sort of Salazar manqué. A professor of political economy (although an engineer by training) and minister of commerce and industry for a short period in his native Rumania,[80] he wrote *Le Siècle du Corporatisme* and its companion work, *Le Parti Unique,* after his political career had been cut short and published them in Paris. In the former he not only advanced his cosmic prediction about the ineluctable future of corporatism, but he supported his position with a complex, if schematic, argument—elements of which are strikingly modern.[81]

First Manoïlesco asserts (other corporatist theorists to the contrary notwithstanding) that his conception of this system of interest representation—actually he presents it as a complete system of political domination—has nothing to do, institutionally or ideationally, with an imagined revival of Catholic or medieval practices. Not only does he doubt the existence of natural harmony in such anciens régimes, but he accepts as definitive and desirable the rupture performed by nineteenth-century liberalism and capitalist development. His argument, then, is rigorously secular and, in his view, both progressive and realistic, looking forward prospectively rather than backward nostalgically.

Second, Manoïlesco makes his case on materialist grounds. While convinced, like Durkheim, that properly constructed corpora-

---

[80] For a brief description of his role in relation to Rumanian politics, see Andrew Janos, "The One-Party State and Social Mobilization: East Europe between the Wars" in S. Huntington and C. H. Moore, eds. (fn. 38), pp. 213-14.

[81] In the following summary of his argument I will not cite specific page references, except in the case of direct quotes, since the elements of his position are frequently scattered rather widely and I have synthesized them freely. All quotes are from the 1936 edition (fn. 1).

tions would provide the answer to overcoming modern man's moral and spiritual malaise, integrating him into society through new communal bonds, the imperative forces leading to corporatization were to be found in the political economy of his time, in the nature of ownership, production and distribution of capitalism itself. In fact, at several reprises, Manoïlesco approvingly cites Marx, although in general he regards him as a theorist of the past rather than the present century.

Third, Manoïlesco denies that corporatism is merely a temporary defense mechanism for the mobilization and/or protection of class egoism which will somehow fade away when the conjunctural threat has passed. Rather, he presents it as a permanent institutional form, not intrinsically beholden to any social class or even to the maintenance of the status quo, capable of subduing particular interests to overriding national goals and eventually of transforming the capitalist basis of society itself.

In contemporary parlance, Manoïlesco was a theorist of "external dependence." While he occasionally hints at essentially internal political conditions, for example, "premature" radicalization of the working class through ideological diffusion, fragmentation and loss of nerve on the part of the bourgeoisie, urban-rural tensions, decline of local and regional loyalties, that might contribute to provoking a corporatist response, its essential "reason for becoming" lies in the system of unequal international exchange.

> Just as Marx's theory leads us to understand the social phenomena of the capitalist world and especially that of exploitation *by classes,* this theory of international exchange makes us understand the inequality *between peoples* and relations of exploiter and exploited that connect them.[82]

Corporatism, as he understood and advocated it, is an institutional-political response to a particular process of transformation that the world political economy and its attendant system of international stratification is presently undergoing. Its "dominant cause" lies in the relations between *peoples,* rather than between *classes* within national units. In fact the latter are conditioned, if not determined, by the former. The entire spectrum of political forces has shifted: "The Nineteenth Century knew the economic solidarity of *class.*

---

[82] *Ibid.,* p. 30.

The Twentieth will know the economic solidarity of *nations*."[83]

According to Manoïlesco, the dynamic element in this process of world economic transformation consists of a radical "national" demand for restructuring the international division of labor and its distribution of benefits. Peripheral capitalist nations are becoming increasingly aware of the disparity in returns generated by their exchange of raw materials and foodstuffs for the manufactured goods produced by the advanced, earlier developing economies and are beginning to implement new national economic policies, especially ones aiming at import-substituting industrialization and control of foreign trade. This diffusion of industrialization and policy techniques was greatly accelerated by World War I, but is an autonomous secular trend which can be expected to continue on throughout the century. In essence and embryo, Manoïlesco anticipated the general arguments and even many of the specific points of what twenty years later came to be known as the ECLA (Economic Commission for Latin America of the United Nations) doctrine or, even later, the UNCTAD (United Nations Conference on Trade and Development) position.

To this, he added a second, more static observation: the end of territorial expansion. The twentieth century, he felt, would see the exhaustion of both open internal frontiers and manifest external imperialism. While he by no means could be credited with foreseeing the formal decolonialization of Africa and Asia (his perspective was strictly Eurocentric), he did see that the international system had in a physical sense filled out existing space. Borders and loyalties were becoming fixed; territoriality from being a variable had become a constant. Economic, social and political problems would have to be tackled and especially organized within constant, zero-sum parameters.

These compound changes in international relations—the collapse of the prewar liberal economic order, the rising demand for equality of benefit and status between nation-states, the definitive demarcation of territoriality — provided the materialistic (and speculative) foundations for Manoïlesco's ideology of defensive, nationalistic modernization from above. Each national unit, each state, must henceforth act exclusively as its own agent in its own interests and with its own resources, bargaining continually for survival and self-advantage in a dangerous and unstably equili-

---

[83] *Ibid.*, p. 35.

brated international system. Nineteenth-century assumptions about liberty and initiative in the pursuit of individual self-interest and the benevolent, self-corrective operation of free and competitive markets and political processes were no longer valid. As a consequence of these new tensions between central and peripheral capitalisms and between all autarkically minded nation-states, the twentieth century would impose new conceptions of justice and forms of political organization.

Corporatism, he argued, would be one of, if not *the* institutional response to these *impératifs de l'époque*. It alone would permit the state to fulfil the new functions which were being thrust upon public policy by external exigences. It would emerge first where those imperatives and tensions were the strongest, the southeastern and southern periphery of Europe, but once successful there, it would compel similar transformations in the organizational structure and policy practices of the earlier developing, liberal-pluralist systems.

But why corporatism? Why this particular set of *sous-instruments de l'Etat* as Manoïlesco unflinchingly called them? His arguments are multiple, if not equally convincing and consistent:

1) Such corporations would fill out a continuous hierarchy of authority, thereby providing the isolated and impotent individual with a set of well-defined intermediary ranks and loyalties "dragging him into society" à la Durkheim and offering the political system the means "to resolve from a unitary and logical point of view all the specialized problems posed by the complex relations between the individual and the state."[84] To do this, Manoïlesco noted, these new units of representation would have to be *integral*, not just cover economic interests as in Fascist Italy, but spiritual and moral ones as well.

2) The functional specialization of corporations would be "technologically self-determining" dividing the polity into vertical units of interest aggregation which in turn would enhance the role of technical expertise, depersonalize leadership and bring out naturally balanced interdependencies between issue areas. Most importantly and specifically, they would facilitate the expanding role of the state in national economic planning and international economic bargaining.

3) By devolving authority from the state to "neatly defined,"

---

[84] *Ibid.*, p. 74.

"never contradictory" and "preestablished" interest hierarchies, the state would be relieved of decisional and implementational responsibility over "nonessential" matters (welfare, health, etc.) and could then devote more attention and effort to such "essential" tasks as internal security, external defense, foreign affairs, and national propaganda. In addition,

> The multiplication of economic, cultural, intellectual and social functions of the state and the plurality of sources of public power creates a new function (or gives greater scope to a function already existing in embryonic form) which is the *function of arbitration and coordination of all national activities*. . . . The imperatives of our time oblige the state to recognize these [conflicts of collective interests]; they even oblige it to solve them. And they make the state the most active and solicited of arbitrators . . . [Even more] the state must have [its own power of initiative]. It must anticipate these conflicts of interest; it must have the initiative over all general decisions facilitating the coordination of national activities. Initiative becomes a new function unknown by the individualist state and embracing all manifestations of national life.[85]

4) Corporatism through its compartmentalized vertical pillaring and internal hierarchy of authority would provide an antidote to the "spirit of class." This latter, outmoded form of "horizontal consciousness" would be replaced by the new spirit of national solidarity and functionally interdependent organization.

> Despite the fact that corporative consciousness is presently weak, it will always triumph in the end. Because in the limited world we are entering today, where solidarity and organization are imperatives for survival, there will be no place for *artificial* social differences. Or, differences of class are mostly *artificial* and *temporary*, linked to the exceptional circumstances of the nineteenth century.[86]

While Manoïlesco implies that this "benevolent" ninety-degree switch in the polarities of group consciousness would begin in the periphery and come as the result of, rather than the prerequisite for, the forceful implantation of state corporatism, he hints that it will

---

[85] *Ibid.,* p. 131. This is the same author who thirty pages before had claimed: "Between the corporatist conception of the state and the pure individualistic one, there is a certain coincidence in outcomes. Both systems result (*aboutissent*) in a minimal state"!! (p. 101).

[86] *Ibid.,* p. 107-8.

be subsequently transmitted to the center where its adoption will be more spontaneous and voluntary:

> In Western Europe, the owning class and the working class will draw together, impelled by the common danger they both face equally of witnessing the collapse of the industrial superiority from which they have both benefited.[87]

Tactically speaking, Manoïlesco observes that in the short run "the best way to vanquish the actual antagonism of classes is to recognize it," that is, to incorporate "separate but equal" (*paritaire*) representations of owners and workers within the same corporation, but in the long run it will no longer be necessary to provide even such a simulated equilibrium, given the projected disappearance of class identification.[88]

5) One reason Manoïlesco was able to soft-pedal the coercive, authoritarian aspects of the transition to state corporatism was his belief that the twentieth century would see a major change in "the scales of moral and social values" held by citizens and subjects. The past century's ideals of individual equality and liberty would be replaced by new collective goals of *social justice*, based on differential rights and obligations according to the functional importance of one's role in society; and the goal of organization would replace consensual restrictions on mutual activity in return for security and higher productivity. Both of these new *idoles de l'époque* would, of course, have to be made compatible with and subordinate to the highest ideal of all, that "indisputable criterion," which Manoïlesco exclaimed in a burst of totalitarian rhetoric to mean that: "All that conforms to the national interest is just; all that is contrary to that interest is unjust."[89]

As complex and suggestive (if schematic and deformed by wishful thinking) as these hypotheses may be, Manoïlesco is much less explicit about the politics and the specific decisional sequence involved in the transition toward this new form of interest representation. Pure (read, societal) corporatism, he conceded three years later, can only be attained *after* the widespread development of "corporative consciousness" and such a high degree of national

---

[87] *Ibid.,* p. 108, fn. 1.
[88] *Ibid.,* pp. 108-9.
[89] *Ibid.,* p. 110.

integration that "old" and "artificial" class and partisan loyalties had been eradicated or, at least, severely eroded. This, he admits, is a long way off and, in the meantime, those "imperatives of the epoch" demand action, especially in the periphery. There, subordinate corporatism is the only answer: "It is natural that the corporations must be held in tutelage. The indicated tutor . . . is the single party . . . for a transitory period."[90]

In the present absence of comparative case studies, it is not easy to evaluate the merits of Manoïlesco's prototheory of the emergence of state corporatism, or to elaborate further upon it. In a very general way, there seems to be a correspondence between the context of peripheral, delayed-dependent capitalism; awareness of relative underdevelopment; resentment against inferior international status; desire for enhanced national economic and political autarky; extension of state control through regulatory policies, sectoral planning and public enterprise; emergence of a more professionalized and achievement-oriented *situs* of civil servants; and the forced corporatization of interest representation from above. Manoïlesco's belated remarks on the specific instrumentality responsible for this change have been less well confirmed. In no case was the single ruling party the primary or exclusive tutelary agent. Rather, state executive and administrative bodies tended to act directly in both establishing and subsequently controlling these new *sous-instruments*. The implantation of state corporatism, in fact, was compatible with a wide range of party contexts—from the no-party systems of Brazil, Greece and Austria, to the weak, reigning but not ruling, single-party systems of Spain and Portugal, to the strong monopolistic party systems of Fascist Italy and Nazi Germany.

On the surface, state corporatism was implanted much more dramatically, quickly, thoroughly and rationally than was the case with the hestitant, uneven, experimental, incremental, "creeping" pattern of its societal cousin. "Born at the stroke of the legislative baton," as one French critic put it,[91] overnight immense organizational hierarchies with sonorous names were created, covering all interest sectors and all levels of the polity with impressive symmetry of representative and equality of access. Subsequently, these monu-

---

[90] Mihaïl Manoïlesco, *Le Parti Unique* (Paris, 1937), p. 134.

[91] Emile Coornaert, *Les Corporations en France avant 1789,* 4th ed. (Paris, 1941), p. 293.

ments of political architecture persisted for years virtually without juridical or formal modification.

However, detailed analyses[92] have not only revealed the fictitious physical existence of many of these sonorous organizations and their marginal influence over public policy, but have also unmasked their pretence of class symmetry and equality of access. Moving ruthlessly to suppress all preexisting worker associations and to fill the resulting organizational vacuum as quickly as possible with the maximum number and most widely dispersed set of new compliant worker *sindicatos*, the state corporatists acted much more cautiously and "understandingly" with respect to producer and owner interests. Preexisting, voluntaristically supported associations were tolerated or incorporated with their leadership and functions intact; strategically placed elites were granted special organizational privileges and exemptions, for example, the right to form specialized national associations independent of the general sectoral hierarchies; rural landowners, except for those cultivating certain export crops, were left largely untouched, and associations for rural workers, where allowed to exist, were placed under their local control; no serious attempt was made to transform such preexistent, premodern corporations as the Church and the universities; corporatization of civil servants was expressly prohibited, as well as other forms of associability for this *situs;* finally, either no attempt was made to create "uniclass" peak associations of employers and workers (Brazil) or, where the attempt was belatedly made (Portugal), the resultant *corporações* have been run by and for employers. In short, what appear at first sight to be architectonic monuments of great scope, foresight and symmetry turn out upon closer inspection to be just about as limited, improvised and lopsided as those of their societally corporatist relatives.

Some of Manoïlesco's prototheoretical assumptions about the political functions and policy consequences of state corporatism seem to have been confirmed by its subsequent praxis. It has been associated with the extension of state control over export commodities, sectoral policies of import substitution and attempts to exert greater influence in international economic negotiations. While by no means successful in eradicating horizontal (class)

[92] This and the following generalizations about the praxis of state corporatism draw on my case studies of Brazil and Portugal (fns. 19 & 26). The Italian Fascist case, however, does not appear to differ markedly. See Roland Sarti, *Fascism and Industrial Leadership in Italy, 1919-1940* (Berkeley, 1971).

forms of consciousness, its imposition of verticalized decisional hierarchies and fragmented interest categories has definitely undermined the cohesion and capacity to act of the proletariat and even of the bourgeoisie with respect to general policy issues. It has advanced *pari passu* with an expansion in the role of technocratic expertise and impersonal (if not to say faceless) leadership styles. Most importantly, it has greatly advanced and facilitated *verselbständigte Macht der Executivgewalt*, that "process whereby state executive power becomes progressively more independent" from accountability to organized social groups, that Marx so long ago suggested was the crucial element in modern authoritarian rule.[93]

Otherwise, Manoïlesco's specific functional hypotheses have not stood up so well. Horizontal consciousness shows no sign of disappearing no matter how suppressed. Class inequalities in access and benefit have not been erased; they have been institutionalized and augmented. The decision-making load on the state has not been lightened but burdened by the proliferation of dependent functional hierarchies; far from being freed to pursue bold and innovative national policies, the corporate state has been trapped in a fantastically complex network of fiscal prebends, sectoral exemptions and entrenched privileges which ties it closely to a stalemated status quo. Popular demands for individual freedom and equality have yet to give way to respect for organizational hierarchy and acceptance of differential justice. Most striking, however, is the total lack of confirmation in praxis of Manoïlesco's assertion of pious hope that corporatism from above would result in a secular decline in the rate of profit, a devaluation of the role of entrepreneurial risk-taking, a diminution of the power of private property and the emergence of a new social or collective mode of production. So far, state corporatism has produced the contrary and one rather suspects it was always intended to do so.

V

"*Kuppo!*" said the Shah, shaking his head.
Khashdrahr blushed, and translated uneasily, apologetically.

[93] The expression is from Marx's *The Eighteenth Brumaire*. For a further development of these ideas, see August Thalheimer "Über den Faschismus" in O. Bauer *et al., Faschismus und Kapitalismus* (Frankfurt, 1967), pp. 19-38; H. C. F. Mansilla, *Faschismus und eindimensionale Gesellschaft* (Neuwied u. Berlin, 1971); and Nicos Poulantzas, *Fascisme et dictature* (Paris, 1970); also my "The Portugalization of Brazil?" (fn. 19).

"Shah says, 'Communism.'"

"No, *Kuppo!*" said Halyard vehemently. "The government does not own the machines. They simply tax that part of industry's income that once went into labor, and redistribute it. Industry is privately owned and managed, and co-ordinated—to prevent the waste of competition—by a committee of leaders from private industry, not politicians. By eliminating human error through machinery, and needless competition through organization, we've raised the standard of living of the average man immensely."

> Kurt Vonnegut, Jr.,
> *Player Piano* (p.28)

If we accept Manoïlesco's belief in centennial longevity and my hunch that it all began during and immediately after World War I, then we are presently right smack in the middle of the century of corporatism and hence condemned to live with it for another fifty or so years. Kurt Vonnegut's poetic imagination offers us the "comforting" thought that full corporatization will only come in the aftermath of a third major world war. Nevertheless, barring his vision of a future global conflagration precipitating further change, and adopting a more surprise-free scenario, we may question whether corporatism, state or societal, will manage to fill out its century.

State corporatism is everywhere revealing itself more and more costly to maintain through repressive measures and less and less capable of providing the accurate information, semivoluntaristic compliance and contractual complicity needed for managing the modern capitalist state. The obvious answer, an institutional shift from the imposed, exclusionist to the invited, inclusionist type of corporatism, has yet to be made peacefully and incrementally. But the transition to societal corporatism seems to depend very much on a liberal-pluralist past, involving the following: a history of autonomous organizational development; authenticity of representation; protracted encounters between classes and sectors which acquired distinct self-images and loyalties and, eventually, a measure of mutual respect; the presence of competitive party and parliamentary arenas to which wider appeals could be addressed; and, perhaps most importantly, on a previous pattern of relative noninterference by the state which only gradually came to expand its role—and then usually at the request of organized private interests.

Countries locked into state corporatism at an earlier stage of development are likely to find it much more difficult to evolve toward such a consensual solution. There the established pattern is one of asymmetric dependence, unauthentic and fragmented representation, weak associational loyalties, suppressed or manipulated conflict, little mutual respect among groups, no effective means of appealing to wider publics and pervasive state bureaucratic control.[94] Under these conditions, it is difficult to imagine a politically continuous transformation toward societal corporatism; rather, one suspects that the state-corporatist system must first degenerate into openly conflictful, multifaceted, uncontrolled interest politics—pluralism in other words—as appears to be happening in contemporary Spain.

Established, societally corporatist systems are also facing new tensions which they, too, seem incapable of resolving.[95] They are being bombarded with demands for more direct and authentic forms of participation, undermining both the stability of their established internal hierarchies of authority and their claims to democratic legitimacy. More importantly, they are being bypassed with increasing frequency by broad social movements on the one side and specific spontaneous protest actions on the other. The very values and assumptions about society upon which corporatism ultimately rests, functional specialization and hierarchical organization, security and *prévision*, "productivism" and efficiency, economic growth and mass consumption as ends in themselves, are being called into question by these movements and actions. Here, the prospective associational answer is certainly *not* further societal corporatization, *nor* a reversion to past pluralism, *nor* even less a regression to state corporatism, but may be some experimentation with the sort of dispersed, nonspecialized, nonhierarchic, "hived-off," voluntaristic units, autonomously responsible for allocating their values and resolving their conflicts, an interest system which we earlier tentatively identified as syndicalist. Again, however, the

---

[94] These conclusions about the difficulties inherent in the transformation from one type of corporatism to the other are based on the study I have conducted on Portuguese corporatism and are discussed more fully therein; see "Corporatist Interest Representation and Public Policy-Making in Portugal" (fn. 26).

[95] These and other tensions and contradictions of advanced societal corporatism are explored in Christopher Wheeler, "The Decline of Deference: the Tension between Participation and Effectiveness in Organized Group Life in Sweden," unpublished MS, Beloit College, 1972. Also Ruin (fn. 22).

peaceful and incremental route to such a systemic transformation has yet to be found.

*   *   *

Marx once suggested that societies only recognized the problems they stood some chance of resolving. From this optimistic perspective, renewed awareness that we may still be in the century of corporatism should contribute to making it the shortest century on historical record.

The next century, that of syndicalism, already awaits its Lord Keynes or its Mihaïl Manoïlesco!

A WORKING BIBLIOGRAPHY ON CORPORATISM:
ca. 1800-1950

The following is a list of approximately 100 works dealing with the doctrine and/or practice of modern, i.e., nonmedieval, corporatism up to and including the 1930's and 1940's.

I—*Original works dealing primarily with the theory or doctrine of corporatism.*

Charles Anciaux, *L'Etat Corporatif* (Bruxelles, 1935).
Joaquín Aspiazu, *El Estado Corporativo,* 5th ed. (Madrid, 1952).
Raoul Andouin and P. Lhoste-Lachaume, *Le Corporatisme pseudoremède contre l'étatisme* (Paris, 1962).
Eduardo Aunós Pérez, *El Estado Corporativo* (Madrid, 1928).
Guido Bortolotto, *Diritto Corporativo* (Milan, 1934).
Giuseppe Bottai, *Esperienza Corporativa (1929-1934)* (Florence, 1934).
M. Bouvier-Ajam, *La doctrine corporative,* 3d. ed. (Paris, 1941).
Jean Brèthe de la Gressaye, *Le syndicalisme, L'organisation professionnelle et l'Etat* (Paris, 1931).
Jean Brèthe de la Gressaye, "La corporation et l'Etat," *Archives de Philosophie du Droit et de Sociologie Juridique* (1938), pp. 78-118.
Martin Brugarola, *Régimen Sindical Cristiano* (Madrid, 1948).
Marcello Caetano, *Lições de direito corporativo* (Lisbon, 1936).
Marcello Caetano, *O sistema corporativo* (Lisbon, 1938).
António de Castro Fernandes, *Princípios Fundamentais da Organização Corporativa Portuguesa* (Lisbon, 1944).
G. D. H. Cole, *Self-Government in Industry* (London, 1920).
J. Manuel Cortez Pinto, *A Corporação,* 2 vols. (Coimbra, 1955-6).
J. Pinto da Costa Leite (Lumbrales) *A doutrina corporativa em Portugal* (Lisbon, 1936).
Raymond Devrient, *La corporation en Suisse, ses principes et ses méthodes* (Neuchâtel, 1935).
Léon Duguit, *Traité de Droit constitutionnel,* 5 vols. (Paris, 1924-27); vol. II.
Émile Durkheim, "Préface," *De la division du travail social,* 2nd ed., (Paris, 1902).
Anne Fremantle, ed., *The Papal Encyclicals* (New York, 1956).

Otto Von Gierke, *Deutsches Genossenschaftsrecht,* 4 vols. (Berlin, 1868).
Georges Guy-Grand, "Vue sur le corporatisme," *Archives de Philosophie du Droit et de Sociologie Juridique* (1938), pp. 7-26.
Maurice Hanriou, *La Théorie de l'Institution et de la Fondation* (Paris, 1925).
S. G. Hobson, *National Guilds* (London, 1919).
Pierre Jolly, *La mystique du corporatisme* (Paris, 1935).
W. E. von Ketteler, *Ausgewählte Schriften,* ed. J. Humbauer, 3 vols. (Kempten-München, 1911).
John Maynard Keynes, *The End of Laissez-Faire* (London, 1926).
Rudolf Kjellén, *Der Staat als Lebensform,* 4th ed. (Berlin, 1924). Original Swedish edition in 1916.
Harold Laski, *Studies in the Problem of Sovereignty* (New Haven, 1917).
Harold Laski, *Authority in the Modern State* (New Haven, 1927).
Bernard Lavergne, *Le gouvernement des démocraties modernes,* 2 vols. (Paris, 1933); especially vol. I, pp. 176 *et seq.*
Ramiro de Maeztu, *La Crisis del Humanismo,* 2nd ed. (Buenos Aires, 1951). Originally published as *Authority, Liberty and Function* in 1916.
Ramiro de Maeztu, *Un Ideal Sindicalista* (Madrid, 1953).
Henri de Man, *Corporatisme et Socialisme* (Bruxelles, 1935).
Mihaïl Manoïlesco, *Le parti unique* (Paris, 1937).
Mihaïl Manoïlesco, *Le siècle du corporatisme,* "Nouvelle édition," (Paris, 1936). Original edition in 1934.
Eugène Mathon, *La corporation, base de l'organisation économique* (Paris, 1935).
Charles Maurras, *Oeuvres Capitales. Essais Politiques* (Paris, 1973).
Giuseppe di Michelis, *World Reorganisation on Corporative Lines* (London, 1935).
David Mitrany, *A Working Peace System* (Chicago, 1966). Originally published in 1943.
Robert von Mohl, *Politische Schriften,* ed. by Klaus von Beyme (Köln u. Opladen, 1966).
Adam Müller, *Die Elemente der Staatskunst,* 2 vols. (Wien/Leipzig, 1922). Originally published in 1809.
Albert de Mun, *Discours,* 7 vols. (Paris, 1895-1904).
Albert de Mun, *Ma vocation sociale* (Paris, 1909).
Auguste Murat, *Le Corporatisme* (Paris, 1944).
——————, *L'organisation corporative* (Angers, 1935).
Sergio Panunzio, *Stato nazionale e sindicati* (Milan, 1924).
Giuseppe Ugo Papi, *Lezioni di economia politica corporativa,* 5th ed. (Padua, 1939).
Joseph-Paul Boncour, *Le Fédéralisme économique,* 2d. ed. (Paris, 1901).
Pedro Teotónio Pereira, *A Batalha do Futuro,* 2nd. ed. (Lisbon, 1937).
François Perroux, *Capitalisme et Communauté de Travail* (Paris, 1937).
José Pires Cardoso, *Questões Corporativas. Doutrina e factos* (Lisbon, 1958).
Gaétan Pirou, *Essais sur le corporatisme* (Paris, 1938).
Gaétan Pirou, *Néo-Libéralisme, Néo-Corporatisme, Néo-Socialisme* (Paris, 1939).
A. Prins, *La démocratie et le régime parlementaire, étude sur le régime corporatif et la représentation des intérêts,* 2nd ed. (1887).
Pierre-Joseph Proudhon, *De la capacité politique des classes ouvrières* (Paris, 1873).
Walter Rathenau, *La triple révolution* (Paris, 1921).
Georges Renard, *L'Institution* (Paris, 1933).
Henri de Saint-Simon, *Oeuvres,* esp. Vol. XIX, (Paris, 1865-73).
Henri de Saint-Simon, *L'Organisateur* (Paris, 1966).

A. de Oliveira Salazar, *Discuros,* 4th. ed. (Coimbra, 1948), esp. Vol. I.
A. de Oliveira Salazar, *Une révolution dans la paix* (Paris, 1937).
Louis Salleron, *Naissance de l'Etat corporatif* (Paris, 1942).
Louis Salleron, *Un régime corporatif pour l'agriculture* (Paris, 1937).
Friedrich Schlegel, *Schriften und Fragmente,* ed. by E. Behler (Stuttgart, 1956).
Adérito Sedas Nunes, *Situação e problemas de corporativismo* (Lisbon, 1954).
J. C. L. Simonde de Sismondi, *Etudes sur les constitutions des peuples libres* (Paris, 1836).
Georges Sorel, *Matériaux d'une théorie du prolétariat* (Paris, 1919).
Othmar Spann, *Der Wahre Staat,* 3rd ed. (Jena, 1931).
Ugo Spirito, *Capitalismo e corporativismo,* 3rd. ed. (Florence, 1934).
Ugo Spirito, *I fondamenti della economia corporativa* (Milano-Roma, 1932).
Marcel Tardy and Edouard Bonnefous, *Le corporatisme* (Paris, 1935).
J. J. Teixeira Ribeiro, *Lições de Direito Corporativo* (Coimbra, 1938).
M. de la Tour de Pin, *Vers un ordre social chrétien: jalons de route (1882-1907),* 6th. ed. (Paris, 1942). Originally published in 1907.
M. de la Tour de Pin, *Aphorismes de politique sociale* (Paris, 1909).
Union de Fribourg, *Réimpression des thèses de l'Union de Fribourg* (Paris, 1903).
P. Verschave, "L'organisation corporative aux Pays-Bas" in Semaine Sociale d'Anger, *L'organisation corporative* (Angers, 1935), pp. 465-482.
F. Vito, *Economia politica corporativa* (Milan, 1939).
Karl von Vogelsang, *Gesammelte Aufsätze über sozialpolitische und verwandte Themata* (Augsburg, 1886).
Max Weber, *Economy and Society,* ed. by G. Roth and C. Wittich, 3 vols. (New York, 1968); especially vol. I, pp. 40-56, 292-299, 339-354 and vol. III, pp. 994-1001, 1375-1380, 1395-1399.

II.—*Works discussing Corporatist theorists.*

Ralph H. Bowen, *German Theories of the Corporate State* (New York, 1947).
Richard L. Camp, *The Papal Ideology of Social Reform* (Leiden, 1969).
Edouard Dolléans *et al.,* "Syndicalisme et corporations," Ed. spéciale de *L'Homme Réel* (Paris, 1935).
Hal Draper, "Neo-corporatists and Neo-formers," *New Politics* (Fall, 1961), pp. 87-106.
Matthew H. Elbow, *French Corporative Theory, 1789-1948* (New York, 1966).
G. Jarlot, *Le régime corporatif et les catholiques sociaux. Histoire d'une doctrine* (Paris, 1938).
Walter Adolf Jöhr, *Die ständische Ordnung; Geschichte, Idee und Neubau* (Leipzig-Bern, 1937).
P. Keller, *Die korporative Idee in der Schweiz* (St. Gallen, 1934).
Peter Cornelius May-Tasch, *Korporativismus und Autoritarismus* (Frankfurt, 1971).

III—*Works dealing primarily with the practice of corporatist institutions (often however heavily ideological):*

Max d'Arcis, *Les réalisations corporatives en Suisse* (Neuchâtel, 1935).
Firmin Bacconnier, *Le Salut par la corporation* (Paris, 1936).
Louis Baudin, *Le Corporatisme: Italie, Portugal, Allemagne, Espagne, France* (Paris, 1942).
Georges Bourgin, *L'Etat corporatif en Italie* (Paris, 1935).

Simone Comes, *L'organisation corporative de l'industrie en Espagne* (Paris, 1937).

Emile Coornaert, *Les Corporations en France avant 1789*, 4th ed. (Paris, 1941).

Freppel Cotta, *Economic Planning in Corporative Portugal* (London, 1937).

Fritz Ermath, *Theorie v. Praxis des fascistisch-Korporativen Staates* (Heidelberg, 1932).

J. Félix-Faure, *L'Organisation professionnelle aux Pays-Bas* (Paris, 1938).

Antonio Ferro, *Salazar: Le Portugal et Son Chef* (Paris, 1934).

José Figuerola, *La colaboración social en Hispanoamérica* (Buenos Aires, 1943).

Herman Finer, *Representative Government and a Parliament of Industry* (Westminster, 1923); especially pp. 3-34, 210-230.

Daniel Guerin, *Fascisme et grand capital*, 2nd. ed. (Paris, 1945).

Carmen Haider, *Capital and Labor under Fascism* (New York, 1930).

J. E. S. Hayward, *Private Interest and Public Policy: The Experience of the French Economic and Social Council* (London, 1966).

Camille Lautaud and André Poudeux, *La représentation professionnelle. Les conseils économiques en Europe et en France* (Paris, 1927).

Jean Lescure, *Etude sociale comparée des régimes de liberté et des régimes autoritaires* (Paris, 1940).

Emile Lousse, *La société d'ancien régime* (Bruxelles, 1943).

Jean Malherbe, *Le corporatisme d'association en Suisse* (Lausanne, 1940).

Jacques Marchand, *La renaissance du merchantilisme à l'époque contemporaine* (Paris, 1937).

Fr. Oliver-Martin, *L'organisation corporative de la France d'ancien régime* (Paris, 1938).

F. Pereira dos Santos, *Un Etat corporatif: La Constitution sociale et politique portugaise* (Paris, 1935).

Roland Pré, *L'organisation des rapports économiques et sociaux dans les pays à régime corporatif* (Paris, 1936).

L. Rosenstock-Franck, *L'économie corporative fasciste en doctrine et en fait* (Paris, 1934).

L. Rosenstock-Franck, *L'Expérience Roosevelt et le milieu social américain* (Paris, 1937).

Martin Saint-Léon, *Histoire des Corporations de métier depuis leurs origines jusqu'à leur suppression en 1791*, 4th ed. (Paris, 1941).

Carl T. Schmidt, *The Corporate State in Action* (London, 1939).

William G. Welk, *Fascist Economic Policy* (Cambridge, 1938).

Corporatism and Latin American-United States Relations

Fredrick B. Pike

Latin America and the United States: The First Third of the Twentieth Century

In the latter part of the nineteenth century, as a few republics began to enjoy more prolonged moments of political stability, Latin American leaders developed a mania for economic progress. Under the influence of a heterodox form of positivism and in many instances inclined to emulate United States social and economic models, progress-oriented Latin Americans looked upon classical liberalism and the bourgeois, individualistic, profit ethic as the keys to success. Traditional paternalistic devices were repudiated in the interest of converting all members of society who were capable of the transformation — considerable doubt prevailed as to whether Indians, Blacks and various mixed bloods were capable — into competitive, individualistic capitalists whose success in attaining self-reliance and economic independence would propel their nations onward.

The attempt to force the masses, who through the ages had been largely inert in a paternalistic system, to become individualistic and self-reliant virtually overnight, and to compete with others on a basis of liberty and equality, was largely self-defeating. It left the masses isolated and impotent before privileged men who had long since learned how to take advantage of the opportunities afforded by untrammeled individualism. In fact, the new procedures intended to bring about development invited a form of social and economic exploitation more heartless than the periods of colonialism and early independence had known. The situation was exacerbated by the urbanization already under way in many republics before the end of the nineteenth century. Arriving in the mushrooming cities at a time when laissez-faire principles had gained supremacy in a stage of incipient industrialization, emigrants from the countryside discovered none of the paternalistic safeguards that had at least guaranteed them subsistence in a manorial setting.

Out of the worsening social problems that appeared in most

Latin American republics as the twentieth century began there emerged a full-fledged challenge to the legitimacy of the established order. Alarmed by the signs of discontent and fearful of a leveling social revolution, elements within the ruling classes longed for a return to an idealized past in which, as they viewed it, harmony had prevailed among the various components of society.

In the classic corporate social structure that had been a hallmark of most of the Spanish colonial period — though some of its features were challenged and undermined by the eighteenth-century Bourbon reforms — all society had been divided into semiautonomous local and regional associations and also into compartments determined by function and social status. More important than the compartmentalization of society in maintaining social peace and solidarity had been the dichotomized nature of each and every compartment or corporation. Within each corporation was a *patrón* sector, made up of those who gave the orders, who were to some degree independent and self-reliant and individualistic, and also a sector comprised of those who depended for subsistence upon the benevolence of the *patrones*. However large the number of compartments, then, all society was divided into two basically distinct but — theoretically — harmoniously related, interdependent cultures, one dominant, the other subordinate.[1]

Most of Latin America's *hispanistas* or venerators of Spanish culture and legacies attribute corporate traditions to the Iberian background. On the other hand, *indigenistas* often point with pride to the Indian background as the cradle of what essentially is a corporate system—even though they do not customarily call it by that name. Thus the Peruvian Luis E. Valcárcel and the Bolivian José Antonio Arze stress the two-culture aspects of the Inca empire. Both contend that Inca communism or socialism existed only for the lower masses who, although paternalistically protected against various types of calamities and disasters, were allowed by the state apparatus to benefit from their own efforts and labor only to the degree necessary to meet basic needs. In contrast, an Inca elite was to a considerable degree economically independent and given to practices of conspicuous consumption. Moreover, just as the Spanish masses had identified with their

---

[1] For a fuller development of these themes, see my *Spanish America 1900-1970: Tradition and Social Innovation* (New York, 1973).

own particular corporation or functional group, so the Indian masses had identified with their crafts association or with their *ayllu,* an area of land collectively utilized by tribally related families. In both instances the masses remained devoid of the class consciousness that could be dangerous to the interests of an elite. The conclusion reached by Valcárcel, Arze, and numerous other *indigenistas,* is that today's descendants of the high native civilizations of South America — who exhibit overwhelmingly the characteristics of the masses rather than the leaders in the Inca empire — are culturally and spiritually unattuned to the liberal, individualistic, self-reliant, capitalist life styles. If they are to become truly assimilated into the national reality, then, the argument runs, that reality must be one that rejects — at least so far as the lower classes are concerned — liberal capitalism and individualistic democracy.[2] The approach of Valcárcel and Arze suggests that some *indigenistas* at least are just as elitist in their views of the proper social and political organization and just as dubious about society-wide capitalism as are their traditional adversaries. the *hispanistas.**

---

[2] See Valcárcel, *Del ayllu al imperio* (Lima, 1924) and Arze, *Sociografía del inkario: ¿Fue socialista o comunista el imperio inkaico?* (La Paz, 1952). Touching in many of its pages on these corporatist aspects of preconquest Andean life is the superb article by Karen Spalding, "*Kurakas* and Commerce: A Chapter in the Evolution of Andean Society," *The Hispanic American Historical Review,* LIII (1973), 581-599. Spalding also intimates that during the course of the colonial period, Indian life developed along a two-culture pattern. Indian masses often retained a collectivist style of life within their *comunidades,* while a class of Indian *principales* or important men became successful private capitalists. Often the *principales* served as a bridge between the collectivist *comunidad* and the outside, European, capitalist marketplace. Therefore, the collectivism below, capitalism above dichotomy, an important feature of the old as well as the new Iberian corporatism, has an important reflection in Indian culture of the colonial period. In regard to Latin American-United States relations, the significant point is that the Hispanic past and the Indian past mutually reinforce incompatibility with North American liberal models.

* The dichotomized society, with the leading classes relatively independent and self-reliant (in their international relationship to that society at least) and caught up to some extent in capitalist operations while the masses remained dependent and subsistence oriented, may well be the principal feature of corporatism as it has existed and re-emerged in the Iberian and Ibero-Indian cultures. This is why the Cuban endeavor, under Fidel Castro, to eradicate private capitalism altogether and to construct essentially a one-culture society is so totally revolutionary and unprecedented within the Iberian context — and also why it is not destined, in my view, to have many emulators elsewhere in the Iberian world. Many of the non-Iberian forms of corporatism referred to by Philippe Schmitter in the preceding essay seem

At a point generally rather early in the twentieth century, although the precise date differs considerably from country to country, the Latin American ruling classes began to experiment with new variants of corporatism in order to restore social solidarity and reassert their claims to political legitimacy. In line with this, they abandoned the attempt to inculcate the masses with the competitive, individualistic, "money-grubbing" bourgeois ethic, for this very endeavor had already brought about the dangerous alienation of a high percentage of the masses. Beyond this, the success of a very few members of the lower classes in adapting themselves to the new values and indeed becoming successful individualistic capitalists, in command of private capital resources and therefore economically independent and self-reliant, had threatened to bring into being a new class that could conceivably, if it grew sufficiently, resist co-optation and challenge the elite for political control. If the traditional elite was to prevail, apparently it could do so only by eschewing rapid economic development, which seemed to depend on transforming those among the masses who were capable into successful capitalists while eliminating, through a survival-of-the-fittest struggle, those who were not capable.

As Latin American leaders groped toward a new form of corporatism they generally came to rely upon a more centralized structure than had existed in colonial times. Within the political-social structure that gradually evolved as the twentieth century advanced, the internal dichotomy within each corporate association was less apparent than in bygone centuries. Instead of each of society's compartments clearly containing representatives of the two cultures, the role of the *patrón* vis-à-vis each compartment began to be taken on more and more by the state. The masses comprising the dependent culture were grouped into various associations, such as labor unions, and many middle-sector groups

---

to me to manifest less clearly the two-culture aspect of Ibero-Indian corporatism, an aspect — incidentally — that has exercised a far greater molding force on Catholicism than Catholicism on it. The issue, then, is not settled (at least not for me) as to whether certain characteristics of corporatism are associated with the general cultural milieu of the Iberian and Ibero-Indian civilizations throughout their historical trajectories. Indeed, the issue faced here may never be resolved with any greater finality than the heredity vs. environment debate, or the question as to whether Spanish disinclination toward liberal capitalism arose basically from the character of the people or from legal restrictions and other existential factors.

were also encouraged to form professional organizations; each association was ultimately dependent upon the central government for a variety of fringe benefits — such as subsidized housing, free education, paid vacations, retirement pensions, medical services, and the like. Members of each organization derived not only material benefits and security but also a sense of belongingness and participation; and they were apt to identify with their particular group, rather than with a class. Thus they remained largely divided and the only bond they shared was a common dependence upon the favors and concessions of central government.

In their twentieth-century reaction against liberalism, laissez-faire economics and the Latin American version of positivism, leadership groups in most republics disavowed the entire bourgeois ethic. The reason is obvious. The development-obsessed leaders of the late nineteenth century had, in effect, been seeking to carry out a bourgeois revolution, through which individualistic, competitive, capitalist values — the whole life style that traditionalist Catholic spokesmen of the Hispanic world through the years associated with the Protestant ethic and so rejected as heretical — would be imposed upon all members of society, from a traditional elite that had customarily prided itself on lack of materialism, right on down to the masses. Out of this, however, there had come a social problem and in turn a challenge to the whole established order. It seemed clear, then, that the way to avoid social upheaval was for the ruling classes to set a proper example to society by renouncing materialism and taking up the humanistic pursuit of higher values. A ruling class thus purified would be in a better position to exhort the masses to abandon concern with individual material aggrandizement. Essentially, the nonmaterialistic leaders who liked to pose as true humanists were promising to the masses security within a system that "took from them according to their means and gave to them according to their needs." With their needs satisfied by the aristocratic elite that ran the state, the masses, purportedly, would be liberated from the competitive scramble for security based on self-reliance and private possession of capital surpluses. Thus they would be able to concern themselves with the higher values of life — nonmaterial rewards — through which they could achieve fulfillment and content.

The effort of ruling sectors in much of Latin America to keep the masses nonmaterialistic in a life style that attached a premium to dependence and submissiveness while discouraging capitalist incentives hampered economic development, even though it contributed enormously to social stability. Similar results accompanied the upper-class repudiation of the bourgeois ethic, an ethic toward which it had been inclining in the late nineteenth century. In the changing ideological environment of the early twentieth century, an economically productive, materialistic bourgeoisie was to be tolerated as a necessary evil in order to give to the economy some element of viability; but the ruling classes hoped ultimately for the co-optation of the more successful practitioners of the bourgeois arts into the aristocracy's world through associations of various types, often cemented by marriage. This would seriously impede the continuity of economic development, by periodically siphoning the ablest and most productive capitalists into the nonproductive and parasitical world of a traditional aristocracy. At the same time it would prevent a reappearance of the revolutionary pressures generated by the nineteenth-century attempt to bring about the *embourgeoisement* of all society.

As they entered the new century Latin American leaders, in many ways, turned toward the elitist values and corporate models of the past—a past that whether in its Hispanic or Indian guise had not been characterized by undue concern with progress. As a result they faced a serious dilemma. If in the interest of guarding against social revolution they discarded an obsession with economic expansion and development, how could they generate the capital with which to finance the new forms of state paternalism on which their legitimacy was coming to depend? In other words, how could they raise the money to pay the premiums on their new insurance policies against social revolution?

In the colonial period a vast and complex system of social security had been administered by the Church. To finance it, the Church had relied on the profitable operation of its extensive rural properties and its urban business pursuits. In addition, it had relied on the interest earned by massive loans extended through the generations to the members of a largely noneconomic aristocracy. These capital transactions were not referred to as loans, for the Church opposed usury; but loans essentially are what they were. In short, much of the Church's capital for social projects derived from the forced savings of the upper classes. However, as

the twentieth century began, the ruling classes had long since repudiated this form of forced savings, and they hoped to avoid
contributing directly in any way to the new programs of state
paternalism.

For a time, before the population explosion and the "revolution
of rising expectations," it seemed that foreign capital, and especially United States capital, could provide the ruling classes with
a good part of the funds needed to preserve a traditional social
order. Between 1919 and 1929, United States direct investment
in Latin America rose from $1.89 billion to $3.5 billion.[3] Economically, the overall effect of such direct investment may have
been a draining one; this is, at least, the dogma to which all Latin
American economic nationalists subscribe. More obviously, loans
had a long-term capital-draining effect, assuming they were amor-
tized according to contract agreements. Still, considerable United
States capital resources did remain in Latin America, even in the
1919-1929 period when governments were notoriously lenient in
taxing foreign enterprise. If they paid very little in the way of
direct taxes, the foreign firms paid something. More significantly,
the export taxes, on which Latin American governments had traditionally relied for the major portion of their revenue, were paid
increasingly by foreign firms as they came to acquire control over
extractive industries and commercial agriculture. Already by a
point fairly early in the twentieth century there was developing
what leftist writers like to describe as a "symbiotic relationship"
between foreign capital and a Latin American oligarchy. Already,
the "internal domination" by the oligarchy rested upon its "external dependence" — to employ more of the jargon revered by
leftist authors. (Actually, such a situation had developed in seventeenth-century Spanish America. Owners of large rural estates,
for example, were even then dependent upon the external, capitalist market, upon credit from churchmen and merchants, and
upon infusions of new capital acquired through marriage with
successful and relatively recently arrived Spanish entrepreneurs,
for the funds needed to assure their control, paternalistic or otherwise, over their labor forces.)

Early in the twentieth century, the Latin American ruling
elites had begun to utilize the presence of United States capital

---

[3] See Raymond Mikesell, *Foreign Investments in Latin America* (Washington, D.C., 1955), p. 11.

in their quest to preserve a traditional society and to avoid what they perceived as the revolutionary consequences of penetration by United States political culture. The political culture of the United States represented to them the very embodiment of the materialistic, individualistic, competitive bourgeois ethic; it symbolized the conscious endeavor to create a society in which all citizens were to be self-reliant and independent. From the viewpoint of the Latin American ruling classes, nothing was to be more staunchly resisted than the introduction of the Yankee way of life, a way of life which they believed could be brought to Latin America only through leveling revolution.

As the twentieth century began, Latin American statesmen and intellectuals were turning into zealous cultural nationalists in their attitudes towards the United States; by and large, though, they had not yet begun to become economic nationalists. They were hostile to the Colossus of the North not so much because they feared its political imperialism — this fear was relatively insignificant among the major powers of *South* America — as because they feared that penetration of its cultural values would herald social revolution. The Latin American directing classes were not yet economic nationalists, because they saw the need of United States capital if they were to block North American cultural penetration and preserve the area's basic social identity as a two-culture society. And until the post-World War II period it did seem that the Latin American leaders might succeed in utilizing in their defense of the traditional society some of the capital resources generated by the citizens of a country whose nationalistic credo and myth-fantasy and whose sense of mission rested on rejection of the dichotomized, two-culture, corporate society and on the desire to banish that sort of society from the American hemisphere and perhaps from the entire world.

The United States and Latin America:
The First Third of the Twentieth Century

In its relations with Latin America — and with the rest of the world, for that matter — the United States has been motivated primarily by security and economic considerations. This trite observation could scarcely provoke challenge, although authorities have disagreed heatedly through the years over whether it is security or economic interests that have been paramount. Frequently it is alleged that economic considerations assumed primary im-

portance in the "Dollar Diplomacy" conducted by William Howard Taft's administration. In his policies toward Latin America,
however, Taft seems to have been interested in far more than
immediate profit-making opportunities for private United States
capitalists. What he wanted besides was the "regeneration" of Latin
Americans, to be achieved by teaching them how to become
successful capitalists and to live according to the rules of what is
often described as the Protestant ethic. In a way, Taft was simply
seeking to expand upon policies that President John Quincy Adams
(1825-29) had hoped to implement in his dealings with Latin
America. Adams apparently had believed that no real good could
come of his country's economic relations with Latin America unless together with its goods and capital the United States introduced its religious principles. Thus he had hoped to use commercial treaties with the lands to the south as the means for inducing them to accept the principle of religious toleration,[4] an
entering wedge for the ultimate triumph of Protestant values
throughout the hemisphere.

Taft had expressed some of his ideas on Latin American regeneration in a speech delivered on October 1, 1906, at the National University of Havana, just as the second United States
occupation of Cuba was getting under way. He reasoned that if
United States capitalists were encouraged to offer Cubans the
example of their enlightened expertise, then Cubans would in
time begin to develop along the same lines that had made the
United States great. The main lesson, as Taft saw it, the Cubans
would learn from their United States political and economic
tutors was that:

> The right of property and the motive for accumulation, next to
> the right of liberty, is the basis of all modern, successful civili-
> zation, and until you have a community of political influence and
> control which is affected by the conserving influence of property
> and property ownership, successful popular government is im-
> possible.[5]

---

[4] See Wilkins B. Winn, "The Efforts of the United States to Secure Religious Liberty in a Commercial Treaty with Mexico, 1825-1831," *The Americas,*
XXVIII (1972), 311-332.

[5] Quoted in Ralph Edwin Minger, "William Howard Taft and the United
States Intervention in Cuba in 1906," *The Hispanic American Historical
Review,* XLI (1961), 80.

Developing these ideas further, Taft in his 1906 address advised Cubans to foster a lively interest in the acquisition of material wealth. He lamented that too many young Cubans were not sufficiently infused with the mercantile spirit. If they would only develop this spirit, form great enterprises, and then turn their attention to politics, Cuba would become an ideal republic, for, as was clearly implied, it would thereby become like the United States.

For Taft, the acquisition of skills and the character-building involved in becoming successful in business fostered the virtues and wisdom necessary for citizens to function responsibly and wisely in a democratic body politic. Democracy and political stability, he was convinced, could come to Cuba only after the islanders had adopted the bourgeois ethic and taken up the quest for economic gain and self-sufficiency through the competitive struggle. His successor, Woodrow Wilson, seemed in this respect in total accord with Taft, as he devised his policies not only for Cuba and the Caribbean but for Latin America in general.

Through New Freedom reforms in the United States, Wilson hoped to restore the propitious climate for individualistic capitalism that had been temporarily contaminated by the viruses of monopolistic exclusivism. Beyond this, he hoped that reformed United States capitalism could, by vastly expanding its operations in Latin America, set an example that would help to spread the individualism of the New Freedom throughout the hemisphere. Wilson seemed to think that only United States capitalism, once he had implemented the few simple remedies that were required, could be relied upon to bring in its wake an entire political culture conducive to the regeneration of the Latin American masses. European capitalism, thought by the president to be hopelessly sordid in motivation, could not be trusted to do the job.[6] Once converted into self-reliant, successful capitalists with private control over monetary resources, Latin Americans would, Wilson

---

[6] As Arthur Link puts it, "Wilson and Bryan meant to undertake a new policy and hasten the day when the New World would be free from European financial exploitation." See Link, *Woodrow Wilson and the Progressive Era* (New York, 1954), p. 79. In a way this harked back to the "large policy" advocated by Thomas Jefferson which aimed at excluding all European influence from this hemisphere. The essence of the "large policy" subsequently found its way into the Monroe Doctrine and the various additions to it. See Arthur P. Whitaker, *The United States and the Independence of Latin America, 1800-1830* (New York, 1964), p. 43.

believed, become customers for United States manufacturers; beyond this, they would acquire the character and decency needed to make the democratic form of government function.

Little wonder, therefore, that Wilson was enthusiastic about the arguments used in 1914 by Robert Lansing, then a counsellor for the State Department, in suggesting a bold new Latin American policy. In what must surely figure among the longest English-language sentences, Lansing, in a memorandum to the president, had asked:

> Should a new doctrine be formulated declaring that the United States is opposed to the extension of European control over American territory and institutions through financial as well as other means, and having for its object, not only the national safety and interests of this country, but also the establishment and maintenance of republican constitutional government in all American states, the free exercise by their people of their public and private rights, the administration of impartial justice, and the prevention of political authority from becoming the tool of personal ambition and greed, the chief enemies of liberal institutions, of economic development, and of domestic peace?[7]

The president's interest in regenerating Latin Americans by transforming them into self-reliant individualistic capitalists capable of participating intelligently in democratic processes accounts for much of his policy toward Mexico as that country struggled along in the early stages of its Revolution that had erupted in 1910. By 1914 Wilson was convinced that the Constitutionalists, under the leadership of Venustiano Carranza and others, were intent upon encouraging free-enterprise, individualistic, competitive capitalism. To Wilson it seemed that the Constitutionalists, whose northern power base could lay historical claims to being the home of Mexican individualistic enterprise, had discarded the paternalistic interventionist doctrines associated with Iberian Catholicism (and also with the Indian background), according to which the docile dependence of the masses attested to their virtues rather than their vices. It followed that the Constitutionalists could be

---

[7] *Foreign Relations of the United States: The Lansing Papers, 1914-1920,* II (Washington, D.C., 1940), p. 464. Responding to the Lansing suggestion, Wilson wrote: "The argument of this paper seems to be unanswerable, and I thank you for setting it out so explicitly and fully. This will serve us as a memorandum when the time comes, and the proper occasion, for making a public declaration of policy on this important matter." See *ibid.,* p. 470.

expected to encourage the presence of United States private capital so that it could play a role in achieving not only material development but also the moral uplifting of the Mexican populace. Assured by some of his own agents in Mexico, and by Luis Cabrera who was sent on a special mission by Carranza and his associates to enlist the support of the United States government, of the Constitutionalists' intentions, President Wilson threw all his efforts into assuring their triumph.

Among leftist-inclining writers it is a commonplace that United States policymakers, because of their overriding concern with protecting the economic interests of their fellow citizens, can never sympathize with revolutionary aspirations in Latin America. In the case of Wilsonian diplomacy, and of a good deal of subsequent diplomacy as well, these writers miss the point altogether. Wilson wanted to guarantee a safe climate of operation for United States capitalists in Mexico precisely because he was convinced that they could play a role in bringing about a truly profound revolution: a revolution that involved ending the traditional dominant-subordinate two-culture society by transforming virtually all citizens into competitive, self-reliant capitalists who would then be able to parlay their economic self-sufficiency into political self-rule.[8] To a major degree, Wilson's quarrel lay with Mexican traditionalists of many varieties. The anticapitalism of many of these traditionalists, that helped endear them to leftist analysts in the United States, sprang far more from historical precedents and patterns than from Marxism.

As it turned out Wilson, as well as many Constitutionalists, were thwarted in their hopes. Mexicans basically out of sympathy with the free-enterprise credo gained control of the Constituent Assembly that gathered in Querétaro in 1916 and produced a constitution that was promulgated in 1917. By sharply curtailing the practice of classical, liberal capitalism, by providing for massive doses of state intervention in the social and economic spheres, the new Mexican Constitution created the legal basis for perpetuating a basically two-culture society in which the masses would remain both economically and politically dependent. At the time, United States business interests and government officials, misunderstanding events

---

[8] Because of his lack of understanding of Latin American culture Wilson, even as a later president, John F. Kennedy, probably did not realize how profound a revolution would have to be carried out in order to attain his objectives.

as much as most leftist observers, grumbled that the 1917 Constitution, because of the statism and paternalism it prescribed and its acceptance of a collectivist rather than an individualistic political culture for the masses, was "un-American." The truth is that the Mexican Constitution reflected origins, both Spanish and Indian, that were far older in America than the individualistic, noncorporate approaches that had evolved in the United States.

By being themselves, as in many ways they returned to traditional modes through revolution, the Mexicans fashioned a system that limited some of the immunities previously enjoyed by foreign capital and forced it, as the price for its continuing presence, to contribute a greater share of profits to the Mexican government. By gaining a larger share in the earnings of foreign enterprises, the Mexican government found some of the revenue needed to maintain the masses in a state of security but at the same time in one of dependence. As the 1930's began, however, the governing elites in most of the other Latin American countries had not yet devised the means to increase their share in the earnings of foreign capital. As a result their position was precarious, all the more so as the effects of the world depression began to be felt. This is the background against which the emergence of the Good Neighbor Policy must be viewed.

The Good Neighbor Policy

At the sixth Pan-American Conference held in Havana in 1928, the Latin American delegates had by no means presented a solid front in urging the United States to desist once and for all from intervention in the internal affairs of its sister republics in the hemisphere. In fact, the representatives of host-country Cuba and of Peru had spoken eloquently in defense of intervention, picturing it, under certain conditions, as the only means of preserving civilization and decency. It was a different story, however, at the seventh Pan-American Conference, held at the end of 1933 in Montevideo, Uruguay. There the Latin American delegates lined up unanimously to press Secretary of State Cordell Hull, personally representing the Franklin D. Roosevelt administration, to subscribe to the principles of absolute nonintervention.

It is rare indeed that the Latin American republics achieve a united front on any issue. What was responsible for the unanimity with which they supported the nonintervention doctrines in 1933 (and again in 1936 at a Buenos Aires Conference of American States)? Basically, I think, the answer lies in the economic adversity resulting from the great depression.

The depression rendered vulnerable, perhaps as never before, the position of the ruling elite. With foreign loans no longer available, with foreign investment having virtually ceased, and with revenue from export taxes declining precipitously because of plummeting world prices for raw materials, the governing classes no longer had available to them the funds to finance the modest social programs they had begun to introduce, in many countries at least, and on which their continuing ability to remain in control seemed to depend. They might still retain their power, however, if the United States government did not prod them too insistently to resume payment on defaulted foreign debt obligations and if it permitted them to renegotiate arrangements with private United States investors so as to obtain greater tax yields and overall benefits. In short, they saw their ability to survive in terms of being able to treat foreign private capital—primarily United States private capital—to some extent as they saw fit, without fear of diplomatic intervention by the United States government in defense of the economic privileges of its citizens.

At the Montevideo Conference, Mexico's Foreign Affairs Minister José M. Puig y Casauranc delivered one of the most important addresses. Puig argued that the basic concern for the American hemisphere was shifting toward socioeconomic considerations and away from the old political issues. The primary challenge facing the hemisphere, he declared, was to provide social justice. He concluded that the inter-American movement was doomed if it could not meet this challenge. Throughout much of his speech, Puig seemed rather clearly to be implying that Latin American governments must be allowed to increase, without fear of retaliation, the share accruing to them from foreign investment so as to be able to finance social justice projects.[9] Shortly, the Mexican's stand was backed by a rising tide of economic nationalism in Latin America, with most of its exponents making much of the various studies conducted during the 1930's—some of them by the United States Congress—that indicated the degree to which North American

---

[9] The Chilean newspaper *La Nación* (Santiago) commented favorably on the Puig y Casauranc address in its December 17, 1933, edition. Its commentary was typical of the Latin American response to the message of the Mexican Minister of Foreign Affairs.

capitalists had in the past avoided paying a fair share of earnings to host-nation governments.

Economic nationalists at this time aimed at *increasing* Latin American dependence on the United States and thus they stand in stark contrast to a later group of their breed which would raise the demand for reduced economic dependence. Revisionist writers of the New Left have been quite mistaken in attributing the continuing "containment" and dependence of Latin America during the Good Neighbor Policy days exclusively to the self-serving schemes of United States economic interests in league with powerful national political figures. Their mistaken view arises largely from the fact that their research centers on policies formulated in Washington and ignores factors that have actually been more influential in determining relations between Latin America and the United States: namely, factors produced by the internal Latin American situation.

The Good Neighbor Policy scored its initial gains because, in the first place, it repudiated the sort of moral crusading through which Woodrow Wilson and others had hoped to regenerate Latin Americans in line with United States values. Also contributing to success was the fact that, even though corporatism was "probably less well known in America than the geography of Tibet,"[10] the United States government in its desperate search for remedies to the depression leaned toward the use of corporatist tactics in the early days of the New Deal; therefore it could respond with tolerance and forebearance when Latin American governments introduced corporatist and/or socialist experiments (often the two cannot be distinguished) as they moved toward "statism" and controlled economies. Beyond this, success resulted because those who devised and at first implemented the Good Neighbor Policy seemed willing to allow Latin Americans a much freer hand in dealing with the economic interests of United States citizens. Thus, the Roosevelt administration refrained from directly assisting the Foreign Bondholders' Protective Council in its efforts to force Latin American governments to resume payments on foreign debts. What is more, the State Department seemed inclined to permit Latin Americans to increase their share in the profits of United States capital-

---

[10] This was the appraisal of *Fortune* made in a 1934 edition (X, p. 45) devoted to an analysis of the Italian system; it is quoted by John A. Garraty, "The New Deal, National Socialism, and the Great Depression," *The American Historical Review*, LXXIV (1973), 914.

ists. A point of contention remained, however, when it came to defining what constituted a fair share. Without going into detail, it can safely be said that as the European crisis intensified and the threat of United States involvement in war became more imminent, the share that the Washington government was willing to permit the Latin American governments rose steadily.

As the 1940's began, then, the policy enunciated in 1933 by Puig y Casauranc seemed to have prevailed. It appeared that Latin American governments were relatively free to set their own policies in dealing with foreign capital, and that they could demand from it a far larger yield than the Roosevelt administration would have been prepared to tolerate in its early days. Partially as a result of this, the position of the ruling elites in many republics was somewhat more secure as World War II began than it had been at the inception of the Good Neighbor Policy. But there were clouds on the horizon. Latin America's governing groups hoped Washington's permissiveness would be permanent. On the other hand, the good neighbors in Washington fretted over the degree of goodness that wartime exigencies had forced on them and desired a return to what they considered a more rational and normal form of neighborliness.

An additional source of future trouble had appeared as the 1930's drew to a close. At issue was the problem of defining not fair share and neighborliness but rather the concept of development.

The year 1938 was a historic one in United States-Latin American relations, for it witnessed the granting of a development loan to Haiti by the Export-Import Bank. The United States had now embarked upon a policy of committing public funds to Latin American development. (Secretary of State William Jennings Bryan had once suggested such a policy, but President Wilson had rejected it in horror.) Ever-present security considerations accounted in part for the new approach, which was shortly expanded with development loans to Mexico, Brazil, Ecuador and Bolivia, among other republics. Behind the approach there also lay the conviction that the more economically developed Latin America was, the more economically beneficial it would become to the United States. The rationale for entering into a new type of relationship with Latin America was set forth by Assistant Secretary of State A. A. Berle, Jr., in 1941:

. . . we have shifted our entire point of view. Instead of being anxious to find a place where a group of people who have privately saved money can secure a private stream of profits, we are anxious rather to find opportunities for sound development which may add to the general safety, security, and well-being of the Western hemisphere. . . . First, we are both morally and economically better off as the American nations strengthen their economic position. Any rise in their standard of living we consider a direct benefit to our economy and to our hemispheric security. Second, the steady and continued development of other American countries is in the economic interest of the United States as well as of those countries.[11]

Even more succinctly than Berle, President Roosevelt described the guiding concept of the new relationship to Latin America. In June of 1943 he stated: "I do want to get across the idea that the economy and social welfare of Jesus Fernandez in Brazil does affect the economy and social welfare of John Jones in Terre Haute, Indiana."[12]

To Berle, Franklin Roosevelt, and also to Nelson Rockefeller who as the Coordinator of Inter-American Affairs backed the fresh approach, development necessarily implied the use of United States models. It entailed contributing to the economic self-reliance of the masses by turning them into capitalists with their own purchasing power so that they could acquire United States manufactured goods and obtain the happiness that supposedly accompanied the satisfaction of consumer wants. Thus the use of public money would result in better long-term opportunities for private United States business and contribute to political stability in Latin America.

Conceived in the spirit of nonintervention, the Good Neighbor Policy by 1938 had, in a way, taken on an interventionist aspect that bore some parallel to the sort of moral crusade Woodrow Wilson had sought to wage in the hemisphere. Between 1938 and 1942 the men who directed the policy clearly hoped to regenerate Latin America by uplifting the masses to the levels of values and of purchasing power that were deemed indispensable for the proper functioning of business and the attainment of human dignity.

Recipient Latin American republics welcomed the loans from Washington, but their rulers in general had in mind dramatically

---

[11] Address of Berle, June 24, 1941, to the fourth Conference on Canadian-American Affairs in Kingston, Ontario, quoted in David Green, *The Containment of Latin America: A History of the Myths and Realities of the Good Neighbor Policy* (Chicago, 1971), p. 82.

[12] Quoted in *ibid.*, p. 129.

different concepts about what development entailed. Above all they did not want to see the masses converted into self-reliant capitalists in possession of significant amounts of private capital resources. Should the masses gain economic self-reliance, they would inevitably come to demand political self-reliance, and thereby threaten the corporatist-based social stability that elites had been seeking to reestablish, in most republics, since the early part of the century. To the governing classes of Latin America, development was most likely to mean two things: (1) enhancing economic opportunities for the tiny minority of the population permitted by the traditional system to function as self-reliant, independent citizens; and (2) increasing government revenue in order to make possible social-justice programs designed to maintain the dependence of the masses on the state and prevent them from acquiring the individualistic incentives of capitalism.

The United States-Latin American confrontation that seemed inevitable because of profoundly differing concepts of development did not take place in the era of the Good Neighbor Policy. The reason for this was that the demands of World War II forced the United States to abandon the commitment of public funds to Latin American development projects. The confrontation, therefore, was delayed and did not really begin to shape up until the end of the 1950's.

A Post-World War II Period of Transition in United States-Latin American Relations, 1945-1960

Even as the war was beginning, Dr. Eduardo Villaseñor, director-general of the Bank of Mexico, spoke for many Latin Americans as, in effect, he warned the United States that its private capitalists must expect to pay an increasing proportion of their profits to Latin American governments so as to contribute to social programs intended to placate the masses. Villaseñor stated:

> Foreign investment should make a firm stand for a certain measure of social reform in the country. . . . Perhaps the paradise in which all the protection is given to the capitalist and no protection to labor will one day be discovered to be a fool's paradise when labor, organized or not, will break out in violence to get by force and violence what law has not provided for them.[13]

[13] Quoted in W. Feurlein and E. Hannan, *Dollars in Latin America* (New York, 1949), p. 117.

This spirit was far more apparent as the war came to an end; and it surfaced conspicuously in the draft resolution introduced by the Cuban delegation to the Conference of American States that assembled at Chapultepec, Mexico, early in 1945. The resolution stipulated that "investment of capital and economic resources should be made, under the supervision of the state, under terms and conditions most favorable to the development of the countries benefited." Quite clearly the Cubans had in mind obtaining a larger proportion of foreign capital's earnings.

To the United States delegation at Chapultepec, however, increasing demands on foreign capital smacked of statism and suggested the insidious kind of "un-American" ideologies associated with the vanquished Axis powers—and, as the Cold War took form, with communism. Experiments outside the mainstream of liberalism were no longer to be tolerated by policymakers in Washington, at least not to the extent they had been in the early days of the Good Neighbor Policy. Assistant Secretary of State Will Clayton told the Latin Americans at Chapultepec to put their faith in free trade and private free-enterprise capitalism while avoiding the pitfalls of state interventionism.

Laurence Duggan, who had played an important role in molding the Good Neighbor Policy, was also present at Chapultepec. One of his sharpest impressions at the meeting concerned the degree to which fear of communism gripped most of the Latin American delegates.[14] Actually, this fear was more feigned than real. In the mid-1940's the Latin American ruling classes in general did not perceive an immediate threat in communism. What most concerned them was the threat posed by power-seeking rivals within the oligarchy, as well as the menace of domestic revolutionaries not affiliated with international communism. In order to remain in power, the incumbent regimes, whose representatives at Chapultepec spoke of the communist menace, recognized the need to assure their acceptance by the masses through means of state paternalism. Hoping to obtain from United States sources, both private and public, some of the funds needed to finance state welfare, they sought to frighten the State Department with the specter of communist takeovers if massive assistance was not forthcoming.

---

[14] Duggan, *The Americas: The Search for Hemispheric Security* (New York, 1949), p. 117.

However, United States representatives were not ready to be pressured by such methods—not yet.

Beginning at Chapultepec, and continuing throughout the 1950's, Latin Americans urged the United States to resume the commitment of public funds that had been a feature of the Good Neighbor Policy between 1938 and the beginning of 1942. To these pleas, Washington administrations consistently turned a deaf ear, admonishing Latin Americans all the while to seek development through the wise use of private capital. Spruille Braden, for a brief time, after the war, assistant secretary of state in charge of Latin American affairs, expressed the official policy in words that William Howard Taft and Woodrow Wilson might well have been proud to utter:

> I wish to emphasize that private enterprise is the best and in most circumstances the only really sound means to develop the known or unknown resources of a new country. . . . The institution of private property ranks with those of religion and the family as a bulwark of civilization. To tamper with private enterprise . . . will precipitate a disintegration of life and liberty as we conceive and treasure them.[15]

The Republicans' John Foster Dulles was almost as enthusiastic as the Democrats' Braden in extolling liberal capitalism as the panacea for Latin American problems. Furthermore, he too, even as Taft, Wilson, and Braden, saw a connection between liberal capitalism and liberal, individualistic democracy. In addition, Dulles looked to the nourishing of individual liberty, both economic and political, as the best means for combating the communist menace. In June of 1946 he stated that Soviet leaders were intent upon spreading their system throughout the world because of "their honest belief that individual freedom is a basic cause of human unrest and that if it is taken away it will promote world-wide peace

---

[15] U.S. Department of State, Inter-American Series No. 32, *Private Enterprise in the Development of the Americas: An Address by Assistant Secretary Braden Before the Executives' Club of Chicago, September 13, 1946* (Washington, D.C., 1946), pp. 2-3. Braden's position, similar to that of Taft and Wilson, was also in line with views expressed by Henry Stimson in his 1927 book, *American Policy in Nicaragua* (pp. 122-123): "The intelligent leaders in Nicaragua . . . realize that Nicaragua today lacks one of the principal foundations for a democratic government in that she has no well-developed middle class. . . . Such a middle class cannot come into existence until the industries of the country are developed. These industries cannot be developed without capital, and capital can be obtained only by foreign loans. . . ."

and security."[16] Dulles found it well-nigh impossible to understand the ruling classes of Latin America; for, in their attitude toward the masses of their countries, they were in accord with Soviet thinkers. The Latin American rulers were convinced that, so far as the masses were concerned, individual freedom was indeed a basic cause of human unrest and that denying it would promote the peace and security of the ruling classes and the general stability of the political order. This is why they turned to methods of statism to preserve the masses in their accustomed dependence, hoping all the time that the United States would help finance these methods.

Between the end of World War II and the conclusion of the Korean War in 1953 most Latin American countries enjoyed a period of relative prosperity, owing largely to the generally high world prices commanded by their exports. Only with the recession of the mid-1950's would it become urgent for Latin American leaders to obtain an increasing flow of United States funds in order to preserve their traditional social structures. Only then would there come into clear focus the opposing views of United States and Latin American leaders on what was basically involved in securing development and stability while containing the threat of Marxist revolution.

As early as 1948, however, at the Bogotá (Colombia) Conference that gave birth to the Organization of American States, some of the dimensions of the impending clash had become discernible. At that meeting the Latin American representatives, whenever economic matters came up for discussion, stressed public capital and government-controlled development corporations as key elements in achieving progress. It was quite apparent that the classes they represented hoped to prevent the spread of individualistic capitalism among the masses, and thereby to block the penetration into their countries of the type of democracy venerated by most United States intellectuals and statesmen with a penchant for "nation building." On the other hand the United States delegation at Bogotá, seeing progress and stability as attainable only by emulation of their country's historical experience, insisted that private capital, whether domestic or foreign, would have to be relied on for development. The difference in approach could scarcely have been more profound. The Bogotá Conference, in fact, witnessed a preliminary attempt to synthesize two basically incompatible ideologies; and the

---

[16] Quoted in Green, p. 277.

virtual impossibility of effecting such a synthesis has underlain many of the subsequent failures in hemisphere relations.

In late 1954 the first Economic Conference of the Organization of American States convened in Petropolis, near Rio de Janeiro. With Raúl Prebisch, secretary of the United Nations' Economic Commission for Latin America, in the forefront, the Latin American delegates urged government-to-government aid upon the United States, insisting that private foreign investment was, in its long-term consequences, draining their national economies. Their arguments produced no effect. What is more, at a subsequent economic conference held in 1957 in Buenos Aires, United States spokesmen still stood firmly on their customary ground. They pointed out that United States-owned companies operating in Latin America paid salaries of approximately one billion dollars to 609,000 employees and delivered another one billion dollars in taxes to Latin American governments.[17] In addition they maintained that private investment was on the increase (standing at $3.5 billion in 1929, it would climb to between $8 billion and $9 billion by 1959, representing about 30 percent of the total of private United States capital invested abroad). In their view there was no need for the United States to consider expanding the economic base of its relations with Latin America.

Although it was not apparent at Buenos Aires United States policy toward Latin America was already in the process of change by 1957. In fact, experiments which would help shape a new economic policy had been under way with Bolivia since 1953. The experiments were now about to be expanded to encompass more of Latin America. The reason for this could be traced in large part to the serious recession that gripped most of the hemisphere's republics. As the recession worsened, it became imperative to reconsider the assumption that private investment constituted an adequate stimulus to economic progress.

---

[17] The statistics on which the United States position at the Buenos Aires Conference was based are found in U.S. Department of Commerce, *United States Investments in Latin America* (Washington, D.C., 1960). According to this work, United States companies, while employing a little over 1 percent of the labor force in Latin America, accounted for roughly 10 percent of the area's gross national product and paid one-fifth of all taxes and one-third of all direct assessments on income. See also the July, 1963, issue of the *Quarterly Review*, published by the Bank of London and South America, Ltd., which was reprinted in the U.S. Congress Joint Economic Committee hearings entitled, *Private Investment in Latin America* (Washington, D.C., 1964), pp. 442-451.

Influential in making policy for Bolivia, Dr. Milton Eisenhower had by 1957 come to accept the need for the United States to begin to employ public funds in alleviating social problems in much of Latin America, lest these problems lead to communist takeovers. Eisenhower has explained his viewpoint in his book, *The Wine Is Bitter*:

> I was stimulated to reach certain convictions by Pedro Beltrán of Peru, who made an eloquent plea for U.S. help in social development. . . . What we were doing in Latin America, he said, was well and good, but it was not enough, and it was doing too little for the people who needed housing, better diets, education, and health services. He urged that we finance such social projects in Latin America.[18]

A typical representative of the more reactionary elements of the Latin American oligarchy, Pedro Beltrán at least had the foresight to see that the traditional social order was threatened unless a vast amount of additional spending was channeled into social projects. Above all, though, he wished to spare the native oligarchies the burden of contributing their own funds to social spending. Therefore he directed his "eloquent plea" to the United States, pointing constantly to the rising communist menace to bolster his arguments —and often fabricating communist threats through the irresponsible journalism characteristic of his influential Lima daily *La Prensa*.

Milton Eisenhower still entertained certain reservations, for he wisely perceived that the Latin Americans themselves remained hesitant to commit their own funds to essential reforms: "They were concerned only about more money from abroad for social projects."[19] Nevertheless, a crisis seemed at hand. Guatemala had barely been saved, so it seemed to United States observers, from a communist takeover in 1954 through the covert intervention of the C.I.A. Then in September of 1958 Salvador Allende, backed by Marxian Socialists and Communists, missed winning the Chilean presidential election by less than 40,000 votes. In May of the same year the hostile reception accorded Vice President Richard M. Nixon in Peru and Venezuela had shocked many United States officials into an awareness of the need for a revised Latin American

---

[18] Milton Eisenhower, *The Wine Is Bitter* (Garden City, N.Y., 1963), p. 205.

[19] *Ibid.*, p. 206.

policy. At the very end of the critical year Fidel Castro came to power in Cuba, and soon Milton Eisenhower would write: "There can be no doubt that Castro's wicked influence in the Hemisphere was spurring us onward. . . ."[20] By now the president's brother had become wholeheartedly converted to the notion of using United States public funds to bring about social reform in Latin America. Furthermore, an increasing number of Washington officials was experiencing a similar conversion.

In the spring of 1960 President Eisenhower made a tour through Argentina, Brazil, Chile, and Uruguay, and was duly impressed by the stories of rising communist influence told him by representative figures of the ruling classes in those countries. The following September the third Economic Conference of the Organization of American States convened in Bogotá. By now the United States was ready to accept the position urged on it by Latin Americans since the end of World War II. Subscribing to the Act of Bogotá, the Eisenhower administration agreed in principle to commit public funds to social reform projects in Latin America. Even before the Act of Bogotá, moreover, Congress had approved an appropriation of $500 million to establish a special Inter-American Social Development Fund to deal with such matters as agrarian reform, housing, medical and education facilities.

Those shaping the new policies for the United States expected the commitment of public funds to be a stopgap measure; they saw these funds as providing an incentive to recipients to take steps, including tax and agrarian reforms and anti-inflation programs, that would quickly reduce their dependence on outside economic resources—even if not reducing their dependence on United States markets for imports. Here was a point for future contention, as President John F. Kennedy would discover. In the early 1960's economic nationalism, as most frequently expounded by the Latin American oligarchy, still rested on the hope of increased long-term dependence on the United States.

The United States and Latin America, 1960-1973

The Alliance for Progress, launched by President Kennedy in March of 1961, was defined in greater detail in the Charter of Punta del Este (Uruguay), signed the following August. The

[20] Quoted by R. Harrison Wagner, *United States Policy Toward Latin America: A Study in Domestic and International Politics* (Stanford, 1970), p. 147.

Charter called for a vast cooperative program in the Americas to raise standards of health, housing and education (goals that appealed particularly to Latin Americans, as they were to be pursued in part through United States funds) and to improve tax-collection processes and achieve better income and land distribution (goals that appealed particularly to United States officials). To help meet Alliance objectives, the United States pledged $11 billion over the course of ten years, two-thirds to be provided by public funds, one-third by private investment. The understanding was that assistance would be rendered only to those governments that introduced adequate reforms.

In the view of Kennedy administration officials who shaped and sought to implement the Alliance, social stability and economic progress in Latin America were essential in order to end the communist menace and also in order to render the area more economically advantageous to the United States. Stability and progress, it was assumed, could best be achieved by increasing the participation of the masses both in the gross national income of the Latin American countries and in their political processes. When it came to containing communism, there was no significant distinction between the approach of the Democratic officials then in power and that of John Foster Dulles. Dulles, it will be recalled, had noted that the Communists believed individual freedom was a basic cause of human unrest; therefore, by taking it away they hoped to promote peace and security. It followed in the Dulles view, and in that of the Kennedy administration as well, that the way to combat communism was to maximize individual liberty and freedom throughout the world. This conclusion emerged from the belief that the United States, precisely because of its widespread enjoyment of individual freedom, presented the most hostile climate possible for the spread of communism. Other areas of the world could likewise be immunized against communist infection if their leaders could be persuaded to emulate United States political, social, and economic models. Looking toward Latin America, then, the Kennedy administration prepared to take up a Woodrow Wilson-like crusade to spread a variant of the New Freedom.*

---

* In his essay in this collection, Howard Wiarda suggests that United States pressure, as applied immediately after World War II and intensified in the Alliance for Progress era, was largely responsible for Latin America's renewed experiments with liberalism and rejection of corporatism. In line with my own general conviction that Latin America responds primarily to an

Two, among the many, agencies through which the Kennedy team hoped to accomplish Alliance goals in Latin America were organized labor and the Peace Corps. AFL-CIO officials were enlisted in the cause of training Latin American union leaders to seek autonomous power, to think in terms of demanding increased real wages for the rank and file, rather than remaining abjectly dependent upon government for the extension of various paternalistic fringe benefits that brought no genuine economic power to the working classes. The Peace Corps, through "community development" projects (often integrated into broader scope USAID programs and military "civic action" ventures), was to organize the poor and to help them achieve an input into the political system. In the early days of the Peace Corps, I personally listened rather incredulously as experts preached the Alliance doctrine, assuring young volunteers that through mastering the techniques of community development they could change the face of Latin America in a few years. To their credit, many of the volunteers expressed

---

internal dynamic rather than to foreign pressures, I tend to view United States influence as relatively unimportant in causing the temporary shift of its southern neighbors back to liberalism. A contrary interpretation seems to assume too large a degree of United States omnipotence. The shift under discussion represents to me simply another incident in Latin America's perennial identity crisis. In reacting to this crisis Latin America identifies sometimes with liberalism, especially as it is preached even if not practiced in the United States, and at other times with the corporatism of the Iberian and also—in the case of Indo-America—the Indian past. The prosperity occasioned by World War II, and fed later by high export prices occasioned by the Korean War, encouraged Latin American leaders to believe that "statism" and the managed economy were less essential than in the decade of the 1930's. Further, a relatively quiescent social scene encouraged governing groups to imagine they could discard some of the paternalistic burdens that had seemed essential to prevent upheaval at an earlier period. Not until Latin America as a whole fell into the throes of a depression, as it had by 1957, and social problems had acquired a frightening intensity, did a shift back to corporatism seem imperative. In general, it can be hypothesized that in eras of economic optimism, especially if during these eras the social problem seems manageable in proportions, Latin America will incline toward liberalism. In times of economic uncertainty, however, and especially on those occasions when explosive social problems bring widespread and immediate fear to accommodated sectors, the shift is toward corporatism. If, then, the Alliance for Progress was conceived at least partially in the hope of spreading liberalism in the republics to the south, it came into being at one of the least propitious moments in Latin American history. For an excellent study of factors originating in the United States that contributed to the Alliance's failure, see Abraham F. Lowenthal, "United States Policy Toward Latin America: 'Liberal,' 'Radical,' and 'Bureaucratic' Perspectives," *Latin American Research Review*, VIII (1973), 3-25.

doubts about the morality of such cultural intrusion. Such doubts apparently seldom gave pause to the brash, arrogant and supremely ethnocentric officials who conceived and directed the Alliance for Progress.

The spirit of the Alliance, with its emphasis on transforming the Latin American masses into economically self-reliant (so they could purchase more goods from the United States and be in a better position to resist the blandishments of communism) and politically participating citizens, found its way into the 1966 Foreign Assistance Act. The Act stipulated that all United States economic aid programs should encourage the development of "democratic private and local governmental institutions" in the recipient countries by using their "intellectual resources" to stimulate "economic progress and social progress" and by supporting "civic education and training skills required for effective participation in governmental and political processes essential to self-government."[21]

Underlying the entire Alliance for Progress approach was the assumption that the United States possessed sufficient economic resources and also sufficient expertise to solve social problems and to build nations in Latin America according to blueprints of the United States society. Underlying the approach also was the conviction that through its increasing economic presence in Latin America, the United States would acquire the political leverage needed to insist upon enactment of basic reforms. In line with this, there was a concerted attempt to woo the Latin American military into patterns of "right thinking."

As the 1960's began, Latin America's leaders on the whole also believed that the United States possessed sufficient funds (if not necessarily the expertise) to solve, or at least to ameliorate, the area's social problems. At the same time they hoped that, as in the past, they could use the economic resources obtained from the United States to safeguard and preserve the established order. By the time of Kennedy's death, however, they had grown increasingly apprehensive, for never before had the United States moved so insistently to apply pressure for a basic alteration of the established order.

Latin America's ruling classes hoped to attain internal stability and to minimize the risk of communism and other movements of

---

[21] Quoted by Ernest W. Lafeber, "Moralism and U.S. Foreign Policy," *Orbis*, XVI (1972), 403-404.

radical change precisely by keeping the masses without individual freedom, by perpetuating their dependence upon a benevolent state. Rather than income redistribution, which would bring some power and self-reliance to previously marginal citizens, the elite envisioned a program of increased fringe benefits that would heighten the dependence of recipients on their benefactor—the state and those who ran it. If the Washington administration continued to make such a nuisance of itself by insisting on its approach to development and containment of communism, then the traditional economic relationship to the United States, that of external dependence, would have to be reconsidered.

By 1966 some observers, on both sides of the Rio Grande, had grasped that a basic assumption under which both Washington officials and Latin American leaders had proceeded was no longer valid: in the light of Viet Nam commitments, internal problems, and a balance of payments crisis, it was becoming clear that the United States did not have adequate funds either to engage in nation-building schemes in Latin America or to make substantial improvements in the area's social conditions. Visiting Bolivia in 1966, Senator Allen Ellender explained that the United States would have to limit economic assistance to all nations, including Bolivia, because of its large foreign debt and balance of payments difficulties. President René Barrientos responded on the front page of the leading La Paz daily: "We have to stop believing that we can live forever from foreign aid. . . The approach [has] . . . passed which accustomed us to throw stones at the American Embassy and say, 'There is Communism here and if you do not help, Bolivia will go under.' "22

In the early 1960's, then, United States assistance had first become onerous to Latin Americans because of the increasing number of strings attached. Subsequently, in the latter part of the decade, it had become apparent, especially in view of the worsening Latin American population problem, that neither United States aid, provided through public funds, nor the yield from taxes on private North American firms could possibly suffice to meet the social overhead bills that had to be paid if the traditional society was to be preserved. In the new set of circumstances, "external

---

22 Quoted by James W. Wilkie, *The Bolivian Revolution and U.S. Aid Since 1952* (Los Angeles, 1969) p. 37.

dependence" no longer guaranteed an elite its "internal domination."

In the light of this situation, Latin American leaders increasingly recognized the need to do what the Mexicans had begun to do in the aftermath of their Revolution: to become skilled practitioners of capitalism themselves so that, relatively on their own, they could generate at least a significant portion of the capital necessary to finance the social projects essential to maintaining the dependence of the masses. No longer would it be possible for the gentlemanly classes to remain parasitical and to disdain bourgeois behavior patterns and economic activity as beneath their dignity; no longer would it be possible for them to enjoy accustomed immunity from taxes. The ruling classes of Latin America, the men at the top of the dominant culture, had to disavow the aristocratic set of values that was the legacy of the colonial period and of their initial "symbiotic relationship" to United States capital and they had to embrace the bourgeois ethic; otherwise, it would be impossible to maintain the essential features of the dichotomized, two-culture, corporate society. Development, as masterminded by national entrepreneurs, bureaucrats and technocrats had now begun to replace external dependence as the key to internal domination by an elite.

No longer, in the changing times, could foreign capital be allowed a relatively free hand within the Latin American countries. In the old days it had seemed comparatively unimportant if foreign capital had not contributed adequately to overall development and if its principal long-term effect had been to drain the local economies. In the old days the draining effects and the distorted patterns of development resulting from foreign capital investment had not seemed of crucial significance, so long as the investment resulted in at least some immediate increase in government revenue that would facilitate the financing of minimal social programs—to say nothing of financing the military and other agencies of security and repression. But, in the 1960's and the 1970's, with social costs expanding dramatically, it became essential for Latin American governments to discipline foreign capital to the fullest degree possible, short of driving it out of the region altogether, in order to derive from it the maximum contribution to local needs. Time had caught up with the prophetic utterances made by Eduardo Villaseñor at the outset of World War II.

An example of the new approach to foreign capital, which

harks back in some ways to the experiences of the Mexican Revolution, is provided by the foreign investment code agreed to by the Andean Republics (Colombia, Ecuador, Peru, Bolivia, and Chile) in 1971. It restricts new foreign investment to areas not competitive with domestic enterprise, limits reexport of capital to the original investment when the firm is sold or liquidated, and provides for establishment of local majority control and ownership of all business—though exceptions are possible—within a stipulated period of time: fifteen years in Colombia, Chile and Peru, twenty years in less developed Bolivia and Ecuador.[23]

By the late 1960's "external dependence" had not only ceased to serve the purpose of "internal domination"; it had in some instances become actually counterproductive to that purpose. This was owing to the rise of virulent nationalism in Latin America and the fact that its most appealing point had come to be denunciation of Yankee capital and the native *vendepatria* (sellers of their country) *oligarquía* that had historically benefited from foreign capital's presence. With the veritable explosion of a new type of economic nationalism characterized by a denunciation of dependence, the relationship between Yankee capital and a Latin American oligarchy was no longer a source of strength to local elites.

The New Struggle for Elite Legitimacy in Latin America and the Importance of the Third Position

In the colonial period, an age of religious faith in which there was little questioning of the mutual interpenetration of the divine and the temporal, the legitimacy of political rulers had depended to some extent on the degree to which they also basked in an aura of divinity—a situation that found a striking parallel among the more highly developed preconquest civilizations. This aura of divinity proceeded largely from the control that political leaders exercised over the Church and from the widespread belief that their mission was to frame laws, with the advice of theologians and other men of God, in harmony with the divine will. In the present-day secular age, the legitimacy of political ruling classes in Latin America depends upon their ability to discharge the paternalistic

---

[23] See Edward S. Milenky, "Developmental Nationalism in Practice: The Problems of Progress of the Andean Group," *Inter-American Economic Affairs,* XXVI (1973), 49-58, and Kenneth A. Switzer, "The Andean Group: A Reappraisal," *ibid.,* 69-82.

obligations once assumed by the Church and to gain acceptance as the agents for achieving national destiny, rather than for fulfilling the divine will.

In the past, political leaders, intimately associated with and sometimes one and the same as religious leaders, conferred upon the masses not only the material rewards of paternalism but also significant nonmaterial gratifications; for they assured the masses of equality in the next world. Today, ruling classes are tending more and more to rest their claim to authority not only upon the central government's social security programs but also upon the assurance that all people are equal, even though they must perform different functions, in the struggle to achieve a proud national destiny by discarding dependence upon the United States. In a way the United States is now being used to accomplish for Latin America's dominant culture what Protestantism helped accomplish for the rulers of the sixteenth- and seventeenth-century Hispanic world. The Counter-Reformation brought to the masses of the Hispanic world a sense of involvement and participation in a noble crusade and rewarded them with a feeling of equality with their rulers in contributing to that crusade. Thus, the Counter-Reformation was in its time vitally important to Spain's upper classes in preserving a two-culture society within which the masses, relishing their sense of mission, remained unquestioningly committed to their leaders. In contemporary Latin America, anti-Yankeeism is serving a similar purpose: it is bringing about the "mobilization" of the masses without necessarily increasing their "participation," to revert to the terms used by James Malloy in a preceding essay.

Most Latin American nationalists, beginning particularly with the initial Juan Domingo Perón regime in Argentina (1946-1955),[24] and continuing with the Christian Democrats of Chile

---

[24] The ideology of Peronism, known as justicialism, laid stress on finding the proper balance between individualism and collectivism. There can be no doubt that it envisioned individualism primarily for elite groups and collectivism specifically for the masses. Walter Little makes the following judicious assessment: "Justicialism was not designed to radically transform the national economic and social structure, but it is ironic that its conservative tendencies were lost upon the conservative critics of the regime, who saw only the illiberalism which accompanied it. The Peronists were overthrown by those who objected to their apparent radicalism and who did not understand how truly conservative their vision of society was. The novelty to which they objected lay in the fact that while Peronism required the support of the common people the mediatory role normally performed on their behalf by the political parties was now to be

(1964-1970) and with the military officers governing Peru (since 1968), Bolivia (since 1964)[25] and Ecuador (since 1972),[26] have embraced what they commonly refer to as a Third Position; and it is likely that the Chilean regime succeeding the overthrown Salvador Allende (1973) will follow in this pattern. By the Third Position, most Latin American nationalists mean one that is neither capitalist nor communist. Current developments indicate that the Third Position in Peru, Bolivia and Ecuador, and also in Argentina with the return of the *peronistas* to power in May of 1973, entails essentially the preservation of a two-culture society.[27] Within this

---

performed by the State." See Little, "Party and State in Peronist Argentina, 1945-1955," *The Hispanic American Historical Review*, LIII (1973), 661.

[25] Similarities between the corporatist patterns of the military government in Peru and the policies of the military rulers of Bolivia are revealed in Bolivia, Ministerio de Planificación y Coordinación, *Estrategia socio-económica del desarrollo nacional*, 2 vols. (La Paz, 1970), and Salvador Romero Pittari, "Bolivia: sindicalismo campesino y partidos políticos," *Aportes*, No. 23 (1972), 62-100. See also footnote 40 of the Malloy essay.

[26] For background material see George Pope Atkins, "La Junta Militar Ecuatoriana (1963-1966): los militares latinoamericanos de nuevo tipo," *Aportes*, No. 24 (1972), 6-21, and John D. Martz, *Ecuador: Conflicting Political Culture and the Quest for Progress* (Boston, 1972). On the similarity of the program of the Ecuadorian military to Peruvian models see *Latin America*, VII (September 28, 1973), 309-310.

[27] The United States press tended to hail Brazil's economic success after the military overthrew President João Goulart in 1964 as proof that liberal, laissez-faire approaches still worked. The fact of the matter seems to be, though, that the Brazilian economic miracle has been based less on liberal than on corporatist models, a matter discussed by Howard Wiarda and touched on by Philippe Schmitter in their essays. Douglas Chalmers, moreover, provides a persuasive appraisal in his discussion of authoritarian politics in Riordan Roett, ed., *Brazil in the Sixties* (Nashville, 1972), esp. p. 52. He argues that Brazil is developing into a "sort of flexible corporate state in which politics takes place essentially within nominally administrative structures" and that politics is based on vertical structures of patron-client relationships. Whatever the current situation may be, it is clear, as Wiarda argues, that Brazilian development and political patterns during the Getulio Vargas regime (1930-1945) were largely based on corporative models. Here, in fact, is a classic example of how a Latin American country used a close economic relationship with the United States to strengthen its own, un-United States-like traditions. For all of his success in this, however, Vargas continued to be apprehensive that economic dependence on the United States would in the long run limit Brazil's freedom of action, a point properly stressed by Ronald E. Rady, *Volta Redonda : A Steel Mill Comes to a Brazilian Coffee Plantation* (Albuquerque, 1973).

A significant difference between corporatism under Vargas and under the military is readily apparent, and it reveals a great deal about the nature of the new corporatism not only in Brazil but in all of Latin America. In his approach to corporatism, Vargas relied heavily on the Catholic Church and acknowledged the ideological inspiration of its doctrines. In the corporatism that has emerged

society, the dominant culture is to be largely capitalist in orientation. Its members will be to some extent individualistic and competitive, although considerably hedged about by government regulations, and they will be at least partially self-reliant, possessing private capital resources as a result of which they are not altogether dependent on state benevolence. In contrast, the members of the subordinate culture are to be socialist in outlook. Rather than being competitive, individualistic and self-reliant, they are expected to depend upon a government that takes from them according to their abilities and means—ostensibly utilizing what it takes to advance the cause of national destiny—and gives to them according to their needs. Beyond material security, the masses—at least so the emergent elites of a new but also quite traditional Latin America hope—will seek nonmaterial compensation and will prize the sense of community and dignity that results from sharing in the decision-making process of various local, regional, and functional organizations. If politicized at the grass-roots level the masses will, the members of the dominant culture hope, contentedly leave decision-making at the higher, national level to an elite that exercises a moderating power over the body politic.

With the rise of a new nationalism in Latin America and its skillful use by elites to preserve the essence of a two-culture, corporate society, United States hopes to "regenerate" its southern neighbors by remaking them in the North American image seem more implausible than ever before. Perhaps this is one reason why United States interest in Latin America languishes in the early 1970's.

Power wielders in today's Latin America are no more anxious than their counterparts of bygone generations to see the masses respond to the kind of advice that Richard Nixon gave his fellow

---

under military aegis since 1964, the Church is not only a thoroughly insignificant factor but it is also locked in a serious confrontation with the government. On this see Thomas C. Bruneau, *The Political Transformation of the Brazilian Catholic Church* (Cambridge, England, 1973) and "Power and Influence: Analysis of the Church in Latin America and the Case of Brazil," *Latin American Research Review,* VIII (1973), 25-51. Even though elsewhere in Latin America the new corporatism has not produced a Church-state confrontation, Catholicism does not exercise the ideological influence it did in the 1930's, the last era in which homage was widely and openly paid to corporatism. The secular, "this-worldly" religions of developmentalism and nationalism have gained the upper hand and governments tend to rely on nonmaterial rewards distinct from those provided by religion to keep the masses appeased and quiescent.

citizens in his 1973 second presidential inaugural address: "Let each of us ask—not just what will government do for me, but what can I do for myself." The message that Latin America's rulers hope the masses will take to heart is contained in Fidel Castro's twenty-sixth of July address of 1970: "Today the citizen feels that the state should solve his problems. And he is right. This is really a collective mentality, a socialist mentality. . . . Today it is not possible to depend on individual efforts and means as it was in the past."

Castro, of course, would like to see his prescription for collectivism applied to every member of society. In short, he would like to forge a one-culture society. This may also be what many sectors associated with the ill-fated Allende government in Chile (1970-1973) had in mind. But in the rest of Latin America ruling groups seem overwhelmingly committed to confining application of the Castro prescription to the lower classes, to the subordinate culture. This is what their legitimacy seems to them to demand; and this is what the Third Position means to them. Understandably, then, elites and would-be elites are rediscovering the usefulness of corporatism and eschewing the social, political, and economic beliefs, values, and goals that have stamped the political culture of the United States.

Conclusion

Anti-Yankeeism, expressed in terms of cultural nationalism, appeared in Latin America in a more robust form than ever before around the turn of the century. To a large extent it stemmed from ruling class fear of social upheaval and from the conviction that the United States cultural influence, if allowed penetration into Latin America, would inevitably foment that upheaval. By and large, United States imperialism was not the cause of, but merely a contributing factor to and a rationale for, anti-Yankeeism. Basically, this frame of mind arose from internal conditions within Latin America. Almost regardless of what Latin American policy it had pursued, the United States could not have snuffed out the hostile sentiments among its neighbors. Accomplishing this would have required the United States, among other things, to alter its entire domestic culture so as to bring it into line with the objectives and values of the Latin American political culture.

In the 1960's and 1970's the anti-Yankeeism gripping Latin

American elites—and not just radical agitators and Marxist intellectuals—is motivated once again by a rising fear of social upheaval, and by the conviction that the United States is not doing and perhaps cannot do enough to help contain the menace—and that what the United States would like to do, if able, would add to the menace. The anti-Yankeeism of the present era, expressed often in terms of an economic nationalism that denounces dependence, probably cannot be dramatically curbed by any policy that the United States could reasonably be expected to adopt. In order to reduce vastly the present feeling of hostility to it, the United States would have to abandon a good deal of the capitalist, free-enterprise, liberal ethic and also become a far more generous dispenser of charity for the Latin American masses than its means permit and than it chooses to be for its own masses.

The history of inter-American relations teaches that Latin American leaders, intent upon safeguarding their own authentic national identity, are just as ill-disposed toward cultural spillovers in the hemisphere as are most United States leaders. A lesson no less clear is that when United States policies facilitate the quest of Latin Americans to be themselves, these policies are likely initially to meet a cool response among would-be nation builders of the North American intelligentsia and perhaps among the public in general, because of the abiding—although happily often latent—concern for uplifting those imagined to be less happy and less endowed.

In carrying out a bourgeois revolution from above, Latin American elites have chosen methods, including developmentalist nationalism and paternalistic corporatism, aimed at maintaining lower class dependence. These methods, even if only minimally successful, could buy considerable time for a traditional society that, although extensively modified, is still basically two-culture in composition; while doing this, they could promote stability, prevent revolutions from below, and contain the threat of Marxism. Such end results would prove equally appealing to Latin American elites and to the United States "establishment"—however bitterly they would be lamented by those whose vantage point is the New Left.

The prevalence of guerrilla activity during the 1960's in Latin America and the widespread fear, both there and in the United States, of uncontainable upheavals from below, doubtlessly persuaded some United States policymakers to veer away from the onetime interest in promoting liberalism south of the border. It had become apparent that if the masses were to be regenerated and rescued from marginalization the process was more likely to take place within a Marxist than a capitalist system—owing in part to the fact that the Latin American subordinate culture has historically been far more attuned to a system that demanded of them according to their abilities while giving to them according to needs than they were to the workings of individualistic liberalism. As this became apparent, United States security considerations dictated abandonment of the old liberal vision, shaped by regenerationist and economic hopes, of transforming Latin American masses into politically self-reliant purchasers of North American consumer goods. In the light of new developments, Latin America's traditional two-culture corporatism seemed best suited to the security interests of the United States which have always prevailed (and quite properly so), when there is a conflict, over purely economic and moral uplift goals.[28]

Perhaps the dawning comprehension in Washington of what a new breed of leaders to the south hopes to accomplish through corporatism explains why recent United States neglect of Latin America has been relatively benign. Perhaps, too, this comprehension accounts for attempts to forget the Hickenlooper Amendment and other relics of a not distant past when it was widely believed by those shaping United States policy that only from widely diffused

---

[28] Melvin Burke and James Malloy, "Del populismo nacional al corporativismo nacional (El caso de Bolivia, 1952-1970)," *Aportes* (October, 1972), 67-96, argue that the United States aid policies had already shifted from promotion of liberalism to acceptance of corporatism by the latter 1950's in the case of Bolivia. The primary reason for this they trace to the classic dilemma of whether to stress rising consumption for the lower classes as an essential political objective, or to pursue strictly economic goals which, in the interest of capital formation that does not weigh heavily upon middle classes, demand limiting the consumption of the masses. In effect, the authors seem to argue that United States planners abandoned once cherished dreams of spreading liberalism, accepting instead a situation in which the masses would be dependent for their subsistence upon the willingness of a new capitalist elite to assume the burdens of paternalism. In this, United States policymakers have acted in accord with one-time populist movements in Latin America whose leaders had initially emphasized increased consumption for the masses. When faced, however, with a choice of increasing purchasing power among the masses or pursuing economic goals that would primarily benefit a new bourgeoisie, both United States "nation builders" and Latin American populists chose the second approach. In line with this decision, corporatism has been accepted, tacitly at least, as the proper development formula.

private, individualistic capitalism, whether at home or abroad, did all blessings flow.

For the moment, at least, corporatism lives anew—or still—in the Iberian world, in part because it is perceived to be the best method for containing social revolution. Beyond this, the reasons for corporatism's continuing viability are not clear. Does corporatism—whether in its "natural" or in its more authoritarian military guise—live because it serves the cause of nationalism among states seeking to establish cultural independence from both the capitalist and socialist worlds? Is corporatism, as Howard Wiarda maintains, an intrinsic part of the Iberic-Latin tradition? Or, is current corporatism in part the product of the Iberian world's delayed development, as Philippe Schmitter hypothesizes? One might go beyond this question to inquire if delayed development could be caused by the attitudes and values that in turn have historically inclined the Iberian world more toward corporatism than liberalism.

All the while, there are ample grounds for concluding, in line with Ronald Newton's analysis, that the vogue of natural corporatism in Spanish America will prove ephemeral because this system is inadequate to cope with the complexities and pressures of even semimodernized states. James Malloy demonstrates that the Peruvian military have encountered formidable problems and suffered important setbacks as they turn toward a more authoritarian variant of corporatism; their system of rule scarcely seems a panacea. If Peru and also Ecuador and Bolivia are able to muddle through in the years ahead, it will probably be owing less to their system of government than to the success of foreign enterprise in locating more petroleum reserves. Similarly, Brazil's recent successes are based to a considerable degree on the inpouring of foreign capital, while foreign capital as well as tourism have been essential ingredients in Mexican—just as in Spanish—progress. But Mexico's corporatist system, once widely heralded as the hope for the future of all Latin America, has in recent years become the despair of many observers. Finally, Spanish corporatism of the Franco era presents certain symptoms of serious malaise.

Perhaps, though, the inadequacies of corporatism, in whatever guise, are not of overriding importance in assessing its future in the Iberian world. No system, after all, really works, except during brief and rare moments in history when fortuitous circumstances operate in a particularly benign manner. Nor are the people of the

Iberian world characterized by an obsession with the workability of systems, having never developed a deep commitment to the pragmatic notion that truth is something that happens to an idea. Leaders of that world might well continue to cling to the values, attitudes, prejudices, myths and fantasies encompassed by corporatism—even nonauthoritarian corporatism, whose proponents view the present-day intimate relationship between corporatism and authoritarian militarism as a temporary aberration—regardless of the demonstrated real-life shortcomings of the system. Undoubtedly they could muster convincing arguments that corporatism works as well as liberalism (bolstering their contention by the recent spectacle of the United States as a "banana republic"), populism or communism. And they could point, by way of justification for what many critics might consider their irrational, romantic obstinacy, to the remarkable endurance of the liberal credo in the United States—where people are supposed to demand that ideas work—regardless of how long ago the failures of liberalism were becoming apparent to astute observers.

In contrasting two of the celebrated poets of the English language, a noted literary critic has observed: "Byron lacked Shelley's remarkably forgiving nature, with its urbane awareness that in mere actuality no one can long approximate any ideal whatsoever."[29] In regard to corporatism, those who shape the destinies of the Spanish- and Portuguese-speaking world may well react more like Shelley than Byron, remaining undismayed by the fact that men cannot prove steadfast and unselfish in the attempt to approximate corporatism's ideals. Such human frailty will not necessarily render those ideals less appealing, or cause them to be perceived as less authentic and natural within the context of national experience. Through the operation of similar processes, liberalism in the United States could be saved for years to come as a value system and as an expression of broadly shared aspirations.[30]

---

[29] Review by Harold Bloom of Bernard Grebanier, *The Uninhibited Byron: An Account of His Sexual Confusion*, and Leslie A. Marchant, *Byron, A Portrait, New York Times Book Review*, November 22, 1970, p. 8.

[30] It is instructive that the counterculture's assault against the United States system, still ensconced behind the façade of liberalism, was no more successful in the 1960's and early 1970's than the attack of Latin American guerrillas against their increasingly corporatist establishments. Today the "greening" of the United States seems no more likely than the successful upheavals from below that only a short time ago were widely predicted for Latin America by many journalists and even those purporting to be serious scholars

Should this be the case, North Americans and their neighbors to the south will continue to fantasize destinies that are basically distinct and even incompatible.

—myself among those at the head of the list.

Admittedly one must not claim too much for corporatism as *the* means for defusing revolutionary explosions. Perhaps the least corporatist of any of the major Latin American countries, Venezuela is also among the most stable. In December of 1973 no less than 85 percent of the voters, in a presidential election that has been hailed as a model of honesty, rejected extremes of right and left in giving their support to the two candidates of moderate parties committed to reform but opposed to revolution. Undoubtedly many factors which account for the Venezuelan situation escape this writer. Certainly, though, the country's comparatively—for Latin America—advanced degree of development, based largely but by no means exclusively on petroleum production, as well as its lack of racial prejudice has some bearing on the matter. Owing to a complex set of factors in its historical development, Venezuela is probably the country in all Latin America, Brazil included, that is the least contaminated by racism. Not led by racial bias to fear and despise the masses, Venezuela's ruling classes have felt little need to resort to corporatism in order to keep the masses essentially depoliticized and immunized against individualism. On the other hand, Colombia is by no means a model either of economic development or racial tolerance. Yet in the past few years it seems to have achieved greater political and social stability with what appears to be only a minimal reliance on the methods of corporatism. I suspect, though, that Colombia is more corporatist than some observers recognize. Having disavowed its flirtation with liberalism and returned in many ways to its corporatist traditions with the Conservative restoration of the mid-1880's, Colombia in recent times has not had to introduce publicized crash programs of corporatism in the endeavor to safeguard elites and maintain stability.

The New Corporatism in Franco's Spain and Some Latin American Perspectives

Fredrick B. Pike

Background: Turn-of-the-Century Spain and a Renewed Commitment to Corporatism

The most fundamental issue that Spaniards confronted at the end of the nineteenth century was by no means a new one: it revolved about the role that capitalism should play in their nation's future. The history of Spain had witnessed the consistent failure of the capitalist ethic to establish itself as the prevailing value system and myth-fantasy. And—to look briefly ahead—the renewed failure of capitalism to capture the national fancy at the turn of the century goes a long way toward explaining the basic tone of Spanish history from that time until the post-Civil War period. This renewed failure strengthened a national life style that Spain, or more properly Castile, had embraced in the early sixteenth century.

When Spain, with Castile in the forefront, began to achieve national solidarity under the Catholic monarchs Ferdinand and Isabella, the key to unification lay in the mounting commitment to religious uniformity and religious intolerance. Concomitantly, Spain moved toward social solidarity through a different, but related, type of uniformity and intolerance. In the social field, Spain's uniformity manifested itself in the intolerance, shared by nobility and peasants alike, of bourgeois values associated first with the Jews and *conversos* (Jews recently baptized as Catholics) and later, as the Counter-Reformation began to absorb national energies, with the individualistic, materialistic, capitalist acquisitiveness that Spanish Catholics from the very outset ascribed to a Protestant ethic.

In turning their backs yet again on a bourgeois-oriented society and the life styles associated with liberalism and capitalism, Spaniards at the beginning of the present century were in a way reasserting their faith in many of the basic features of the paternalistic, harmonious, noncompetitive, corporate society. This type of society, instead of waning at the close of the Middle Ages as elsewhere in Europe, had actually gained strength as the modern period began;

171

and, in spite of the pleas for Europeanization or liberalization raised by many leaders of the "Generation of 1898," Spaniards, as they mused upon the lessons of their disastrous war with the United States, were little inclined on the whole to repudiate certain basic traditions of the national reality.

By the end of the nineteenth century, Spain had undergone considerable development.[1] Yet self-sustaining economic progress based upon robust domestic capitalism remained as much as ever an elusive goal. Much of Spain's mineral wealth, a good deal of its railroad capital, and many of its chemical firms were in the hands of foreigners. At the end of the century, the national iron and steel industry used only about 10 percent of the ore extracted in Spain. Furthermore, the country suffered from a consistently adverse balance of trade. More basic still as an indicator of the weakness of Spanish capitalism was the "disproportion between production and consumption."[2]

The poverty of the labor force, still overwhelmingly agricultural in 1900 (68 percent), accounted in large measure for this disproportion. Joaquín Costa, perhaps the most perceptive observer of the contemporary scene, seemed to have this in mind when he wrote at the end of the 1890's: "The workers are the only Indies which remain to Spain; she must not lose them also."[3] As a result of its defeat at the hands of the United States, Spain had lost most of her colonial markets; and she could not survive, Costa seemed to be saying, if she lost the market potential of her own workers by allowing them perpetually to exist in a precapitalist stage in which they lacked purchasing power. As it turned out, however, this continued for several subsequent generations to be the fate of the working classes. A major reason for this lies in the fact that Spain's directing classes and many of her social and economic critics, including Costa

---

[1] See Jaime Vicens Vives, with the collaboration of Jorge Nadal Oller, *An Economic History of Spain,* trans. Frances M. López-Morillas (Princeton, 1969), esp. pp. 607-745, for an authoritative summary of nineteenth-century economic development. Greater detail is often provided by Gabriel Tortella Casares, *Los orígenes del capitalismo en España: banca, industria y ferrocarriles en el siglo XIX* (Madrid, 1973). Valuable insights on the nineteenth century are also found in Santiago Roldán *et al., Formación de la sociedad capitalista en España, 1914-1920,* 2 vols. (Madrid, 1973).

[2] Introduction by María Carmen García-Nieto to her edited work, *Restauración y desastre, 1874-1889: Bases documentales de la España contemporánea* (Madrid, 1972), p. 16.

[3] See Costa, *Oligarquía y caciquismo, Colectivismo agrario, y otros escritos,* an anthology edited by Rafael Pérez de la Dehesa (Madrid, 1967), p. 198.

himself, basically feared transforming the masses into genuinely participating capitalists with effective purchasing power.[4]

Early in 1901 Costa read in the Ateneo of Madrid what was to
become a celebrated report. It bore the title, *Oligarquía y caciquismo
como la forma actual de gobierno en España: urgencia de cam-
biarla.* Following its presentation, the Ateneo solicited comments on
the report from a total of 171 Spanish intellectual, social, and political leaders. One of those responding was Lorenzo Benito de Endara,
a professor of law and the vice-rector of the University of Barcelona.
The most important thesis he developed in his commentary was that
all efforts to end *caciquismo* (a system of political corruption manipulated by a complex network of bosses or *caciques*) and all attempts
to educate the masses would fail so long as the masses remained
"without capital."[5] In urging, essentially, that the Spanish masses
be transformed into capitalists, that they be inculcated with ambitions for personal gain and given the means to satisfy these ambitions
so that they could become effective purchasers, Endara was advancing a position that had precious few adherents among Spanish
middle and upper classes—even though a similar position had been
advanced, beginning in the early seventeenth century, by a handful
of reform advocates known as the *arbitristas.* In the 1890's, and in
the immediately ensuing decades, the overriding concern of the vast
majority of Spain's accommodated sectors was to prevent the lower
classes from becoming capitalists. Even the minimally successful
capitalist was, after all, a person who was to some extent economically independent, a person whose security rested to some degree on
the individual possession of capital savings, rather than upon the
paternalism of a *patrón* class. And the Spanish middle and upper
classes remained convinced that if the masses became economically
independent they would inevitably demand political independence
and in the process threaten the existing, hierarchical structure with
the sort of social revolution that many alarmists, dismayed by a rising
tide of proletariat violence, feared might be imminent.

As early as 1884, an important spokesman for Spanish labor had
recognized that the political dependence of the masses was the con-

---

[4] On the aversion of Spain's petit bourgeoisie to the spread of capitalism
among the masses, see my "Capitalism and Consumerism in Spain of the 1890's:
A Latin Americanist's View," *Inter-American Economic Affairs,* XXVI (1972),
esp. 32-38.

[5] Quoted in Manuel Tuñón de Lara, *Medio siglo de cultura española, 1885-
1936* (Madrid, 1971), p. 140.

sequence of their economic dependence.[6] The accommodated classes also recognized this connection and, unlike the labor spokesman, they wanted to maintain both the economic and political dependence of the lower classes. This meant quarantining the masses from the individualistic, profit incentives of capitalism. How to achieve such a quarantine without altogether stifling economic development?

In some of his best-known writings Costa praised Spain's collective rural traditions that "altogether lacked a parallel in any other European country."[7] Costa, I believe, was impressed by rural collectivism because he saw in it the means of preventing the infusion of capitalist values among the Spanish agricultural labor force; hence, his preoccupation with restoring the communal lands that had gradually been seized from the municipalities, in part because of the desire of an earlier generation of would-be reformers to achieve progress by forcing rural laborers to live as competitive, individualistic capitalists. A revival and strengthening of collectivist economic traditions would, Costa apparently believed, stifle the individualistic aspirations of rural Spaniards, encourage them to place the good of the collective unit above self-gain, and accustom them to seeking security in dependence upon the collective association rather than in the amassing of private goods and wealth.

At the same time that collectivism was used to shield the rural peasantry against the temptation to gain private profits, capitalism, in the Costa view, was to be encouraged among an urban bourgeoisie whose members purportedly understood how to achieve economic progress. According to Costa's formulas, however, the smooth functioning of capitalism required that it be confined to the urban bourgeoisie—and specifically to the lesser bourgeoisie that Costa hoped to see replace the noneconomic oligarchy. The masses, if allowed

---

[6] See Agrupación Socialista Madrileña, *Informe a la Comisión de Reformas Sociales* (Madrid, 1884), pp. 1-6. The *Informe* was the work of Jaime Vera and represents the first closely reasoned critique of the capitalist system, from the basis of Marxian analysis, to be written by a Spaniard. See also Vera *et al.,* *La clase obrera española a finales del siglo XIX* (Madrid, 1973). Among the best studies of Spanish labor during this period are Manuel Tuñón de Lara, *El movimiento obrero en la historia de España* (Madrid, 1972); Clara E. Lida, *Antecedentes y desarrollo del movimiento obrero español, 1835-1888: textos y documentos* (Madrid, 1973); and Josep Termes Ardevol, *Anarquismo y sindicalismo en España: la Primera Internacional, 1864-1881* (Barcelona, 1972).

[7] Rafael Pérez de la Dehesa, *El pensamiento de Costa y su influencia en el 98* (Madrid, 1966), p. 102.

to participate privately in the gains of national economic development would disrupt the development process; for, as they came into possession of economic power they would demand a share of political power and thereby jeopardize the complex development mechanism which, purportedly, only an elite could operate. Accordingly, Costa advocated rural collectivism, which in a country that was overwhelmingly agricultural would encompass the vast majority of the lower classes, and urban, bourgeois capitalism. This would result, he affirmed, in a unique Spanish middle way between communism and individualistic capitalism.[8] Without doubt, Lázaro Cárdenas made a similar appraisal when he served as president of Mexico (1934-1940); and this appraisal profoundly influenced his policies[9] —generally described as revolutionary but actually highly traditional in their objectives.

Many Spaniards in addition to Costa, among them both liberals and conservatives, desired at the turn of the century to establish collective worker groups not only in the countryside but in the cities as well.[10] They looked back in a way to the old medieval guild

---

[8] These ideas can be found in Costa, *Colectivismo agrario* (Madrid, 1898), esp. pp. 66-67, 315, 228-242. See also my *Hispanismo, 1898-1936: Spanish Conservatives and Liberals and Their Relations with Spanish America* (Notre Dame, 1971), p. 57, *passim*.

[9] One of the best and most succinct accounts of the development of Mexican corporatism under President Cárdenas is Arnaldo Córdova, "La transformación del PNR en PRM: El triunfo del corporativismo en México." (Paper presented to the IV International Congress of Mexican Studies in Santa Monica, California, October of 1973.)

[10] On the vogue of corporatist ideology among both liberals and conservatives in turn-of-the-century Spain see my "Making the Hispanic World Safe from Democracy: Spanish Liberals and *Hispanismo*," *The Review of Politics*, XXXIII (1971), 307-322; "Spanish Origins of the Social-Political Ideology of the Catholic Church in Nineteenth-Century Spanish America," *The Americas*, XXIX (1972), 1-16; and *Hispanismo*, esp. pp. 255-258. On the basis of my research I must question the contention of Philippe Schmitter in his essay in this collection. Schmitter writes: "Those who advocate corporatism in the Iberian and Latin American areas unabashedly and unashamedly import their ideas from abroad." While it is interesting that one of the very few Spaniards Schmitter cites in his bibliography, Eduardo Aunós Pérez, derived the bulk of his corporativist ideas from Italian sources, the great majority of Spanish corporatists found their inspiration in their country's authentic traditions. This was as much true of the liberal secularists, among them Costa and Adolfo González Posada, as it was of the conservative Catholics, whose major spokesmen included Jaime Balmes, Juan Donoso Cortés, Antonio Vicent, and Juan Vázquez de Mella. It is equally instructive that the great Spanish Conservative statesman Antonio Maura and the equally distinguished Liberal leader José Canalejas did not require recourse to foreign influences in reaching accord that a cor-

system, and also prophetically ahead to the corporate state that many critics of the established order throughout Europe began in the post-World War I period to hail as a panacea. These Spaniards hoped to suppress the desires of the masses for capital accumulation and individual advancement by guaranteeing them security within appropriate functional collectivities that would administer social security and mutual assistance programs for all members. Such a system would guarantee social peace. And against the background of social peace, a skilled, capitalist bourgeoisie could achieve national economic development. The proponents of such a system desired to superimpose the structure of bourgeois capitalism upon a corporative base of noncapitalist laborers.

If, on the one hand, Spain's accommodated sectors generally believed that the masses must be prevented from developing into self-reliant capitalists, and if, on the other hand, they believed that a social problem must be prevented from reaching an explosive level, then it was essential to devise an effective system of paternalism for ministering to the essential needs of the proletariat. To at least a limited degree the Catholic Church did succeed in parts of agricultural central and northern Spain in fashioning a paternalistic system that rested on clergy-controlled, guildlike associations that administered various social assistance programs. Elsewhere, however, paternalism had by the turn of the century failed to provide any adequate degree of security for the impoverished masses. As a result, the social problem continued to pose the threat of revolution.

The paramount reason for the failure of paternalism can be traced to the highly charged clericalism-anticlericalism issue. The Church claimed the right to supervise and conduct charitable programs in Spain, in line with traditions firmly established in the Middle Ages. Churchmen resisted those programs that called for government bureaucrats, allegedly tainted in many instances by liberal heresies and Masonic aberrations, to administer charity to the masses. Basically, the clergy saw in church-controlled paternalism

---

poratist restructuring provided the only avenue to Spanish stability in the early twentieth century.

Corporatism, in a distinctive Spanish mold, was a key element in the attempt of Spaniards to establish closer cultural ties to Spanish Americans and to stiffen Spanish Americans in their opposition to United States values and life-styles. In my mind, there is little doubt that Spanish American corporatist *pensadores* derived their concepts largely from Spanish sources which in turn owed very little, except by way of occasional refinement and emphasis, to non-Spanish sources.

the means of combating the secularist trend among the masses. For their part, many government figures, dedicated to liberalism and its Spanish variant known as *Krausismo*,[11] saw in state-controlled paternalism the means of spreading a secularist spirit among the masses and freeing them from the alleged superstitions of the traditional faith.

Churchmen and their *Krausista* adversaries among Spanish liberals did agree upon the need to bestow nonmaterial rewards upon the masses. Both schools insisted that the attempt to resolve the social problem merely by conferring greater material rewards would arouse an insatiable craving for more and more in the way of material goods and lead ultimately to social revolution. In the importance which they attached to nonmaterial rewards, churchmen and *Krausistas* were in basic accord that the masses must not be infused with the capitalist spirit. At this point, however, agreement ended. Churchmen insisted that only in the traditional faith could the masses find the nonmaterial satisfactions that would effectively curb their revolutionary leanings, while *Krausistas* rested their hopes upon the nonmaterial gratifications to be provided by nondenominational humanism and pantheism, and by an elevation of the cultural level of the lower classes. The bitter competition between traditionalists and liberals, clericals and anticlericals, churchmen and *Krausistas* contributed significantly to the situation in which the masses remained, throughout much of Spain, without either material or nonmaterial rewards.

By the beginning of the twentieth century, in large measure because they were terrified by lower-class violence and the specter of revolution, Spain's directing classes had, almost *in toto*, abandoned the dream that earlier schools of reformers, beginning in the seventeenth century, had entertained of hastening economic development by encouraging the rise of popular, grass-roots capitalism. Not even the urgent need to acquire new markets, a need that was clearly recognized by the so-called *regeneracionistas* following the loss of Cuba, Puerto Rico and the Philippines in the war with the United

---

[11] Among the more recent studies on the impact of *Krausismo,* named after the German philosopher Karl Christian Friedrich Krause (1781-1832) are Elías Díaz, *La filosofía social del Krausismo español* (Madrid, 1973); Juan José Gil Cremades, *El reformismo español: Krausismo, escuela histórica, neotomismo* (Barcelona, 1969); A. Jiménez Landi, *La Institución Libre de Enseñanza y su ambiente,* Vol. I, *Los orígenes* (Madrid, 1973); and Juan López Morillas, *El Krausismo español: perfil de una aventura intelectual* (México, D.F., 1956).

States, was enough to induce Spanish leaders to seek means of spreading purchasing power among the masses. As a result, capitalism maintained a precarious existence, consumerism continued at a minimal level, and development languished. Between 1906 and 1930, the increase in annual per-capita income averaged only 0.95 percent;[12] and it would have been much lower had it not been for the notable growth experienced during the Miguel Primo de Rivera dictatorship (1923-1930) and, more significantly, had it not been for the remittances of Spanish emigrants living in Latin America.[13]

Spain had failed to enter the world of capitalism and it had also failed to discover new expedients to render viable its old corporate mode of existence—to which it had in many ways renewed its commitment—through effective paternalism. These twin failures would be rectified only in the post-Civil War period, especially in those years from the 1950's to the early 1970's, when Spain scored spectacular gains in capitalist development and simultaneously strengthened the paternalism on which an elitist, nonliberal, corporate social structure depended.

Economic Development in Post-Civil War Spain

Early in the second half of the twentieth century an eminent French historian of Spain asked: "Which will come out on top in the end, the spiritual and economic archaism of the far-flung country areas, or the seething innovations of port and metropolis?"[14] At the outset of the 1970's, the observer of Spain could no longer raise such a question. The spirit of seething innovations had clearly triumphed, the traditional Spain seemed well on the way to extinction, and in its place there appeared to have emerged just one more successful, bustling, bourgeois country.

Between 1961 and 1970, the period marked by the effects of Spain's first two development plans, the annual growth in per-capita

---

[12] These are the statistics of the Instituto Nacional de Estadística (Madrid), reported in the Madrid newspaper *ABC,* July 12, 1972, p. 21.

[13] On the importance to the national economy of remittances from Spanish emigrants to the New World, see my "Hispanismo and the Non-Revolutionary Spanish Immigrant in Spanish America, 1900-1930," *Inter-American Economic Affairs,* XXVI (1971), 3-30.

[14] Pierre Vilar, *Spain, A Brief History,* trans. Brian Tate (Oxford, London, 1967), p. 3. The translation is based on the sixth French edition of *Histoire de l'Espagne* (1965) and on the Spanish edition (1960).

income averaged 6.45 percent.[15] By 1972 the per-capita income for the country as a whole stood at approximately the $1,000 level, up from about $300 in 1960, while in Madrid, with its population of more than three million, it had considerably exceeded that level.[16] The real growth in Spain's GNP for the decade 1960-1970 was 75.5 percent, the highest in all of Europe and surpassed in the world only by Japan with its increase of 110.5 percent. In the rate of industrial growth Spain also stood at the top of all the countries of Europe. With a base of 100 for 1960, the index of industrial growth registered 296 in 1970. For chemicals, the 1970 index was 395, for automobiles 861.8, and for per-capita consumption of electricity 155.2.[17]

By 1970, not only economically but demographically, Spain could be considered a modern country. Its population of 34,032,801 —up from 18,600,000 in 1900—had gained relative stability with low mortality and birth rates.[18] Between 1960 and 1970 the rate

---

[15] See address of Admiral Luis Carrero Blanco on the occasion of the July 11, 1972, inauguration of the new headquarters of the Instituto Nacional de Estadística, reported in *ABC*, July 12, 1972, p. 22.

[16] See *Anuario Político Español 1969: Cambio social y modernización*, ed. Miguel Martínez Cuadrado (Madrid, 1970), p. 43.

[17] *ABC*, July 29, 1972, p. 49.

[18] Salustiano del Campo Urbano, "Composición, dinámica y distribución de la población española," in Campo Urbano, director, *La España de los años 70*, I (Madrid, 1972), 15-16. This is an extremely valuable study based on the most reliable statistics available and utilizing the most important literature on the subject. The same may be said of the other essays appearing in this admirable work. Another indispensable source on the contemporary socioeconomic situation in Spain, with many statistical charts and containing the official text of the government development plan for the 1972-1975 period is *III Plan de Desarrollo Económico y Social, 1972-1975*, 4th ed. (Madrid, 1972). Also valuable are José Cazorla, *Estratificación social en España* (Madrid, 1973); Manuel Fraga Iribarne, Juan Velarde Fuentes, and Salustiano del Campo Urbano, *La España de los años 70*, Vol. II, *La economía* (Madrid, 1973); *Guía de Fuentes Estadísticas de España* (Barcelona, 1973), a two-volume work prepared under the auspices of the Comisión Mixta de Coordinación Estadística; *Informe anual de la O.C.D.E. sobre le economía española* (Madrid, 1971); Instituto de Estudios Fiscales, *Economía española, 1973* (Madrid, 1973); Arturo López Muñoz, *Capitalismo español: una etapa decisiva. Notas sobre la economía española, 1965-1970* (Algorta, 1971); José María Ordeix Gesti, *España hacia una economía industrial* (Barcelona, 1973); Raimundo Poveda Anadón, *La creación de dinero en España, 1956-1970: análisis y política* (Madrid, 1972); and *Sociología española de los años setente* (Madrid, 1971). Many penetrating studies of contemporary Spain are found in the proceedings of the conference "Spain in the Seventies: Problems of Change and Transition" held in June of 1973 in Washington, D.C., under the joint sponsorship of the Center for Strategic and International Studies, Georgetown University, and the Institute of International Studies of the University of South Carolina.

of increase was a readily manageable 1.12 percent per year. In other ways also Spain had become demographically modern. In 1967 the life expectancy at birth for women was 74.56 and for men 69.23 (higher than in either the United States or the Soviet Union but below the Scandinavian countries and several other nations), up from 35.7 for women and 33.85 for men in 1900. The rapid growth of a middle class pointed in addition to the sort of population generally described as modern. Although estimates vary disconcertingly, depending upon the criteria used, it is widely agreed that by 1970 the middle class comprised better than 50 percent of the population—estimates for the upper classes range from 0.5 percent to 20 percent, and for the lower classes from 28 to 60 percent.[19]

Critics of Franco's Spain like to attribute the country's economic development less to shrewd domestic economic management than to the windfalls of tourism and foreign investment.[20] Such a view is not lacking in justification, although without some sound planning it is unlikely that vast numbers of tourists and huge sums of foreign capital could have been attracted to Spain. In any event, in tourists and foreign capital Spain has found the sort of bonanza that statesmen of the imperial age hoped, in vain, would result from the colonization of America.

In still another way, Spain has been able to take advantage of the affluence of foreign lands in order to build up its domestic economy. In the 1960's the emigration of Spaniards abroad continued to be as important as it had been in the turn-of-the-century period. However, significant differences had developed. In the earlier period Spanish emigrants came mainly from the northern, the north-

---

[19] See FOESSA (Fomento de Estudios Sociales y de Sociología Aplicada), *Síntesis del Informe sociológico sobre la situación social de España 1970*, 2nd ed. (Madrid, 1972) p. 546. Collaborating in the preparation of this valuable work were Armando de Miguel, Jesús M. de Miguel, Amparo Almarcha, Jaime Martín Moreno, Benjamín Oltra, and Juan Salcedo. The complete 1,654-page work, of which the above is a careful abbreviation, is *Informe FOESSA: Informe sociológico sobre la situación social de España en 1970* (Madrid, 1970). See also Juan Diez Nicolás and Juan del Pino Artacho, "Estratificación y movilidad social en España en la década de los años 70," in Campo Urbano, *La España,* I, 395-97.

[20] The importance of tourism and foreign investments is treated by Eric N. Baklanoff, "Spain and the Atlantic Community: A Study of Incipient Integration and Economic Development," *Economic Development and Cultural Change,* XVI (1968), 588-602. The initial stages of Spain's broadening economic contact with the outside world under the Franco regime are described by Arthur P. Whitaker in *Spain and the Defense of the West: Ally and Liability* (New York, 1961).

western and northeastern areas, and they went principally to
America. Once settled there the great majority remained for years,
and many never returned to Spain. In the 1960's Spanish emigrants went in impressive numbers to European countries on a
short-term basis; and, to a large extent, they came from Andalusia.
Instead of becoming anarchists as in the past, the disadvantaged in
today's Andalusia are obviously seeking to resolve their problems by
accumulating capital so as to enter the consumer economy. What
is more, the emigrants of the 1960's, returning relatively quickly to
their native land, tend to exert a greater influence than did their
turn-of-the-century predecessors in stimulating the development process through the savings and newly acquired skills they bring home
with them. Of still greater significance is the fact that Spain, in
contrast to earlier times, has learned to tolerate and even to admire
the money-grubbing small capitalist who goes abroad with very
little in mind other than becoming wealthier; for among the Spaniards remaining at home there is an ever-increasing number who
seem themselves to have little else in mind.

Undoubtedly a major factor contributing to changing attitudes
is the process of urbanization that Spain has undergone in recent
years. The following table provides some of the basic statistics of
urbanization. According to the norms used by the authorities preparing this table, rural inhabitants are those living in centers of less
than 2,000 residents; intermediate, those living in centers with between 2,000 and 10,000 residents; and urban, those living in centers
of more than 10,000.

Rural-Urban Division of the Spanish Population

Year	Rural		Intermediate		Urban	
	Number (in millions)	Percentage of Population	Number	Percentage of Population	Number	Percentage of Population
1900	5.12	27.5	7.5	40.3	5.9	32.2
1970	3.7	11.0	7.65	22.5	22.6	66.5

(Source: Salustiano del Campo Urbano, "Composición, dinámica y
distribución de la población española," in Campo Urbano,
director, *La España de los años 70* (Madrid, 1972), I,
20-21.)

The converse to urbanization is the decline of the agricultural
population. Even more than vegetative growth within the cities, the

migration of rural workers to urban centers has accounted for the dramatic rates of urbanization. Between 1962 and 1970, more than 3.5 million Spaniards were involved in the process of domestic migration, most of them leaving the slowly developing rural areas and taking up residence in Spain's most developed and industrialized cities, especially Madrid, Zaragoza, Seville, and—most recently— Valladolid.[21] Owing to internal migration, between 1950 and 1967 the number of rural workers dropped from 5.53 to 3.7 million, and for 1980 it is projected that the agrarian sector will have an active population of only 2.2 million—less than half of what it was in 1960.[22] With ample justification Juan Diez Nicolás, one of Spain's leading authorities on demography, has written that the greatest population redistribution in Spain's history has taken place between 1960 and 1970.[23]

As the Spanish population has shifted to the cities, the composition of the working force has changed proportionately. The percentage of rural laborers within the economically active population dropped, between 1950 and 1960, from 49.6 percent to 41.7 percent; and between 1960 and 1970 it declined further, from 41.7 percent to 31 percent. Meanwhile, the percentage of the labor force employed in industry rose from 24 percent in 1950 to 38 percent in 1970—with an absolute increment of 2.2 million persons. In the same twenty-year period the number of persons employed in services rose from 2.9 million to 4.7 million, or in terms of percentage of the active population from 27 to 36 percent. In projecting the " 'terciarization' of our economy," Juan José Caballero contends that by 1975 Spain's economy will to a large extent be one of services, in that the services sector will be the most numerous division within the labor force.[24]

Migration into the cities has "mobilized the persons who were most traditional and sedentary"[25] and has helped bring about one of the most significant peaceful agrarian reforms in history. Faced

[21] See Banco del Estado (Banesto), *Anuario de mercado español, 1971* (Madrid, 1971), p. 448, and *Instituto Nacional de Estadística, Anuario Estadístico de España, 1970* (Madrid, 1971).

[22] Juan José Caballero, "Clase obrera y relaciones de trabajo," Campo Urbano, *La España,* I, 609.

[23] Juan Diez Nicolás, "La urbanización y el urbanismo en la década de los 70," *ibid.,* p. 155.

[24] Caballero, "Clase obrera," p. 610.

[25] Alfonso García Barbancho, *Las migraciones españoles en 1961-1965* (Madrid, 1970), p. 20.

with labor shortages, owners of the latifundia have been forced to bargain with rural laborers almost as equals; and they have had to begin to modernize production by introducing technological innovations. In 1957 there were 169 persons in the active agricultural population for every tractor; in 1967 there were nineteen persons for each tractor, and in 1971 approximately eleven.[26] Meantime, those who have moved into cities, a move made possible because of industrialization, have become converts to the capitalist-consumerist way of life and have abandoned the collectivist, anarchist ideas that appealed to many of the south's rural laborers in the late nineteenth and early twentieth centuries.

And what of those who have remained in Spain's rural areas? To a large extent they have been caught up in a process that has "urbanized rural life."[27] A subsistence existence had characterized traditional rural life and had bred a set of values in which miserliness was prized and consumerism eschewed. In an agrarian setting, with its simple, dichotomized stratification, there were relatively few incentives to try to prove, by means of conspicuous consumption, that one belonged to a higher social status; for one's status was largely determined by his birth rather than by what he managed to acquire. In the Spain of the 1960's, however, the rural workers have been assimilated into the urban society with its emphasis on the acquisition of consumer goods. The linkage between urban and rural Spain provided by roads and cars and by the communications media, as well as by migration, has helped make this possible. Above all, however, the acquisition of purchasing power by rural Spaniards and their consequent emergence as consumers have linked them in their values to the city dwellers.

The statistical indications that Spain has become a consumer society are impressive, although it must be remembered that the transition has been most dramatic in Madrid and its environs, in the

---

[26] FOESSA, Síntesis, p. 67.

[27] Roberto Sancho Hazak, "La sociedad rural hoy," Campo Urbano, La España, I, 223. See also José Manuel Narado, La evolución de la agricultura en España. Desarrollo capitalista y crisis de las formas del producción tradicionales (Barcelona, 1971). Richard Herr, in his brilliant study Spain (Englewood Cliffs, 1971), also stresses what in effect is the urbanization of rural life. At one point he writes: "I conclude that the alienation of the common people of rural Spain from the urban groups holding progressive doctrines . . . was the most important cause for Spain's political instability in the last two centuries. This alienation arose after the Enlightenment introduced an ideological schism into the ruling groups, and it is disappearing with the integration of the countryside into modern urban culture" (p. 283).

Basque Provinces, and Cataluña, and that parts of the country still remain isolated in a preconsumer, precapitalist existence.[28] In 1939 an average of 61 percent of the expenditures of Spanish households was allotted to food, 9.4 percent to clothing, 14.6 percent to rent or payments on the purchase of a home, 8.5 percent to household expenditures, and only 7.4 percent to diverse consumer goods. In 1968, 44 percent was allotted to food, 13.5 percent to clothing, 10 percent to rent or home purchase, 8.1 percent to household expenses, and a substantial 23.7 percent to the purchase of diverse consumer goods.[29] In 1969, 27 percent of all Spanish households owned an automobile, in comparison to 12 percent in 1966 and 4 percent in 1960.[30] Moreover, with a base of 100 for the year 1964, the index of total consumption in Spain stood at 106.96 in 1965 and 135.79 in 1969. The index for the consumption of durable goods had risen to 121.65 in 1965 and to 172.87 in 1969.[31]

Clearly, the Spanish masses were acquiring more and more purchasing power. Between 1963 and 1971 the percentage of the national income received by wage-earning and salaried classes rose from 53.3 to 58.8.[32] While the percentage of the total national income that went to wage earners and the salaried classes was lower than in France and Italy in 1964, its increase—within the context of Spain's socioeconomic traditions—has been startling. By 1968, moreover, Spain's wage-earning and salaried groups were earning a greater percentage of the total national income than their counterparts in Italy and were steadily gaining on those in France.[33] The relative success of Spain in comparison to the republics of Spanish America in improving income distribution is striking; and it helps explain some of the differences between the patterns of development, capitalism, consumerism, and corporatism in Spain and in Spanish America.

---

[28] See *Anuario Político Español 1969*, p. 69.

[29] See Instituto Nacional de Estadística, *Contabilidad nacional de España, años 1964-1969* (Madrid, 1970); *Encuesta sobre cuentas familiares, marzo 1958* (Madrid, 1960); *Encuestas de presupuestos familiares, años 1967 y 1968* (Madrid, 1970); and *Encuesta de presupuestos familiares, marzo 1964-marzo 1965* (Madrid, 1965).

[30] FOESSA, *Síntesis,* pp. 91-92.

[31] See Instituto Nacional de Estadística sources cited in note 26.

[32] See Carrero Blanco address, cited in note 13.

[33] A much fuller statistical account of recent Spanish development is found in my "Capitalism and Consumerism in Spain of the 1960's: What Lessons for Latin American Development," *Inter-American Economic Affairs,* XXVI (1973), esp. 3-16.

Capitalism and Consumerism in the Spain of the
1960's: The Basis of a Two-culture Society

In 1919 the Spanish statesman Francisco Soler Pérez proposed that steps be taken to increase the rural population, because this was "the cement of the nation." By inducing migration out of the cities so as to swell the rural population, "the most conservative class in Spain," it would be possible, he asserted, "to produce a social climate not propitious to the agitation that is dangerous to the lives of all nations."[34] In many ways the Soler appraisal reflected the official mentality of turn-of-the-century Spain, a mentality that prevailed up to and even into the era of the Second Republic (1931-1936). Spain's "agrarian myth" rested on the conviction that the rural classes were more virtuous precisely because they had remained isolated from the materialistic, acquisitive, individualistic set of values that was the hallmark of an urban bourgeoisie.

What was most abhorrent to the official mentality of early twentieth-century Spain has come to pass in the 1960's. Spain has become an urban society in which the masses possess purchasing power and have overwhelmingly rejected the values and motives associated with the existence of subsistence and the culture of poverty. Yet this transformation has not led to a leveling revolution and economic change has not yet produced fundamental political change. Instead, the political control exercised by an elite seems to have been strengthened by the entire process of economic development that Spain has undergone since the end of the Civil War. In attempting to explain this situation it is necessary to distinguish between consumerism and capitalism and to show that although the Spanish masses have become consumers only a small elite can be described as capitalists.

The political system evolving out of the Nationalist triumph in the Civil War has been amazingly successful in channeling more money into the hands of the Spanish masses; for in no other way could the economic interests of the financial aristocracy, the industrialists and the producers who exercise vast power over the political system, have been adequately served. With their increased purchasing power, however, the masses have not become independent, either economically or politically. Instead, as a consumer mania has gripped them, they have become subject to the operation of a new type

---

[34] Quoted in FOESSA, *Síntesis,* pp. 161-162.

of "iron law of wages." The more they earn, the more they feel compelled to spend on consumer goods, and the more they feel justified in increasing personal indebtedness so they can purchase still more goods. The result is that no matter how much they earn, they acquire no capital surpluses—and thus no economic independence. With no uncommitted private economic resources they are, even though they may be earning relatively high incomes, dependent in the final instance upon a government that supplies them with a wide coverage of paternalistic protection, including medical, unemployment and retirement benefits as well as generous vacation, educational, and recreational facilities. In a way the economic miracle of post-Civil War Spain has increased the dependence of the masses and prevented what Ortega y Gasset so feared: "the vertical invasion of the barbarians." Spain's lower classes seem little concerned with demanding a voice in national decision-making processes, so long as those in power afford them security through state paternalism, and so long as the power wielders make purchasing power available to them.

Consumerism has stifled the once rampant spirit of anarchism in Spain. Now that they have savored the pleasures of consumerism, Spaniards are disinclined to opt for the lack of individual purchasing power and the life of poverty that were key tenets of anarchism; nor have Spaniards yet had time to become disillusioned with consumerism as have many citizens of countries that underwent earlier modernization.

It may not be easy to perpetuate Spain's social tranquility—indeed its perpetuation for over thirty years seems eerily abnormal. Anarchism still lives, at least in the Spanish periphery if not in its one-time power base of Andalusia. Its survival, however, is not owing to a rejection of capitalism and consumerism but rather to the continuing strength of Basque separatism and Catalan regionalism, which in turn can be traced in part to the racially inspired animosity of peripheral Spaniards that is directed against those of the center, with the former dismissing the latter as racially impure. At this point in history, not even the most successful operation of capitalism and consumerism has thoroughly calmed the tensions of regionalism and racism in countries where these tensions are deeply rooted in the past.

The shortcomings of Spain's social-economic system cannot necessarily be held accountable for the failure to defuse the explosive charges planted just beneath the surface of political events; but that system does face an ever more difficult challenge if it is to continue, as in the past twenty years or so, to minimize the forces of social upheaval. In the final analysis, the continuation of relative tranquility demands a continuing economic expansion adequate to meet the rising consumer wants of the masses, and adequate also to meet the social overhead of lavish government paternalistic programs. At least through the 1960's, the Spanish system worked reasonably well to meet these goals. When the system occasionally malfunctioned— as it seemed increasingly to do in the early 1970's—the governing elite had ample means of repression at their disposal.

Those who command in Spain tend to be capitalists, in addition to being consumers. Either because of their huge resources of wealth, or because they have had the character to liberate themselves to some degree from the compulsion to consume, they have been able to escape an iron-law-of-wages situation that drains off all income. Possessing a capitalist mentality, they think in terms of using money to generate more money, and they appreciate the power that comes from the independent possession of capital surpluses, a power that frequently leads to participation in the political rule of the country— a participation that in turn often facilitates the accumulation of additional wealth.

Thus, Spain's directing elites live in a world of capitalist values, while the Spanish masses have taken up a postcapitalist set of values —as their counterparts in the United States may be doing—in line with which individual economic independence is not prized, money is not saved in order to create more money or to provide security, and a paternalistic state is relied upon to provide the services that the individual cannot purchase himself because of his complete immersion in the habits of consumerism.

According to a classic description much in vogue in the nineteenth and well into the twentieth century there were two Spains: the one was liberal, tolerant, secularist, progressive, development-minded, consumed with the epic sense of life, and Europeanist in orientation; the other was conservative, fanatical, theocratic, archaic, stoic, dedicated to the tragic sense of life, and oriented toward national traditions. The differences between the two Spains, conceived of in these terms, had become blurred by the 1960's, with the country having made considerable progress toward becoming one and integrated. But the gulf separating the Spain of consumerism from that of capitalism was so enormous that one could still justifiably posit the existence of two Spains.

Many of the circumstances under which Spain has achieved its post-Civil War economic development have contributed to the emergence of the two-culture dichotomy. In a penetrating analysis Carlos Moya Valgañón argues that Spanish development under Franco was initially spearheaded not by a new and assertive bourgeois-entrepreneurial-bureaucratic elite, as most theorists have maintained, but rather by the Spanish government, relying first of all upon old-line military technicians who had risen to prominence during the Civil War and upon the traditional aristocracy whose fortunes rested on land and finance capitalism.[35] Only later, as the government sought to rationalize the economic structure, did the new bureaucratic management experts and entrepreneurs begin to attain power. In a way, the government called into being an entrepreneurial elite, and then began to confer political power on its members. Had a development-minded bourgeoisie been forced to turn to the masses for support in fighting a battle against archaic, entrenched interests, then the masses might have gained at least a taste of power. Instead, the Spanish development process has left the masses virtually as inert politically as they were at the turn of the century. One finds interesting parallels to this situation in the industrialization of certain Latin American republics.[36]

Spain's new bourgeois elite came into being not so much because of the thrust and drive of its members as because of the generous inducements that government held out to those who would contribute their efforts to the country's modernization. These inducements were frequently extended through the Instituto Nacional de Industria (similar to many of the *fomento* or development corporations in Latin America), which in the early years of its existence in the 1950's was directed mainly by military personnel. Using public

---

[35] Moya Valgañón, "Las elites económicas y el desarrollo español," Campo Urbano, *La España,* I, esp. 571.

[36] On the parallels in Latin America, see Claudio Véliz, ed., *Latin America and the Caribbean: A Handbook* (London, 1968), pp. xxii-xxiii. In setting forth his interpretation, Véliz, an eminent Chilean intellectual, writes: ". . . the rise of industry in Latin America has not been accomplished against, or in spite of, the policies, attitudes or preferences of the central state; there has not been a confrontation between an industrialising bourgeoisie and a traditional state. Far from it; industrialisation has depended directly on state intervention and success for the entrepreneur is often more dependent on good relations with a governing party than on technical or business efficiency."

money, often in collaboration with private capital, to create firms that in many instances were later turned over in their entirety to private capitalists, the INI presided over the induced birth of large-scale Spanish industrial capitalism.[37] The process led to the ultimate incorporation into the political power base of a new capitalist sector made up of the men who had taken fullest advantage of the favorable circumstances afforded by government. Spain finally had its bourgeois revolution, but it was a revolution from above. And because of the manner in which capitalism has achieved growth in Spain, a traditionalist aristocracy, under the careful protection of the government, has entrenched its power by leaguing itself, economically and often matrimonially, with a new manager-planner-technocrat class.

The INI has been able to obtain the huge sums needed to carry out its ambitious projects in part through the forced savings of the lower classes resulting from an essentially regressive taxation policy.[38] The effect of forced savings on the part of the masses has been two-fold: it has increased the dependence of the lower classes upon the government for various social services; and it has augmented the economic independence, based on private capital surpluses, of the Spanish elite by freeing them to some degree from tax burdens. Much more important in making possible the elite's economic independence has been the degree to which Spain's economy has benefited from the spending of tourists, from foreign investment, and from the remittances of emigrants. In the process of capital formation, therefore, the government has not had to rely primarily upon capturing the resources of the wealthy classes—an unpleasant prospect for the governing sectors that Latin American rulers have had

---

[37] By 1971 the INI, employing over 200,000 persons (almost one-third of the number employed in Spain's vast tourist and tourist-related enterprises), had a total of nearly 6.8 billion dollars invested in the Spanish economy and in just the preceding ten years had helped to bring into being twenty-four important new industrial firms. See *ABC*, July 23, 1972, p. 41.

[38] State reliance primarily on indirect taxes, which tend to weigh proportionately more heavily on the lower classes (except in the case of indirect taxes collected on sale of luxury items), is revealed by statistics found in the *Anuario Político Español 1970* (Madrid, 1971), p. 323.

National Income in Millions of Pesetas, with a value of approximately sixty-nine to the dollar

	1968	1969	1970
Direct Imposts	61,740	71,500	86,096
Indirect Imposts	140,450	150,575	174,651

to begin to contemplate in the critical circumstances of the 1960's
and 1970's.

The Spanish Masses: Consumerism, Paternalism and Nonpoliticization

A 1968 interview of Spanish youth between the ages of fifteen
and twenty-nine reveals that the highest percentage (33 percent)
of those replying to a question concerning why the population was
not politically informed believed that the problems of politics and
government were so complicated as to be beyond their comprehension. Another 17 percent responded that youth was not interested in politics. What is more, 43 percent of the youth inter-
viewed thought that there was enough political liberty at present,
while only 33 percent thought there should be more. Presented
with the question "Speaking in general terms, would you like
changes in important aspects of the political organization of Spain?"
38 percent replied negatively and 28 percent affirmatively, while 34
percent did not express an opinion.[39]

The continuing nonpoliticization of Spanish youth and the
masses in general depends upon keeping the majority of Spaniards
economically impotent and manipulated through a system of consumerism, and also of forced savings, that effectively siphons off
their money as quickly as it is earned. At the same time it is essential
that the state intervene to supply the masses with the services that
they lack the private means to purchase. Under Franco the Spanish
government has unhesitatingly assumed its paternalistic obligations
to the economically and politically dependent masses, thereby moving to perpetuate that dependency—and presenting a striking contrast to the failure of paternalism at the turn of the century.

Large-scale government paternalism was introduced by the
Franco government at the beginning of the first major thrust toward
urbanization, industrialization, and modernization—it began still
earlier in Latin America, between 1903 (Uruguay) and 1930
(Brazil) and has played perhaps an even more important role than
in Spain in preventing the politicization of the masses. Paternalism
was introduced in Spain before the masses had become politicized,

---

[39] The interview was conducted by the Instituto de la Opinión Pública in
May-June, 1968. An excellent article by José Ramón Torregrosa Peris, "Orien-
tacion sociopolíticas de la juventud española," Campo Urbano, *La España*, I,
861-912, is based on this source. See in particular pp. 874, 879, 896, and 903.

and it seems to have been intended to prevent the politicization of the majority of citizens. In the United States and to some degree in the major powers of Western Europe, state paternalism came relatively later in the modernization process. It came after the masses had already acquired some political voice, in part because they had responded to deep-seated traditions of capitalism that stressed private economic independence, without which private political independence will be insecure at best. And, government paternalism in the countries that underwent early modernization has not, at least not yet, altogether silenced the political voice of the masses.

Some indication of the degree to which the Spanish government has assumed the burdens of social responsibility is provided by a breakdown of government spending in 1970. In that year 14,997 million *pesetas* (at an exchange rate of approximately 69 to the dollar) went into education and professional (meaning usually vocational) formation, an expenditure that benefited primarily the poorer classes in view of the continuing tendency of the wealthy to send their children to private schools; 14,690 million *pesetas* were allotted to housing, in the form of subsidies to firms constructing lower-class dwellings and assistance to working-class families to enable them to purchase, and in far fewer instances to rent, homes;[40] and 4,347 million *pesetas* were spent by the government on social security, health, and social assistance.[41] By way of comparison, the government as of 1971 spent slightly over 5,509 million *pesetas* on defense, a figure representing about 13 percent of the budget, down from 23 percent in 1961.[42]

The relatively modest government outlay on social security, health, and social assistance provides only a slight indication of the actual scope of the financing of those programs. Far more so than in other countries, the Spanish government relies on assessments on employees and employers to finance social security. In 1966 government contributions financed 4.2 percent of Spain's social security expenses (down from 10 percent in 1963), while government contributions were 13 percent for Greece, 17 percent for France, 18 percent for Italy, 22.5 percent for Portugal, 49.8 percent for Great

---

[40] See *Anuario Político Español 1969*, pp. 260-261.
[41] See *Anuario Político Español 1970*, p. 317.
[42] *ABC*, July 25, 1972, p. 14.

Britain, 68.8 percent for Ireland, and 72 percent for Denmark.[43]

Spain's social security system, expanded in 1967 to cover sectors of the active rural population, provides retirement pensions and homes for the aged, unemployment insurance, recreation and vacation facilities, and a wide variety of health services. A 1963 amendment to the social security law created an obligatory health insurance institution, the Seguro Obligatorio de Enfermedad, to augment and complement the health services provided by the regular social security apparatus. As a result of the creation of the SOE and various other refinements in the social security program, government health assistance, intended in the 1950's to cover only the proletariat and the very lowest middle classes, extended to 80 percent of the active population in 1968; in 1971, over 28 million Spaniards fell under the protection of one or another social security health program.[44] Surveys show that the lower classes feel they are receiving at least moderately satisfactory medical attention.[45] Undoubtedly this feeling contributes to the legitimacy of an elitist government.

In their dependence upon the government for educational facilities, the Spanish masses—essentially, those Spaniards whose consumer patterns and earnings leave them with no private income for the schooling of their children—have also had some reason to feel satisfaction in recent years. In 1950 the number of Spanish children, ages six through thirteen, not enrolled in any school was estimated at two million. In 1968 it was down to half a million.[46] In the same period the level of illiteracy among the adult population declined from 14 percent—compared to 43 percent in 1900—to about 5 percent. It used to be that the person receiving the bachelor's degree (at the end of secondary schooling in the traditional Spanish educational structure) could expect to be addressed as Don. This custom was abandoned only in fairly recent years as the number of

---

[43] See La economía española, 1971: Anuario del año económico, directed by Juan Muñoz, Santiago Roldán, and José Luis García Delgado (Madrid, 1972), pp. 121-122, 131.

[44] Hoja de Lunes (Madrid), August 21, 1972, p. 13. See also Antonio Perpiñá Rodríguez, Sociología de la Seguridad Social en España (Madrid, 1973).

[45] See FOESSA, Síntesis, pp. 254-255.

[46] These statistics are qualified in ibid., p. 261, where it is estimated that the number of children not actually receiving education, even though enrolled in schools, was over 1.5 million in 1964 and approximately 800,000 in 1968. One of the best sources on the Spanish educational structure is the Libro Blanco de educación (Madrid, 1969). For a sharp criticism of Spanish educational reform plans see Ignacio Fernández de Castro, Reforma educativa y desarrollo capitalista. Informe crítico de la Ley de Educación (Madrid, 1973).

children completing secondary education began to expand dramatically. In 1967 over one million youths were studying for the bachelor's degree, and shortly, according to projections, the number will be up to two million. Very soon, in fact, the number of those completing secondary education will be about the same as those finishing primary studies.[47] The main thrust of education reforms in Spain during the past several years has been toward increasing the number of public secondary schools—a development keenly resented by many leading figures in the Catholic Church which midway through the 1960's still provided secondary education to about two-thirds of those receiving it in Spain.

The expanding of educational services represents one of the key methods by which the Spanish government is increasing the dependence of the consumer-oriented masses upon it, and at the same time sustaining them in the hope that they, or at least their children, will be able to consume still more in the future and thereby enhance their status and *dignidad*. Various sociological surveys have indicated that the majority of Spaniards prize education primarily as a means of augmenting income.

In the past few years the Spanish governing elites have begun to benefit, whether by design or accident, from a process that for years has contributed to the ease with which the ruling classes of Latin America have maintained the masses in a state of dependence: the inflationary process.

Within a system in which the laboring masses lack disposable capital resources, which is the case when consumerism is functioning the way a directing elite intends it to, inflation increases the dependence of the masses by creating just one more instance in which they must turn to the government for protection. At the same time, of course, inflation makes more difficult the task of the governing sectors, for it imposes upon them an additional challenge to meet the aspirations of the dependent masses and creates a further risk of loss of acceptance by the masses. Inflation also increases the pressure upon the directors of the nation's economy to augment production so that rising labor costs will not cut unduly into profits. At least through the beginning of the 1970's the technocrats who had come, by and large, to provide direction to the Spanish economy were proving themselves capable of coping with the problems of inflation and, beyond that, of turning inflation to the advantage of the

---

[47] FOESSA, *Síntesis*, p. 267.

established political system. Whether they can deal successfully with increases of 15 percent in cost of living, as was registered in 1973, remains to be seen.

Occasionally Spanish labor has resorted to strikes in order to pressure government into issuing decrees that authorize wage increases above the rise in living costs. When strikes occur in today's Spain—and they do occur, although prohibited by law—they take the form not of a confrontation with capital, but rather of an appeal to government for redress of grievances. The truly important aspect of a strike in Spain is not that it is illegal, but rather that it is a manifestation, almost an acknowledgment, on the part of labor of its dependence on government. If a strike is a manifestation of dependence it is at the same time a criticism of government. Understanding that a strike will be recognized not only in Spain but abroad as a criticism, the wielders of political power, hoping to save face, tend to respond as the kindhearted father in assuaging the grievances of children and dependents.

The Spanish Elite and the Independence of Capitalism

At this point it is necessary to make explicit a hypothesis that so far has been implicit in this essay: not until a person escapes from the compulsion of consumerism, not until he ceases to be caught up in the workings of a modern-day variant of the "iron law of wages," will he develop interest in gaining his political liberation and come to demand a voice in political decision making at the national level. If this hypothesis is valid, it explains why Spain continues to be a dichotomized society made up of those who are dependent and those who are independent, of those who are passive and those who command. Moreover, if valid, it explains why the directing elites in Spain have been correct in their general assumption that economic development need not lead to democracy—an assumption that sets the leaders of the 1960's clearly apart from those of the turn of the century. Today's elites have all along assumed that the masses would not develop sufficient character to cast off the bonds of consumerism and escape from a status of dependence upon a paternalistic government whose workings remained incomprehensible to them. They have further assumed that within the setting of a modernized society it was the strength of character to gain freedom from consumerism that would separate them, the rulers, from the masses.

Spain has always possessed a superrich class whose members, whether or not they show any strength of character, have enjoyed economic independence and power which frequently they have used to acquire political influence. This class still exists. Since the inception of the Franco regime it has exercised vast power in governing as well as in financial circles. What is novel and striking in post-Civil War Spain is the appearance of a new class of power wielders who have attained their status largely through dedication to the classic capitalist ethic, through their single-minded devotion to using their skills to generate more and more money and to attain higher and higher levels of production, and through their stoic resistance to temptations to squander gains in nonproductive consumerism. The *Opus Dei* religious order provides one of the clearest, but by no means the only, examples of Spain's new capitalist elite and political leaders.[48]

A notable precursor of *Opus Dei*'s approach to matters of economic and moral development was Ramiro de Maeztu, a leading ideologue of Spanish conservatism in the 1920's and 1930's who was assassinated at the outbreak of the Civil War in 1936. The son of a Basque father and an English mother, Maeztu lived many years in England and married an Englishwoman. Always fascinated by the differences between Anglo-Saxon and Spanish culture, he came to admire the "reverential sense" with which men of the English-speaking world approached money and to lament the traditional profligateness of Spaniards. Profoundly influenced by the writings of Max Weber, Maeztu concluded that Spain could never attain eco-

---

[48] In correspondence of March 2, 1973, with the author, Juan J. Linz, a renowned authority on Spanish history and the contemporary scene, expressed some dubiousness about the capitalist ethic, entrepreneur role of the *Opus Dei*. He feels that in its operations the *Opus Dei* often illustrates that political power can become transformed easily into economic power, rather than the reverse. If this is so, then the *Opus Dei*, showing a considerable parallel to the Society of Jesus, demonstrates the workings of a concept that Ramiro de Maeztu has referred to as the "money of power," *i.e.*, the accumulation of wealth through connections with the wielders of power. According to Maeztu, this was the traditional approach of Spaniards to the quest for money. Whatever the truth, it is certain that critics and bitter foes of the *Opus Dei* are legion among Spaniards. Their pressure contributes to the removal of many *Opus Deistas* from high positions in a reshuffling carried out by the Franco regime in 1973. Apparently the *Opus Dei* technocrats suffered a further loss of power in the January, 1974, realignment following the assassination in the previous month of the premier, Luis Carrero Blanco. For a devastating account of the religious order that must be used with caution, see Daniel Artigues, *El Opus Dei en España*, 2nd ed. (Paris, 1971).

nomic development unless its leading classes came to understand that the successful quest of money would strengthen moral virtue and that, in a way, by acquiring capital surpluses and using them to stimulate national economic output they were preparing themselves for heaven. Unlike so many of his contemporary fellow rightists in Spain, Maeztu did not believe that massive capital development would lead to democratic leveling. Instead, he was convinced that a new capitalist elite would, by its success in generating wealth and presiding over the economic modernization of Spain, prepare itself not only for heaven but for unchallenged leadership in the temporal order as well. Thus Maeztu foresaw economic development as a means of strengthening elite rule.[49]

It is in this spirit that the *Opus Dei* operates. Monsignor José María Escribá de Balaguer, founder of this lay religious order in 1928, stresses in his book, *Camino* (1965), that idleness is sinful, that man can best sanctify himself through labor, and that he can most readily find God not by withdrawing from the world but by remaining in it and attaining the greatest possible degree of skill and perfection in the practice of his profession. Members of *Opus Dei* are expected, as a sign of moral strength, to free themselves from the compulsions of consumerism and to dedicate themselves steadfastly to the creation of new wealth, not so much for their own advantage as for the common good of the nation. *Opus Dei* members at the highest level must take a vow of celibacy and turn their earnings over to the order, which then pays them what amounts to an allowance appropriate to the social status they occupy.

In a bygone era in Spain, members of the religious orders dedicated themselves to the efficient working of their lands—and more recently to the efficient management of the industries and urban businesses that they came to own—so as to accumulate the capital that was necessary to carry out vast programs of charity and paternalism among the indigent. The effect of this, in social-political terms, was to bring security to the masses in their status of dependence, and to keep them quiescent within the established system. Members of the new religious order of *Opus Dei* work collectively to maximize their capitalist skills so that the Spanish nation will create adequate wealth not only to permit generous programs of govern-

---

[49] See Maeztu, "El espíritu de la economía ibero-americana," *Revista de las Españas* (Madrid), Nos. 9-10 (May-June, 1927), and Pike, *Hispanismo*, esp. pp. 79, 363.

ment paternalism, but also to spread sufficient purchasing power among the masses and produce sufficient goods so that the masses may in general be kept politically dormant within the life style of consumerism. Not only the members of *Opus Dei* but also their archrivals, the Jesuits, have come to see the values of consumerism in maintaining elite rule. In present-day Spain the Society of Jesus is as active as the *Opus Dei* in trying to inculcate reverence for capitalist skills among the leadership class so that this class will be able to keep the mechanisms of capitalism-consumerism functioning satisfactorily.

The objectives of the *Opus Dei,* and of the Jesuits as well, in the social, economic and political realms have been succinctly summarized by Laureano López Rodó. A leading example of an *Opus Dei* technocrat and one of the guiding spirits behind Spain's development plans, López Rodó states in his book, *Política y desarrollo*:

> One of the urgent necessities of our time is political stability, without which the government cannot comply with its commitment, each day more complex, of directing state action, above all in what bears on socio-economic development. For this it is convenient that the government not be at the mercy of parliamentary debates.[50]

In the Spain of the 1960's and 1970's, there are certain "aristocrats of labor" whose earning power makes it feasible for them to dream of entry into the ranks of the bourgeois elite that controls decision making at the national level and that dedicates at least part of its wealth to the generation of more capital and less consumption. At an earlier time in Spain, and in much of Spanish America as well, middle sectors aspiring to upward social mobility identified with and defended a traditional nonbourgeois aristocracy which they looked forward eventually to joining—and which they frequently succeeded in joining. Thus, although a middle class did exist, according at least to economic criteria, on the basis of values and attitudes its members lacked class awareness, having already been co-opted by the aristocracy. If in today's Spain a lesser bourgeoisie made up of the better remunerated laborers can with some expectation of success look forward to ascending into the bourgeois elite, they will tend to act as watchdogs for that elite. In such circumstances there will be little likelihood that reasonably well-to-do social sectors will join

---

[50] See p. 85 of the López Rodó book (Madrid, 1970).

with marginal citizens in seeking to undermine the privileges of the ruling class.

Through the decades and centuries, Spain and Spanish America have been characterized by a remarkable degree of upward social mobility, and by the openness of the aristocracy, which helps explain the infrequence of truly significant social upheavals. In the traditional corporative structure of the Iberian world, upward social mobility involved not only the passage from a lower into a higher corporation in the hierarchically structured society; indeed, the more important manifestation of upward social mobility was passage from the dependent sector within any corporation into the independent, decision-making sector. If future upheavals are to be avoided, mobility of this type must be maintained, while additional paternalistic mechanisms are devised to cushion the fall of those in a process of downward social mobility.

Education and the Corporate Structure

In maintaining an essentially two-culture society against a background of rapid economic development, Spain has benefited from its educational system and also from the semicorporate nature of its political and economic structure. And, as will be suggested, a close interrelationship exists between education and the new corporatism.

Despite the so-called massification that Spanish universities have undergone with the mushrooming of the middle classes,[51] higher education remains largely the province of the elite. As of 1970, only 6 percent of the university students came from working-class backgrounds.[52] Educational reform programs have recently proclaimed the democratic principle that "no one with capacity shall remain outside of the university." In effect, though, the principle that remains in operation is the more traditional one according to which "no one who belongs to the sectors that have always monopolized access to the university will remain outside of it."[53]

University students understandably view themselves as an elite,

---

[51] See José Juan Toharia, "En torno a la nueva 'contestación,' " *España Perspectiva 1972* (Madrid, 1972), p. 274.

[52] FOESSA, *Síntesis,* p. 273. For an excellent treatment of higher education in Spain as of 1969, dealing in part with its elitist orientation, see Ramón Bela, "Spanish Educational Reform: Three Views," in Stephen D. Kertesz, ed., *The Task of Universities in a Changing World* (Notre Dame, 1971), pp. 353-369.

[53] Toharia, "En torno a la nueva 'contestación,' " p. 274.

and this is why they show much greater political awareness and in general see a need for greater political change than other sectors of Spanish youth. Feeling themselves destined to be the rulers of the country and resentful that their voice is scarcely heeded at the present time, university students vent their frustration through campus disorders and through espousing changes that often strike observers as extremely radical.[54] In their elitist attitudes, however, it seems to this writer that Spain's university students are in the majority altogether conventional and traditional. They may desire change, but—like so many of their counterparts in the United States and Latin America—they assume that this change will have to be carried out under their direction.

At the secondary level the educational reform law of August, 1970, provides measures for safeguarding the hierarchical structure that is obviously desired by the new technocratic elite that since 1957 has been instrumental in shaping the course of Spain's economic and cultural development.[55] The law stipulates, for example, that there will continue to take place at the age of fourteen the qualifying process through which some students are selected for eventual study in the university while others are assigned to further education of a professional or vocational nature. As a result a few students are permitted access to a type of education that will, in theory, impart broad perspectives and enable them to understand the complexities of national and international problems, while the majority are channeled into instruction programs that provide them with skill only to exercise a particular trade or function and do not equip them to see how their trade or function fits into the broad, overall national scene. Students within the first group are expected to acquire the knowledge and wisdom needed to exercise the moderating power— the most important and sensitive aspect of political power within the corporate structure—by means of which they can reconcile the claims of the various functional, organic groups in society so as to achieve a rational synthesis conducive to attainment of the common good. Students of the second group, those steered into professional

---

[54] A decided majority of university students, 75 percent in fact, favor changes in important aspects of the political organization of Spain, compared to only 28 percent of Spanish youth in general. See Torregrosa Peris, "Orientación sociopolíticas de la juventud española," pp. 903-904.

[55] The political shake-up that removed many *Opus Dei* technocrats from high political positions has not changed the elitist outlook of the governing regime; it may, in fact, have strengthened·the commitment to elitism.

or vocational training, may well expect to wield some influence over decisions concerning the operation of their particular functional group; but, convinced that problems of government at the national level are too complicated for them to grasp, they will—so the theory of corporatism goes—contentedly leave the exercise of a moderating power to an elite capable of comprehending the whole rather than just its component parts.

In a way, the nature of the moderating power was described by López Rodó when he wrote: "The function of the state consists in promoting the development of the productive forces and in correcting the imbalances of the economic structure, so as to thereby attain the required economic optimum."[56] A basic assumption of Spain's technocratic elite is that only the man who has liberated himself from the demands of consumerism can acquire the serenity of spirit, the time for study, and the breadth of vision that are required for the wise and proper exercise of the moderating power.

According to the formulas of Spanish corporatism, the working masses, divided and kept distinct within the labor sectors of the twenty-six vertical corporations that correspond to the country's major functional groups,[57] will be allowed some degree of participation in the lower level of decision making within each corporation. The elite in Franco's Spain fully appreciate the value of political participation for the masses in imparting to them the sense of realization and dignity that is essential if they are to remain contented within their particular station in life. However, the Spanish elite hopes to confine mass participation to the less exalted spheres of decision making. The masses, they believe, can attain the full degree of politicization that is appropriate to them by being allowed to participate in directing at the grass-roots level the policies of local institutions, such as town councils and functional syndicates. Undoubtedly the same reasoning lies behind the assimilation of corporatist features into the political economic structure that has emerged since the 1920's in Mexico; it accounts also for the favorable attitudes toward corporatism of many Latin American military regimes of the 1960's and 1970's as well as of a good number of the area's Christian Democrats.

---

[56] *Política y desarrollo*, p. 288. See also p. 300.

[57] The mechanisms of Spanish corporatism are described clearly by Charles W. Anderson in his valuable book, *The Political Economy of Modern Spain: Policy-Making in an Authoritarian System* (Madison, 1970), esp. pp. 66-73.

Corporatism, a recent Spanish sociological survey has suggested, not only accepts inequality but regards it as a positive good. According to the survey, corporatism rests on the conviction "that it is best for those who wield power to recognize the political and social weight which the different social groups have. Political representation will be given in proportion to this weight, not in proportion to numbers."[58] In the final analysis, the corporate formula has functioned with relative success in post-Civil War Spain only because the immersion of the masses in consumerism has decreased enormously the weight which they can deploy in the political arena. Those who are independent, because they are capitalists, have most of the weight; and the corporate structure, with its moderating elite at the top, is a reflection of this fact.

The Spanish working force in the 1960's showed signs of increasing discontent with the functioning of corporatism. Often with the backing of the Church, Spanish labor sought to emerge from the fragmentation imposed upon it by corporatism and to present a united front in pressing demands for higher wages and improved working conditions. In December of 1973, moreover, at about the same time that the funeral was being held for the assassinated premier Luis Carrero Blanco, a group of labor leaders received sentences to long prison terms, precisely for having sought to break out of the corporative mold and to create a broadly based labor movement.

Perhaps these developments do not reflect a basic discontent with Spain's so-called system of organic democracy, or a desire to move toward the Western-style, inorganic democracy of undifferentiated numbers. Perhaps discontent arises basically from the fact that organic democracy is not being given a true chance to operate. Ignacio Camuñas Solis writes in a 1972 publication:

> The best service those who believe in the viability of organic democracy could render would be to put it into practice in depth and to its ultimate consequences. That is to say, to permit a democracy without political parties but in which heads of municipal councils, the presidents of the syndicates and the functional representatives of the third branch in the Cortes all gain office without the need of any ties with power and as the result of being freely elected by their respective bases.[59]

Meantime, whatever its shortcomings, Spain's syndicalist or

---

[58] FOESSA, *Síntesis,* p. 170.
[59] Camuñas Solis, "Introducción," *España Perspectiva 1972,* p. 22.

corporatist system is functioning fairly well as a vital mechanism in bestowing state paternalism upon the laboring classes. Much of the country's social security system is administered on a decentralized basis by the twenty-six syndicates. These syndicates receive a good share of national social security funds by means of which they carry out a broad variety of assistance programs for their members. Thus, the syndicates maintain approximately 125 centers of professional formation in which more than 110,000 students—44,000 of them on full scholarship—were enrolled as of 1970. They run forty-one rest and education centers, handling close to 60,000 residents annually; they arrange vacation tours for over 160,000 workers each year, operate fifty-six parks and sports installations, supervise 14,300 co-operatives of various types with more than 2,300,000 members, and maintain thirty-five sanatoriums and twenty-one consulting centers extending medical services to some five million patients each year. Moreover, as of 1969 syndicates had constructed more than 258,000 housing units; and they administered mutual insurance programs covering more than 6,264,000 workers in 159,000 different firms. The primary purpose of mutualism was to provide pensions for re-tired workers. There were, in 1970, 1,211,383 retired persons on the pension rolls of the mutualism programs operated through the var-ious syndicates.[60] By allotting to the syndicates the administration of important services, the government has acted to increase the im-portance that workers attach to participating in the control of their particular functional association. At the same time the government keeps the labor force fragmented by encouraging workers to identify, in line with old Spanish traditions, with their particular *patria chica*.

Conclusion: Spain and the Spanish New World

Yale University sociologist-political scientist Juan J. Linz has written in one of his many penetrating studies of contemporary Spain:

Are important changes in the economic structure, and with it in the social structure—from agrarian to industrial society, from poverty to relative affluence, . . . — largely independent of political change? Can they take place with only limited changes in the political in-stitutional structure? . . . we feel that ultimately, even when with

---

[60] See *Anuario Político Español 1969*, pp. 508-509, and *Anuario Político Español 1970*, p. 416.

considerable delay, the modernization of the Spanish economy will lead to a convergence of its political institutions with those of the rest of Western Europe.[61]

Here, on the other hand, is a representative sampling of the opinions of some of Spain's technocratic elite. "It is necessary for everything to change in order that everything may continue to be the same."[62] "The ideal . . . has been to assimilate the Western economic models and preserve the specifics of the political and social models that prevailed before the Civil War."[63] "Our economic-social structures are on the way to becoming fully European; our ideological system, the patrimony which we do not wish to renounce, is profoundly Spanish."[64] Finally, Florentino Pérez Embid, one of the most representative intellectuals of the higher circles of *Opus Dei*, laid down some years ago the following formula as his desideratum: "Europeanization in the means and Hispanicization (*españolización*) in the ends."[65]

This is the issue. Is Spain destined, as a result of its economic and social changes, to move irresistibly toward the convergence of its political institutions, and also of its ideological system, with those of the rest of Western Europe? Or, in spite of all that has changed since 1939, can it cling to its traditional rejection of inorganic democracy? If the capitalist-consumerist dichotomy has, to the degree suggested in this essay, forged a two-culture Spain, then Western-style inorganic democracy will continue to find an unpropitious environment in the country.

What are some of the parallels and contrasts between recent Spanish and Latin American developments? For one thing, Latin American leaders in the post-World War II era have largely abandoned the conventional wisdom of most turn-of-the-century elitists for whom economic development that entailed placing purchasing power in the hands of the masses would inevitably bring about social and political upheaval. They are ready, in many instances (as was Juan Domingo Perón in his first period as president

---

[61] Linz, "The Opposition in and under an Authoritarian Regime: The Case of Spain," 1969, mimeo, pp. 69-70.

[62] Antonio L. Marzal, "La participación del trabajo en la sociedad española del desarrollo," *España Perspectiva 1972*, pp. 244, describes this as the ideological formula of the technocrats.

[63] Quoted in *Anuario Político Español 1969*, p. 25.

[64] Quoted in *ibid.*, p. 26.

[65] Quoted in *ibid.*, p. 25.

of Argentina, 1946-1955), to turn to the all-out quest of economic development, satisfied that they can at the same time preserve elite rule—even though the identity of those comprising the elite may have to change. But, development-minded leaders of most Latin American countries lack the economic windfalls that Spain has found in tourism, increased foreign investment, and remittances from emigrants. Hence they face the need to capture increasing amounts of money from the wealthy classes within their particular countries as well as a larger share of the profits of foreign enterprises. And this has led to policies—actually implemented in a few instances but most generally confined to rhetoric—that are often described as Marxist.

Denied many of the advantages—including a low birth rate—that post-Civil War Spain has enjoyed, Latin Americans may not be able to achieve sufficient development to bring the consumer society into being in the immediate future: Mexico, Venezuela, and Brazil stand as the most likely exceptions to this generalization,[66] while Víctor Paz Estenssoro's hopes to transform Bolivia into a consumer society through that country's 1952 social revolution were already thoroughly shattered when he was overthrown by the military in 1964 at the end of a second presidential term. In most Latin American countries, government may have to rely more on state paternalism than on consumerism's new "iron law of wages" to keep the masses quiescent.

Far ahead of other Spanish American republics, Colombia already in the 1880's, led by President Rafael Núñez, had begun a return to many features of the corporative socioeconomic organization that had been dismantled by preceding liberal regimes. To this fact, at least in part, can be attributed the relative social peace that Colombia enjoyed in the early part of the twentieth century. Then, when the country's political stability, increasingly precarious since the World War II period, faced a particularly acute challenge in

---

[66] As of 1970, Mexico's per capita income was estimated by some sources at just below $500, about half of Spain's and not likely to climb dramatically in the immediate future in view of rapid annual population increases. For Venezuela, per capita income registered about $900 as the 1960's ended (by the end of 1973 it was estimated at $1,200, about on a par with Spain), and for Brazil approximately $300. Brazilian planners, buoyed by the rapid development of the late 1960's and early 1970's, anticipate a per capita income of $600 by 1980 and $1,200 by the year 2000. However, according to Hudson Institute projections per capita income by 2000 will be less than $600. See Business International, *Brazil, New Business Power in South America* (New York, 1971), p. 7.

the early 1970's, the Colombian government adopted a wide-ranging renovation of the methods for preserving the established order. While in some ways distinctive, the renovation also brought Colombia in certain respects into line with precedents established in Franco's Spain.

Acting on the advice of Lauchlin Currie (one-time advisor to the Franklin D. Roosevelt administration who became a Colombian citizen in 1959), Misael Pastrana, elected to the presidency in 1970, adopted a development plan that attaches vital importance to raising the purchasing power of the masses. The objective is to increase consumption and thereby eliminate the problem of lagging demand, which Currie views as the crucial constraint on development. The plan also reflects Currie's conviction that "In part the lack of a sense of well-being arises from invidious comparisons of levels of consumption rather than levels of income."[67]

The Colombian development plan calls for the concentration of investment in urban development, particularly in housing. Apparently one reason for this is that surveys taken in Colombia have shown that a key factor in rendering slum dwellers nonradical and relatively content is ownership of their living quarters, regardless of how humble.[68] In this respect, Colombians seem to be following paths explored earlier by the Franco regime in Spain. Subsidized housing projects have enabled an impressively high percentage of lower-class Spaniards to become owners, rather than renters, of homes, thereby fostering in them the conservative attitudes of property owners and at the same time encouraging gratitude toward —and continued dependence upon—the government which has helped to make possible the acquisition of homes.[69] Further in line with Spanish precedents, the Pastrana regime has encouraged and facilitated cooperation between Colombia's technocratic planners

---

[67] National Planning Department (of Colombia), *Guidelines for a New Strategy* (Bogotá, 1972), p. 63, quoted by John W. Sloan, "Colombia's New Development Plan: An Example of Post-ECLA Thinking," *Inter-American Economic Affairs*, XXVII (1973), 56. In his article, Sloan makes a superb analysis of the important Colombian development plan.

[68] J. C. van Es and William L. Flinn, "A Note on the Determinants of Satisfaction Among Urban Migrants in Bogotá, Colombia," *Inter-American Economic Affairs*, XXVII (1973), esp. p. 22.

[69] In 1970, 54 percent of Spanish families lived in homes they owned, in comparison to 36 percent which rented their homes. The statistics for 1966 were 46 percent and 40 percent, respectively. See FOESSA, *Síntesis*, pp. 28-29.

and an important segment of the political elite in implementing the development plan.

Included in the Colombian approach to development is an ingenious set of devices aimed at utilizing the inflationary process even more effectively than it has previously been employed in Latin America[70] and Spain to increase dependence of the lower classes on government. Savings-and-loan agencies, envisaged as an important source of credit for urban development programs, are to be created, with their capital coming to some extent from the savings of the lower classes. To encourage lower-class savings, the Pastrana government in July of 1972 introduced a unit of account called the *Unidad de Poder Adquisitivo Constante* (UPAC). All savings-and-loan accounts as well as savings certificates are to be denominated in terms of UPAC in order to guarantee their constant value even when inflation occurs. As Pastrana explains it: "This will be the first time in the history of Colombia in which the patrimony of the savings, especially that of the poorer classes, will not only be protected against inflation, but will receive ample returns."[71]

The basic importance of the savings plan may well be that it will bring the lower-class savers to rely upon the government to maintain the value of their capital resources. As a consequence, their private savings will not result in the sort of economic self-reliance that elite groups of the Iberian world have traditionally feared would lead to the political independence of the masses and to general social leveling. Instead, savings, in an inflationary setting, will be used, along with expanding social services and the operation of consumerism, to increase the dependence of the masses upon a governing elite. Understandably, an authoritative study concludes that the Colombian development plan "is designed to better living conditions and *not* to change the power structure . . . it constitutes a kind of 'defensive modernization.' "[72]

---

[70] For a particularly acute study of how the inflationary process began initially to be utilized in Chile as a means for increasing the dependence of the masses upon government, see Thomas C. Wright, "The Origins of the Politics of Inflation in Chile, 1888-1918," *The Hispanic American Historical Review*, LIII (1973), 239-259.

[71] *El Siglo* (Bogotá), July 21, 1972, quoted by Sloan, "Colombia's New Development Plan," p. 62. Interest of 5.5 percent is paid on savings accounts guaranteed against erosion by inflation.

[72] Sloan, "Colombia's New Development Plan," p. 65. The emphasis is Sloan's. While Currie himself seems to view the development plan as leading Colombia toward a social system resembling Denmark's, undoubtedly the seg-

Shortly after toppling the Salvador Allende administration in September of 1973, Chile's military leaders announced plans that even more clearly than in Colombia stress the importance of corporatism and call for a type of social organization resembling in many ways the models of Franco's Spain. General Augusto Pinochet Ugarte, head of Chile's military junta, stated that a new constitution for the country would provide for *gremios* (guilds, syndicates, or corporations) as a means of giving citizens "responsible participation" in the life of the country.[73] Chile's principal theoretician of "gremialism," and an important member of the small commission appointed to frame a new constitution, is Jaime Guzmán, a young professor of constitutional law. Apparently he hopes to establish through "gremialism" a type of corporatism similar to that introduced by the military in Peru and described by James Malloy in the third chapter of this book. Moreover, Chilean "gremialism" has been pictured, in terms equally applicable to Peru's social-political experiment, as "a combination of traditional liberalism and a kind of corporatism similar to that practiced in Spain under Generalissimo Francisco Franco."[74] The author of this statement appears unaware of the degree to which Franco's system is itself a combination of traditional liberalism and corporatism.

Although the methods are likely to vary considerably from country to country, an increasing number of Latin American republics could conceivably find the means for accomplishing the goal toward which Spain's technocratic elites have, with remarkable short-term success, devoted their efforts during the past two decades: accommodation between modern times and the essential social features of the traditional, elitist, two-culture, corporate society. In spite of the fact that their rhetoric is often couched in Marxist terms, I sus-

---

ment of the Colombian upper classes presently cooperating in its implementation has far more conservative purposes in mind.

[73] Marvin Howe, "Allende's Middle-Class Foes Winning Power under Chile's Junta," New York *Times,* October 23, 1973, p. 3. See also "Chile: A Corporate State in the Making?" *Latin America,* VII (September 28, 1973), 310-311. Ronald Newton discusses the Chilean case more fully in his essay in this collection.

[74] Howe, "Allende's Middle-Class Foes," p. 3. Corporative prescriptions for Chile are also advocated in Alfredo Alcaino Barros *et al., Participación para una nueva sociedad* (Santiago de Chile, 1973) and were conspicuous in Christian Democratic ideology. See, in particular, George Grayson, *El Partido Demócrata Cristiano chileno,* trans. Adolfo Murguía Zubiarraín (Buenos Aires, Santiago, 1968).

pect that this is what even many leftist proponents of revolutionary change in today's Latin America have in mind.

Spaniards can look with satisfaction upon the members of their *raza* (a term that in Spanish usage customarily denotes ties of culture, language and tradition rather than simply ethnic bonds) in the New World, for Spanish Americans seem to have resisted the lure of Anglo-American models and to have maintained their cultural heritage intact by eschewing liberal inorganic democracy based on society-wide diffusion of individualism. In this situation Spaniards can perhaps find affirmation of their conventional wisdom that liberalism was never more than a passing sickness.

Even intellectuals and statesmen of the Western liberal world seem to have been suffering doubts for a number of years about their system. Perhaps the increasing evidence of the scarcity of basic resources has begun quite recently to strengthen those doubts.

In his brilliant if highly erratic and deeply flawed book, *The Great Frontier* (1952), the late University of Texas historian Walter Prescott Webb advanced a fascinating thesis concerning the origins of liberalism. According to him it was the discovery of the New World—which thereupon became a great frontier for the Old World—that made liberalism possible. By causing the index of goods and things—including land and other resources—suddenly to soar dramatically beyond the index of persons, the richly endowed great frontier made possible a relaxation of many of the Old World's controls and restrictions. As of the early 1970's, however, with the rapid depletion of resources and the startling increase in population—some authorities predict a doubling by the year 2000 of the world's present 3.5 billion inhabitants—the factors that once made liberalism feasible no longer seem to operate.

Repeating and often refining and innovating upon themes that other scholars had anticipated, Karl A. Wittfogel in his book *Oriental Despotism* (1957) hypothesized that the need of early civilizations to control and ration the ever-scarce resource of water made political despotism inevitable. Today, the need to control more and more resources, of which petroleum is only the first to serve dramatic notice to the world of its scarcity, takes its place among the numerous other factors that have for some time caused doubts about the viability of the laissez-faire approach. Such doubts perhaps contribute to the tolerance with which North Americans have quite recently begun to view the nonliberal ways of Spanish Americans.

For years, and even centuries, members of the more highly developed Western world (and also a handful of liberally inclined Spaniards) have been smugly predicting that eventually Spaniards as a whole would become liberal enough to earn the rights of a closer association with polite international society. Today traditionalist Spaniards may with some justification be thinking that eventually the rest of the world will become illiberal enough to merit acceptance by them and by the American members of their *raza*.

Index

Adams, John Quincy, xi, 140
AFL-CIO, 157
Allende, Salvador, 34, 154, 163, 165
Alliance for Progress, 7, 8, 155-158
Andalusia, 181, 186
Andean Republics, 161
Anderson, Charles W., 22
Anti-Yankeeism, 161, 162; and fear of social change in Latin America, 165-166
APRA *(Alianza Popular Revolucionaria Americana)*, 6, 45, 63, 64, 72
Apter, David, 79
Argentina: corporatism, 3, 49; *Peronismo,* 3, 45, 163
Arze, José Antonio, 133, 134
Astiz, Carlos, 30
Authoritarianism: Brazil, 23; and corporatism, 37, 42, 45, 46, 169; and Latin American military, 44; Linz formulation, 9, 53, 58, 59, 75-76, 79-80, 83; and mobilization, 75-76, 80; in the Portuguese monarchy, 16-17; as a regime type, 52, 60; and state corporatism, 105, 106
Autonomous corporate groups. *See* Corporate groups
Azpiazu, Joaquín, 10

Barrientos, René, 159
Beltrán, Pedro, 154

Berle, A. A., Jr., 147-148
Bogotá (Colombia) Conference, 152-153
Bolivia, 77, 78, 204
Bolshevik Revolution, 37
Bourgeois, Léon, 10
Bourgeois profit ethic, 132, 139, 141. *See also* Protestant ethic
Braden, Spruille, 151
Brazil: authoritarianism, 3; *coronelismo,* 28; corporatism, 6, 49; franchise in, 28; military, 27-28, 29; monarchy, 27; unions, 28
Buenos Aires Conference (1936), 145

Cabrera, Luis, 143
Caciquismo, 24, 173
Caetano, M., 12-13, 23, 27
Calhoun, John C., xi
Camuñas Solis, Ignacio, 201
Capitalism: and corporatism, 54, 108-109 ff.; in early development of Portugal, 16; in Latin America, 50, 132, 137, 141-144; and Spanish social structure, 171, 176-177 ff. *See also* liberal capitalism; United States, *and individual countries*
Cárdenas, Lázaro, 175
Carranza, Venustiano, 142, 143
Carrero Blanco, Luis, 201
Castro, Fidel, 155, 165

Development literature, 8
Diez Nicholás, Juan, 182
Dollar Diplomacy, 140
Dominican Republic, 11
Duggan, Laurence, 151
Dulles, John Foster, 151-152, 156
Durkheim, E., 10, 57, 117
Dutra, Eurico Gaspar, 29

Economic development: in Latin
    America, 77, 79; and social
    stability, 132, 137, 148-149,
    152, 156, 174-175, 205-206
Economic nationalism: and for-
    eign capital, 149-150 ff., 160-
    161; in Latin America, 139,
    145-146, 155, 162-163, 165
Eisenhower, Dwight D., 155
Eisenhower, Milton, 154, 155
Elitism: Brazil, 27; functional and
    political elites, 40, 42-43, 50;
    and Latin American masses,
    132, 135, 136, 144, 152, 158-
    159, 164; and Spanish col-
    lectivism, 174-175
Ellender, Allen, 159
Endara, Lorenzo Benito de, 173
Erickson, Kenneth, 29

Faoro, Raymundo, 23, 27
Fascism and corporatism, 7, 38; in
    Italy and Germany, xv, 5, 8,
    9, 11, 85, 104
Ferdinand and Isabella, 46, 171
Ferkiss, Victor C., xi
Foreign Assistance Act (1966),
    158
Foreign capital and Latin Ameri-
    can elites, 138, 144, 150, 160,
    161. See also "Internal domi-
    nation" and "external de-
    pendence"

Foros, 4, 16, 18
Fueros, 42, 46

Galbraith, John Kenneth, xv
Gama Barros, Henrique de, 20
Generation of 1898, 172
Gide, Charles, 10
Good Neighbor Policy, 144-149,
    150-151
Goulart, João, 29
Great Depression, 48, 145-146 ff.
Gremialist movement, 35; in
    Chile, 34-35, 207
Guild Socialists, 36
Guzmán, Jaime, 34, 207

Haya de la Torre, Víctor Raúl, 63
Hickenlooper Amendment, 167
Hispanic tradition of corporatism,
    41, 53, 137, 143, 144. See
    also Iberic-Latin tradition
Hispanistas, 133, 134
Hull, Cordell, 144
Huntington, Samuel P., 75, 80

Iberic-Latin tradition of corporat-
    ism, 6, 7, 9, 11, 31-32, 89-90;
    economic factors in, 16; his-
    toric perspective, 12-24
Inca, 133-134
Indian tradition of corporatism
    in Latin America, 133-134,
    134n, 137, 144
Indigenistas, 133, 134
Individualism, 166-168 ff.; and
    personal liberty, 156
Industrialization, 49, 119, 132;
    and corporatism, xii-xiii, xvii,
    36, 37, 40, 48; and urbaniza-
    tion, 40, 42, 43, 46
Instituto Nacional de Industria,
    188-189